Contents

List of tables and figures

Acknowledgements

Earlier versions of the chapters of this book were presented at a conference held at the Economic and Social Research Council (ESRC) Centre for Analysis of Social Exclusion (CASE) at the London School of Economics and Political Science on the occasion of Howard Glennerster's 70th birthday in October 2006. The authors and editors are very grateful for the comments and suggestions made by the participants in that conference, particularly its chair, Malcolm Dean, and Tony Atkinson, Simon Burgess, Alan Deacon, Carol Propper and Kitty Stewart, who acted as discussants of the papers.

The editors are most grateful to the ESRC for its funding for CASE, which supported this project, and for supporting the inputs of John Hills and Anne Power. Many other members of CASE helped with this project but a particular debt is owed to Anna Tamas, who prepared the whole book for publication. Figures 10.2–10.5 are Crown Copyright and are reproduced by kind permission of the Controller of The Stationery Office and Queen's Printer for Scotland.

All of the contributors owe a large personal debt to Howard Glennerster for his continuing and unfailing support, encouragement and inspiration.

Notes on contributors

Nicholas Barr is Professor of Public Economics at the London School of Economics and Political Science, the author of numerous books and articles including *The Economics of the Welfare State* (4th edition, Oxford University Press, 2004) and *Reforming Pensions: Principles and Policy* (with Peter Diamond) (Oxford University Press, forthcoming), a member of the Editorial Board of the *International Social Security Review* and a Trustee of HelpAge International. He spent two periods at the World Bank working on the design of income transfers in Central and Eastern Europe and has been a visiting scholar at the Fiscal Affairs Department at the International Monetary Fund. Since the late 1980s, he has been active in debates about pension reform and higher education finance, advising governments in the post-communist countries, and in Australia, Chile, China, Hungary, New Zealand, South Africa and the UK.

Tania Burchardt is a senior research fellow at the ESRC Centre for Analysis of Social Exclusion at the London School of Economics and Political Science. Her research interests include theories of social justice, definitions and measurement of inequality and social exclusion, and welfare and employment policy. Recent publications include 'Happiness and social policy: barking up the right tree in the wrong neck of the woods', in L. Bauld, K. Clarke and T. Maltby (eds) *Social Policy Review 18* (The Policy Press, 2006); and *The Education and Employment of Disabled Young People: Frustrated Ambition* (Joseph Rowntree Foundation/The Policy Press, 2005). She is Editor of *Benefits: The Journal of Poverty and Social Justice*.

Jose Harris is Professor of Modern History at the University of Oxford, a fellow of St Catherine's College. She is the author of *Unemployment and Politics* (Clarendon Press, 1974, 1984), *William Beveridge* (Oxford University Press, 1977 and 1997) and *Civil Society in British History* (2003), and editor and translator of Ferdinand Tönnies, *Community and Civil Society* (Cambridge University Press, 2001). She is currently a visiting professorial fellow at the School of Advanced Study, University of London, and is a Fellow of the British Academy.

John Hills is Professor of Social Policy and Director of the ESRC CASE at the London School of Economics and Political Science. His research interests include the distributional effects of tax and welfare systems, social security, pensions, and housing finance. Recent publications include *Inequality and the State* (Oxford University Press, 2004), *A More Equal Society? New Labour, Poverty, Inequality and Exclusion* (co-editor, The Policy Press, 2005) and *Ends and Means: The Future Roles of Social Housing in England* (Centre for the Analysis of Social Exclusion, 2007). He was a member of the Pensions Commission from 2003 to 2006.

Martin Knapp is Professor of Social Policy and Director of the Personal Social Services Research Unit at the London School of Economics and Political Science. He is also Professor of Health Economics and Director of the Centre for the Economics of Mental Health at King's College London, Institute of Psychiatry. His primary research activities are in the areas of long-term care, social care more generally, and mental health policy and practice. Recently he co-edited *Mental Health Policy and Practice across Europe* (McGraw Hill, 2007) and *Long-Term Care: Matching Resources and Needs* (Ashgate, 2004).

Julian Le Grand is the Richard Titmuss Professor of Social Policy at the London School of Economics and Political Science. From 2003 to 2005, he was Senior Policy Adviser to the Prime Minister in 10 Downing Street. His most recent books include *The Other Invisible Hand: Delivering Public Services through Choice and Competition* (Princeton University Press, 2007) and *Motivation, Agency and Public Policy* (revised edition, Oxford University Press, 2006).

Jane Lewis is Professor of Social Policy at the London School of Economics and Political Science. She works on gender regimes and social policies and the implications of family change. Her recent publications include *The End of Marriage? Individualism and Intimate Relations* (Edward Elgar, 2001) and *Should we Worry About Family Change?* (University of Toronto Press, 2003).

David Piachaud is Professor of Social Policy at the London School of Economics and Political Science and an associate of CASE. He was Social Policy Adviser in the Prime Minister's Policy Unit (1974-79) and has been consultant to the European Commission, International Labour Organization, Organisation for Economic Co-operation and Development and World Health Organization. He has written papers and books on children, poverty, social security, social exclusion and social policy.

Anne Power is Professor of Social Policy at the London School of Economics and Political Science and Deputy Director of CASE. She is a member of the Sustainable Development Commission, responsible for regeneration and sustainable communities. She is a visiting fellow at the Brookings Institution in Washington, DC, and with Bruce Katz is developing a Europe-wide and US network of Weak Market Cities, aiming to help regenerate urban communities in a more sustainable way. Her publications include *Jigsaw Cities: Big Places: Small Spaces* with John Houghton (The Policy Press, 2007), *London Thames Gateway: A Framework for Housing in the London Thames Gateway* with Liz Richardson and others (Centre for Analysis of Social Exclusion, 2004), *Sustainable Communities and Sustainable Development: A Review of the Sustainable Communities Plan* (Sustainable Development Commission, 2004), *East Enders* with Katharine Mumford (The Policy Press, 2003) and *Cities for a Small Country* with Richard Rogers (Faber and Faber, 2000).

Tony Travers is Co-Director of LSE London and is based in the Department of Government at the London School of Economics and Political Science. His main areas of research are public finance, local government and urban policy. Recent publications include *The Politics of London Governing: An Ungovernable City* (Palgrave, 2004), *International Comparisons of Local Government Finance: Propositions and Analysis* (Lyons Inquiry, 2005) and *Improving Local Transport: How Small Reforms could make a Big Difference* with Stephen Glaister (Local Government Association, 2006).

Anne West is Professor of Education Policy in the Department of Social Policy at the London School of Economics and Political Science. Her main area of interest is education policy. Her research has focused on market-oriented reforms in education and their impact on equity; financing education; and education policy in a European context. Her recent publications include *Underachievement in School* (RoutledgeFalmer, 2003) and articles in the *Oxford Review of Education, Educational Policy,* the *British Journal of Educational Studies, Higher Education Quarterly* and the *Peabody Journal of Education*.

ONE

Introduction

John Hills, Julian Le Grand and David Piachaud

How to make social policy work? How can policies be designed so as to achieve the aims of government in the social arena? How can these policies be implemented in such a way so as to promote the desired aims but without damaging other aims that we might wish to pursue? Can we ensure that social policies have only those consequences that are intended?

Howard Glennerster, whose work has inspired the contributions to this book, has devoted much of his professional life to answering such questions and the book attempts to build on his contributions. It is thus concerned, not so much with the theory of social policy, but with its practice. The chapters of the book, all written by colleagues of Howard, all distinguished in their own right, focus on the historical development and practical implementation of policy in key areas of social concern. The main focus of the book is on contemporary issues, particularly on the ways in which social policy in Britain has been reshaped in the first decade of the 21st century, the arguments that lay behind those changes, and the issues that they raise for the future evolution of policy.

The structure of the book

The first part of the book looks at the underlying aims of social policy. Jose Harris uses her analysis of the Poor Law to deconstruct some of the mythology surrounding the history of the welfare state. She argues that seemingly quite dated policies and institutions of past eras may contain elements that are constant and universal, or at least recurrent, in many different contexts and epochs, while other apparently 'timeless' models are actually time-specific. She suggests that the Poor Law was less unpopular with poorer classes and not as universally harshly administered than often portrayed. Some at least of the strengths and virtues often ascribed to the welfare state may more properly be seen stemming originally from the Poor Laws, while other, seemingly timeless, aspects of the post-war welfare state, such as its universalism, were in many ways a product of the particular period in which they were introduced. There are lessons to be learned from history about what works; but they may not always be the most obvious ones.

In her chapter, Tania Burchardt emphasises the need to clarify the objectives of policy, especially with respect to social justice, pointing to contradictions in this respect between recent developments in different aspects of policy. She discusses various interpretations of justice – stressing the importance of real-world applications – and concludes by arguing for use of the capability approach pioneered by Amartya Sen. For Burchardt, a conception of this kind has both theoretical and pragmatic advantages: it respects the diversity of human needs, recognises the importance of individual liberty and positive freedom, focuses on ends – outcomes valued in themselves – rather than means, and concentrates on expanding people's capacity for responsibility in general, rather than getting drawn into the "blind alley of devising policies to separate responsible sheep from irresponsible goats".

The second part of the book looks at the ways in which social policies are delivered, focusing on the ways in which policy has changed across a broad spectrum in recent years. Jane Lewis' chapter examines why family issues are so hard for policy makers. She discusses how the increasing pluralism of family form and function poses challenges for state intervention. This is both directly, in terms of family dealings with government officials, and indirectly, via the assumptions that policy makers make, embedded implicitly or explicitly in policies to deliver cash and services. She looks at how recent policy in the UK has 'muddled through' these developments, examining in particular the changes in policy towards the balance between work and family life since 1997. She argues that types of policy intervention that work with the grain of family change are likely to be more successful than those that work against that grain or indeed try to reverse the changes themselves. State interventions cannot be based on assumptions about family form and function that are too far from the reality of people's own ideas, but have to cope not just with the increasing diversity of these ideas, but also the conflicts that may often exist between family members and different types of family.

In her chapter, Anne West brings out some of the tensions that arise when trying to meet different goals in education policy. She describes the evolution of the Labour government's policies towards school education, including the overall level of resources available, their distribution between areas and schools, and particular initiatives focused on schools. The evidence suggests that some of these, such as the numeracy and literacy hours, and 'Excellence in Cities' have had positive results. In general, the expansion of parental choice and school competition have raised overall standards, but the improvements have been mostly concentrated on average and above-average achievers, leaving behind pupils who are low achievers or from disadvantaged backgrounds. There is also evidence of 'cream-skimming' by schools in affecting their intakes, responding to some of the incentives facing them, again to the detriment of the less well off.

Nick Barr's chapter focuses on higher education, looking in particular at the system for financing higher education that had emerged after a series of reforms by 2006. This involves: deferred payment of (variable) fees; what he argues is now a well-designed loans system (with the exception of its subsidised interest rate); and measures to promote access, including restoration of means-tested grants to students from poorer families. He traces the roots of this policy in proposals for 'graduate taxes' in the 1950s and 1960s from the right, in terms of the 'benefit principle', and from the left in terms of redistribution. He then examines the arguments for what has actually emerged – 'income-contingent' loans – in preference to the original graduate tax ideas. He makes the important distinction between strategic policy design, political implementation, and administrative and technical implementation. In many ways, strategic policy design – that most often favoured by academics – is the easy part; the more difficult part is to make policy work on the ground, both in political and administrative terms.

Julian Le Grand's and Martin Knapp's chapters discuss the implementation of market-oriented reform policies in public services. Julian Le Grand examines quasi-markets in publicly funded systems of healthcare, particularly as they have developed in the UK in the last two decades, and concludes that the essential elements of these markets – notably user choice and provider competition – can achieve the ends of healthcare policy, so long as the measures concerned are properly designed. He argues that this means: that there must be mechanisms for ensuring that the entrance for new providers is easy; that exit can take place; that the relevant decisions are immune from political interference; and that patients are given the relevant information and help in making choices, especially the less well off. At the same time, echoing Chapter Five, incentives for cream-skimming should be eliminated, either through not allowing providers to determine their own admissions or through properly risk-adjusting the fixed price system.

Martin Knapp examines fundamental changes that have developed in the delivery of some parts of social care to individuals, aimed at both increasing their choice over service providers, but more recently their control over that choice. He argues that for such policies to succeed requires four elements: a range of services that offers meaningful diversity; accessible and understandable information for service users to make choices between options; empowerment of users and carers to select between services; and control – in some cases with support and monitoring – over those selections. He traces the development of first 'direct payments' to people entitled to support for personal care of different kinds since 1996, and more recently the pilot experiments with 'individual budgets', where service users are using combined resources from a variety of funding streams within what becomes a real, rather than a 'quasi'-market.

Finally in this part, Anne Power looks at the delivery of policy on the ground, in the shape of policies towards neighbourhoods, particularly those with concentrations of households with low incomes. Drawing on long-term work with a number of colleagues in the Centre for Analysis of Social Exclusion (CASE), she examines why neighbourhoods affect social conditions, evidence of recent progress in neighbourhood renewal, and whether more mixed urban communities are likely to emerge as a result of it. Findings from these studies of neighbourhood renewal suggest six issues that can help an area succeed: its location, with advantages to inner, rather than peripheral, areas; special regeneration programmes, particularly those using an incremental approach; selective, 'scalpel' demolition, rather than large-scale clearance; intensive locally based neighbourhood management; keeping neighbourhood conditions in open spaces under control; and the long-term commitment that is needed for renewal to succeed. Such renewal is a foundation stone for creating more mixed-income communities, and is crucial to preserving and repopulating our 'priceless urban assets'.

The third part of the book looks at three dimensions of the distributional effects of policy. David Piachaud reviews the many developments in social security and anti-poverty policy in recent years under the Labour government and shows that both poverty and inequality have fallen. He concludes that the evidence up to 2004-05 shows that 'redistribution works', even if that was not part of the language used by New Labour. However, this success has come at the price of increased complexity, high effective marginal tax rates and a split in responsibility between government departments (the Treasury and the Department for Work and Pensions). Moreover, it is not clear whether this relative success has actually been perceived by the general public, or translated into popular support for the policies concerned. Nor is it apparent what are the next steps that would move poverty rates down below those achieved in 2004-05 to achieve the promised halving of child poverty by 2010, let alone make them among the 'best in Europe' by 2020.

Social policies, particularly pensions policy, also redistribute resources over the life cycle. John Hills' discussion of the major reforms under way in pensions policy emphasises another aspect of workable – and sustainable – social policies: the need to make hard choices, and for those choices to carry popular support. He traces the ways in which perceptions of the pensions problem have changed in the last decade, and why policy responses in the late 1990s proved inadequate. Drawing on evidence collected by the Pensions Commission, which examined the area in detail before making its recommendations (now largely being implemented) in 2005, he looks at public priorities for pensions, but also contradictions in attitudes. People of working age want adequate pensions for their current older relatives and for themselves when they retire. But they underestimate the savings or taxes necessary to fund these, particularly as they (especially younger people) underestimate their own prospective life expectancies. People believe in some form of 'contributory' principle as a way of establishing entitlement to state pensions, but tend to define 'contribution' so broadly as to include almost everyone in the society. Consultation evidence suggests that when people are presented with the issues that drive the need for reform, their preferred responses do mirror the changes now being implemented. However, such support requires information and explanation. One of the side effects of the relatively wide consensus that has developed around the current pension reforms is that their implications are being less debated than they would be if they were more controversial. Their eventual effects may, as a result, come as a shock to many of those who will be affected.

In the final chapter, Tony Travers reviews the development and use of funding formulae for distributing resources geographically between different local jurisdictions in the UK. He traces the historical roots of today's systems back to the ideas of the Webbs and others in the early 20th century, forward to the changes in local government finance proposed in the Lyons report early in 2007. He describes the way resources are distributed for health, education, housing, local government, and between regions and territories. Formula-based grant arrangements for achieving this are more emphasised as policy instruments in England than in many other countries, in part as an attempt to compensate for the relatively high levels of personal income inequality in this country, and because demands for public services that achieve equal outcomes have grown. There is an expectation that the outcomes of schools, hospitals and other public services should as far as possible be equal, that 'postcode lotteries' are an indisputable bad thing, and that public services should compensate for the significant differences in individuals' backgrounds that result from wide personal and territorial income variations. This combination has led to a primacy of universal and equal services that has influenced the very shape of British democracy. However, the advent of quasi-markets, discussed in Julian Le Grand's chapter (Chapter Seven), the need to change behaviour in relation to the environment and the need to provide different incentives for providers may mean that the evolution of equalising funding formulae in Britain has already passed its zenith. Resource distribution in the 21st century is already evolving beyond the settled model of the latter years of the 20th, and the delivery of public services will change accordingly.

The ingredients that make policy work

As well as these issues of specific relevance to each area explored, there are more general themes that emerge from all the chapters on what is needed to 'make social policy work'. The first of these is the necessity for policy makers to have clear goals: to know precisely what are the objectives and priorities of government in the area concerned. Chapters Three and Five illustrate some of the problems that arise when there is a confusion of goals, where goals conflict, and where at different times almost everything is a priority.

Second, it is crucial that providers are motivated to deliver high-quality services. That is, providers must be offered the right incentives – and incentives should not be perverse (Chapters Five and Seven).

Third, there needs to be user involvement and understanding. Without these, services are 'for' people but not 'with' people. Since outcomes in services such as education, health or neighbourhood renewal depend critically on the commitment of parents, patients and local residents, this is essential for services to be effective (Chapters Five, Eight and Nine).

Fourth, there has to be long-term public support, or at least acceptance, of the policy concerned and of its cost. There needs to be a long-term commitment to policy from all sides of the political spectrum. Political footballs soon get punctured (Chapter Eleven).

Fifth, they illustrate the importance of innovation, which in turn requires diversity and experiment. The post-war welfare state was an organisational innovation of its time (Chapter Two), but which then ossified due to lack of effective challenge from exit or voice (Chapter Seven).

Sixth, social policy has to be seen in the wider societal context of changes happening in the family and the economy. In particular, as is argued in Chapter Four, social policy is much more likely to be successful if it goes with the grain of these changes and does not try to reverse them.

Finally, the use of targeted selective responses to tackle greatest needs has to be seen simultaneously in the context of wide inequalities in the UK, but also of the possible damaging effects of the incentives and disincentives particular designs of redistributive policies create for individuals and local organisations (Chapters Six, Ten and Twelve).

Serving humanity better

In addition to these cross-cutting points, there is a yet wider consideration that is reflected both in Howard Glennerster's work and in the chapters of this book. The philosopher Richard Rorty puts it thus:

> I think the time has come to drop the terms 'capitalism' and 'socialism' from the political vocabulary of the left. It would be a good idea to stop talking about 'the anticapitalist struggle' and to substitute something banal and antitheoretical – something like 'the struggle against avoidable human misery.' ... I suggest we start talking about greed and selfishness rather than about bourgeois ideology, about starvation wages and lay-offs rather than about the commodification of labor, and about differential per-pupil expenditure on schools and differential access to health care rather than about the division of society into classes. (Rorty, 1995, p 212)

Or, as Howard Glennerster himself has put it (when considering the untimely death of the disciplinary label of 'social administration'):

> If we had worried less about critical theory and more about cleaning people's rubbish we would have served humanity better.... This is not to say that social administrators should run courses in waste disposal, but it does mean that we should devote more thought to understanding the nature of public sector and non-profit organisations. How do we provide appropriate structures to respond to consumers' demands, and ration scarce resources in ways that reflect political

and professional preferences too? How do we maintain the motivation for efficiency in the absence of profit or the test of competition? (Glennerster, 1987, p 84)

In fact, Howard Glennerster has devoted much of his career to answering questions such as these. He was born in Hertfordshire in 1936 and attended first a secondary modern school, then Letchworth Grammar School. From there he went on to Oxford where he obtained a BA in Philosophy, Politics and Economics. After graduating he worked for the Labour Party Research Department in the period leading up to Harold Wilson's victory in 1964, including work on proposals to create what became the Open University.

He joined the London School of Economics and Political Science (LSE) in 1964, first as a Research Officer in the Higher Education Research Unit, working on the financing of education, including the financing of private schools. He began teaching in the Department of Social Administration in 1968 where he remained until he retired, in name only, in 2001 – by then it had been renamed, despite his 'requiem for social administration', the Department of Social Policy. He progressed from Lecturer to Senior Lecturer to Reader then to Professor of Social Administration in 1984. He is now Emeritus Professor of Social Policy, basing his continuing research in the ESRC Centre for Analysis of Social Exclusion at LSE.

His contributions to the Department of Social Policy and LSE in general have been outstanding. For over 30 years, he was the sure foundation of teaching in the Department, setting the highest standards and leading by example. Not every colleague could quite keep up – as one colleague commented, "one was a little daunted on being told he had taken ten of the latest social policy books on holiday with him". He showed to others what a privilege it is to teach at LSE. Some academics seek celebrity. By contrast, Howard Glennerster is exceptionally modest, polite and unfailingly helpful.

He has carried out research on almost all the social services. Above all he has worked on the finances of social services and the state of welfare. He has contributed a phenomenal amount – perhaps more than anyone in the country, if not the world – to our understanding of these systems and their consequences for people's lives. He has written extensively, having published an array of books and academic articles; those published so far are set out in the Appendix. The range of this work is awesome, covering the history of social policy, education, personal social services, community care, the health service, poverty and social security, public finance, budgeting and planning, quasi-markets and the state of welfare.

Outside LSE, he has, at different times, worked with the Fabian Society and the Labour Party, and has advised HM Treasury and the Department of Health. He has been a Visiting Professor at the Universities of California, Berkeley, Chicago and Washington and a Visiting Scholar at the Brookings Institution in Washington DC. In all his work he has had the outstanding support of his wife Ann who has made her own contribution to generations of pupils and LSE students. Both their children, Rachel and Andrew, have gone on to distinguished academic careers.

Howard Glennerster's work has served to improve the lives of millions who have never heard his name – and it continues to do so. There can be no better tribute for a true scholar of social policy. This book attempts to follow along the path he has cleared.

References

Glennerster, H. (1987) 'A requiem for the Social Administration Association', *Journal of Social Policy*, vol 17, pp 83-4.

Rorty, R. (1995) 'The end of Leninism and history as comic frame', in A.M. Melzer, J. Weinberger and M.R. Zinman (eds) *History and the Idea of Progress*, Ithaca, NY: Cornell University Press.

Part One
The aims of social policy

TWO

Principles, Poor Laws and welfare states

Jose Harris

In writing about the history of social policy, 'Poor Law' principles
have often been unfavourably compared to 'welfare state' principles, as
strategies and social philosophies for distributing services and resources
to persons in need. Poor Law provision has often been associated with
policies of concentrating welfare provision on the 'very poor', with
the exercise of discretion, means testing and character discrimination
in determining who should receive public assistance within any given
community, and with the denial of civic privileges and social respect.
Welfare state provision, by contrast, has been seen as universal in
coverage, deliberately detached from assessments of moral character,
and potentially available to all members of a community – regardless of
wealth, class, economic or social position – as a matter of civic status and
citizen right. Although most sharply emphasised in the historiography
of social policy in Britain, a similar narrative of historical evolution
from archaic Poor Laws to progressive welfare states pervades many
accounts of social welfare provision in other parts of Europe, the British
Commonwealth, Japan and the US (Trattner, 1974; Mommsen, 1981;
Baldwin, 1990; Gould, 1993).

Whether the principles underlying these two models have been
accurately identified, however, and whether the historical progression
from the one to the other has typically been one-way, seems increasingly
open to question. The publication of a volume of essays in honour of
Howard Glennerster, whose work has very often addressed both the
positive and negative relationships between earlier forms of welfare
provision and the imperatives of current policy, seems an apposite
moment for reviewing this dichotomy. In this essay, it will be argued
that familiar portrayals of the key characteristics of the two systems
are in certain respects caricatures; that in real historical settings the
two have often coexisted (and continue to coexist) in tandem; and
that each of them may be seen as complementary to certain wider
economic strategies. In particular, I shall suggest that some at least of
the principles often seen as fundamental to 'progressive' social policy

had their primal origins in the archaic roots of the Poor Laws, although often attributed to the rise of 'modern' welfare states.

★★★

The celebration of Howard Glennerster's 70th birthday in October 2006 coincided with the anniversary of a seminal moment in the history of welfare provision in Britain, and indeed of 'welfare state' thinking more generally, that had occurred almost exactly a hundred years before. In the late summer of 1906, the Royal Commission on the Poor Laws, one of the great path-breaking public enquiries of late-imperial Britain, had met to discuss the question of whether free medical treatment from public funding should be made available to the whole working population, or should be confined merely to those who were technically and legally 'destitute' (this term meaning, in the technical vocabulary of that era, not merely 'the poor' but those wholly without resources for sustaining life and health). The Commission's most celebrated member, Beatrice Webb, recorded that in the midst of this discussion, 'it suddenly flashed across my mind that what we had to do was to adopt the *exactly opposite attitude*'. She suggested instead that medical inspection and medical treatment should henceforth be freely available to everyone who needed them, and that they should at the same time be made 'compulsory on *all sick persons*'. Indeed, all forms of illness and disability were to be treated, not just as an 'individual' problem, but as 'a public nuisance to be suppressed in the interests of the whole community' – a principle that over the next four years Mrs Webb went on to apply to a very wide spectrum of social needs, including not just physical health, but employment, education, housing, environmental services, and family breakdown (Webb and Webb, 1929, vol 2, pp 554-630; Mackenzie and Mackenzie, 1984, pp 44-6).[1]

Social policy over the next half-century, in Britain and many other countries in Europe, and throughout the world, was to follow many paths not wholly approved by Beatrice Webb; but nevertheless her moment of visionary inspiration in 1906 conjured up a cluster of ideas and principles that was to become inseparable from the classic model of a welfare state as it was to emerge in Britain and Europe during the 1940s and 1950s, and that still colours much thinking about public provision for social welfare up to the present day. These ideas and principles were that social services should be preventive as well as curative, universally available even to the most well off, funded by taxation or compulsory state insurance[2], and designed to serve needs that were not merely personal and individual but implicitly public and collective – what Beatrice Webb herself had described as 'the interests of the whole community'. Moreover, so far as Britain was concerned, the evolution of such principles was to dominate historical interpretations of wider developments in social and political history for much of the mid and late 20th century. For many decades, liberal, conservative and socialist historians were to differ to some degree in their evaluation of the merits of these principles and about how and why they had come or were coming about. But their narratives largely concurred in identifying as a central theme of recent history an ongoing systemic transition from individualism to collectivism, from selectivity to universalism, and from social provision as a badge of subordination and stigma to social provision as a tangible embodiment of democratic citizen rights. And within these accounts the story of the evolution of social policy for a time largely crowded out the 19th-century 'Whig' tradition of seeing *legal* and *constitutional* progress as the central commanding narrative of British national history. This newer historiography prioritised the advance of 'fair shares for all' and of 'universalist' social services, rather than the advance of personal, economic and political 'liberty', as the characteristic touchstone of British social, ethical and national identity (Titmuss, 1950; Ginsberg, 1959, Bruce, 1961; Gilbert, 1966, esp pp 448-52).[3] Within this mid-20th-century consensus about the centrality of social welfare, it should be remembered that even such a later critic of extended welfarism as F.A. Hayek – together with many others of a similar 'libertarian' outlook – was initially a supporter of some of the key themes of the 1942 Beveridge Report, such as workmen's compensation and family allowances (Moggridge, 1979; Ebenstein, 2001).[4]

From the standpoint of the early 21st century, however, this early- and mid-20th-century consensus appears to be in terminal decline, with both the guiding principles of the welfare state itself and its salience within the wider national culture seeming ever more contested, contradictory and fragmented. Reformers of the era of Beatrice Webb and William Beveridge had widely assumed that it was possible to design a comprehensive, uniform, one-size-fits-all model of public welfare provision that would adequately meet the needs of the whole community (and in Beveridge's eyes such a model seemed potentially to enhance rather than diminish the idea of personal liberty; Beveridge, 1943, pp 97-9). But this optimistic assumption has been progressively eroded by the competing demands and needs of gender, longevity, ethnic diversity, migration, fast-changing labour markets, new technology, massively rising consumer expectations and the continuously exploding plurality of personal choice, moral values and patterns of family life. Since the 1960s, many practices have crept back into British welfare state provision that were long thought to have largely died out with the 1948 abolition of the English and Scottish Poor Laws (including the revival of some approaches that hark back to Poor Law policies of the pre-Victorian era). And over the same period many new practices have come to the fore that members of earlier generations would have assumed were wholly incompatible with social welfare provision in any shape or form. Market forces, professional management, accountancy and 'targets', for example, have come to play a role in both public and private social welfare schemes that would have been inconceivable, not just in the 1950s' and 1960s' heyday of 'welfare state' provision, but in the earlier decades of the 20th century, when – apart from a small handful of door-to-door insurance agents – the 'private sector' in social welfare had meant, not highly professional private agencies, but loans from neighbours, backstreet moneylenders, charities run by unpaid volunteers, and lower-middle and working-class mutual aid and self-help.

How and why did these changes come about, and what light do they throw on the relation of social welfare provision to wider historical movements? I have never entirely subscribed to the belief of my old doctoral supervisor, Professor Richard Titmuss, that the intrinsic moral character of a nation was to be judged by its purveyance of a particular model of public social services. But I do fully share Titmuss's view, which also infuses much of the work of Howard Glennerster, that the unravelling of the ideas, structures and human relationships entailed in the history of such services can give one a very sharp insight into the complexities and inner dynamics of wider historical change. In this very brief essay, I want to sketch out some of the ways in which the history of welfare provision in Britain may be seen partly as shaping but also as heavily determined by certain wider movements in 19th- and 20th-century social, economic and cultural history.

In the light of these reflections, I want to make three general interpretative comments from the vantage point of the early 21st century. The first is to suggest that the five-act drama of 'from Poor Law to Welfare State', launched by reformist historians, policy makers and political commentators of the 1940s and 1950s, was in many respects something of a myth. When I use the term 'myth' I do not mean this in the crude sense of claiming that it never really happened. I mean 'myth' in the sense that all our understanding of contemporary history, even of the highest quality, is 'mythic'. We do our best to make sense of data about events, expectations, criteria and human peculiarities prevailing at the time, and this is a perfectly genuine part of historical understanding and experience. But since expectations are often falsified and criteria can change, it is scarcely surprising that, in social welfare history no less than in any other branch of history, an interpretation and outlook that seems at one time to be a fast-lane into the future may turn out to be merely a temporary diversion or cul-de-sac. And likewise, the opposite has very often been true: small local experiments, frequently overlooked at the time, have turned out to be important forerunners of much larger structural, normative and policy changes. The family support schemes of the St Vincent de Paul society in the 1840s, the late 19th-century trade union social insurance schemes, the overlap between national insurance and public assistance schemes of the 1920s and 1930s (meant at the time as a purely transient expedient) and more recent developments, such as credit union schemes and shared ownership schemes since the 1990s, are just a few striking examples (see, for instance, Webb and Webb, 1897; Gilbert, 1970; Allen, 1982; Balkenhol, 1999; Layet, 2005, pp 1-46).

In the case of the welfare state, I think it can now be seen that many of the policy innovations of the 1940s – changes that appeared at the time as a fundamental and irreversible rejection of earlier policies and practices – were in fact largely predicated on certain conjunctures in British national history peculiar to that period. These included, not just the dramatic story of wartime social solidarity emphasised by Richard Titmuss in *Problems of Social Policy* (1950); but also – and perhaps more importantly – the quite abnormal and historically unusual character of the British national economy, both during and in the immediate aftermath of the Second World War (Tomlinson, 1997; Geiger, 2004; Edgerton, 2006). The peculiarities of wartime and post-war economic experience were, it now seems, in many ways misinterpreted by policy makers and popular commentators of the period, as an irreversible breakthrough into a new kind of collective human history. Social policy was seen as liberated from the falsely 'individualist', 'selectivist', 'moralistic' and 'underclass' perspectives of past history, and viewed instead as an essential component of the much more egalitarian, redistributive and communitarian ethic believed to have been generated by the war. Such assumptions were to some extent reinforced by the ideological assumptions of the Cold War era, and by the belief among many that, in counteracting the holistic promises of Soviet Communism, 'universalist' and 'comprehensive' approaches to social policy could play an important role in asserting a more ethical, democratic and less coercive, socialist alternative.

Second, I should like to suggest that both the welfare state and the supposedly redundant and outdated Poor Laws were systems designed to meet certain widely differing but nevertheless legitimate needs within the wider society; and that some of the praise heaped on the one and blame poured on the other were to some extent a reflection, not of their intrinsic virtues or demerits, but again of the particular economic, political and international circumstances of Britain in the mid-20th century. The model of universal insurance in the late 1940s and 1950s, for example, may perhaps be seen as complementary to the large-scale industrial expansion, full employment, and expectation of lifetime occupation in a single industry characteristic of many male workers of that era; but it seems less adapted to the more fragmented labour markets of the present day, where much more employment is transient and part time, where individuals move in and out of different jobs with far greater frequency than in the past, and where nearly half the labour force consists of women (always a difficult group to fit into the statistical regularities of contributory social insurance).

Third, I want to draw attention to the fact that, both in the discourse of the 1940s and 1950s, and again in that of the early 21st century, some at least of the virtues and strengths often ascribed to the welfare state may more properly be seen as stemming originally from the Poor Laws. And, conversely, some of the limitations and deficiencies often ascribed to poor relief may perhaps be no less inherent in the structures and practices of modern welfare states. This is not to be understood as in any sense a plea for a return to the pre-1940s Poor Laws. It is meant simply as an attempt to place our understanding of welfare policies at different historical turning-points – in the 19th century, the 1900s, the 1940s and at the present-day – in a deeper historical perspective.

★★★

Let us turn first then to the Poor Law, formally repealed in Britain by the National Assistance Act of 1948, as part of the transition to a new more universalist, solidaristic and 'modern' system of social welfare. The catalogue of the former Poor Law's imputed crimes and misdemeanours is too notorious to need recounting in detail. It stands variously accused in the history books of breaking up homes and families; of berating the poor for lack of civic virtue and thrift, while actively depriving them of their civil rights and petty savings; and of discriminating morally between 'deserving' and 'undeserving', while deploying strategies of stigma, shame and near starvation designed to deter clients from applying for relief in the first place. In economic and political terms the Poor Laws have been variously viewed as a peculiarly inefficient form of pre-capitalist communitarian socialism, as the embodiment of an outdated ethic of Victorian competitive individualism and as a form of institutionalised class oppression (Webb and Webb, 1910, 1927, 1929; Humphreys, 1995; Lees, 1998). And in the eyes of the Webbs and their followers, the overriding fault of the Poor Law was that its policies in all spheres were wholly non-constructive. It was legally empowered to deal with such problems as sickness, malnutrition, loss of employment and family breakdown, *only after they had occurred*, (which meant that well-meaning Poor Law officials who spent public money on trying to *prevent* such outcomes were liable to find themselves legally surcharged and professionally disciplined for wrongful public expenditure).[5]

A consequence of all this was that the repeal of the Poor Laws in 1948 took place within a context, not perhaps of national euphoria, but certainly of general satisfaction that a law long deemed to have outlived its usefulness (like the laws against witchcraft) should be repealed. And behind this repeal lay a widespread popular expectation that a system based on deterrence, discretion and moral discrimination, would henceforth be superseded by one based on universal entitlement to benefits as an automatic citizen right. The story of this heroic transition was to be all pervasive in writings on social policy for the next quarter of a century, eloquently mediated by the famous model of citizenship and social rights set out by T.H. Marshall (1950), and it still survives in many history books and social policy textbooks up to the present day. The grandparents and great-aunts of the author of this chapter were immediate and gratified beneficiaries of this change, and there is no intention here to belittle its material, ethical and symbolic significance.

Nevertheless, after more than half a century, there is surely room for a re-evaluation both of the long-term historical character of the English Poor Law in general and of its role in the welfare revolution of 1948 in particular. Despite the understandable acclaim that greeted the reforms of the 1940s, there is I believe much evidence to suggest, first, that in many spheres and periods the Poor Laws had been far less dreaded and dysfunctional than many early 20th-century reformers implied; and, second, that much of their dreadfulness lay, not in the actual substance of the Poor Laws, but in specific instances of often harsh and inefficient delivery and of failure adequately to implement both the letter and the spirit of the law. Studies of early 20th-century Poor Law hospitals, special schools and old people's homes, for example, suggest that many of these institutions were very far removed from the nightmare scenarios familiar from the Poor Law scandal literature of the early- and mid-Victorian age (Brand, 1965; Crowther, 1978, pp 36-55, 1981). Even so unlikely a defender as Sidney Webb had argued in the 1890s (before his marriage to Beatrice) that the Poor Law system was in many respects actually popular with the British working class because it was seen as embodying certain basic popular rights, and was much less regimented and bureaucratic than comparable social welfare schemes provided on the continent (among which he interestingly cited the universalist social insurance schemes of Bismarckian Germany; Webb, 1902, pp 169-70). Evidence submitted to the 1905-09 Royal Commission on the Poor Laws by lower-class witnesses likewise indicated that, among working people, there were many specific grievances about day-to-day Poor Law mismanagement, but very little suggestion that Poor Law services in general were unpopular and unacceptable. On the contrary, much *more* of such services, more generously administered and funded, but with much *sterner* treatment of a small antisocial minority of abusers of the Poor Law, was what was widely favoured, rather than outright abolition or repeal. Moreover, the Commission found many examples of communities where very poor people, particularly women, moved regularly between work in the labour market, domesticity and poor relief as part of the routine pattern of their daily lives.[6] The mass popularity of the means-tested old-age pensions *outside* the Poor Law introduced in 1908 likewise suggested that it was perhaps the *name* and the past *reputation* of the Poor Law, rather than its actual processes of means testing and personal enquiry that had been the major turn-off for many (Thane, 2000).

The 1920s and 1930s undoubtedly brought a wave of much more bitter working-class reaction against poor relief, and particularly against means testing; but this was closely linked to the fact that prolonged depression brought the Poor Law and 'public assistance' into the homes of many highly skilled and unionised working men (including many former soldiers who had fought in the First World War) who had never before thought of themselves as needing public relief (Gilbert, 1970; Deacon, 1976). Mass unemployment, and official attempts to smuggle Poor Law rules and regulations (particularly those relating to eligibility and means tests) into unemployed relief schemes that were in theory outside the Poor Laws, certainly helped to fuel support for Poor Law abolition, for the 'universalist' agenda of reformers like the Webbs, and for the Beveridge report of 1942. But nevertheless, when eventually introduced as part of the 'welfare state' package in 1948, the act that abolished the Poor Law did not magically transfer the beneficiaries of means-tested benefits lock-stock-and-barrel into the new system of universal insurance. On the contrary, the 1948 act continued with a gradualist process of piecemeal reform that had been going on for several decades. It placed ex-Poor Law institutions (the former workhouses and residential homes) under the control of local authorities, while transferring the recipients of means-tested monetary payments (the former means-tested 'outdoor relief') to a newly named National Assistance Board (NAB). This latter body was now financed by central government, not ratepayers, but in other respects retaining powers, regulations and procedures that remained remarkably similar to those operated by the old Poor Law guardians. In discussions of the time, it was clearly envisaged that the NAB was eventually to be merely a residual service, catering only for a tiny handful of severely disabled persons who could not be absorbed into universal insurance, even under a regime of 'full employment'. But, in the meantime, it had also to cope with large numbers of former paupers, women outside the labour market, old people ineligible for the new insurance pensions and others in need of relief and supplementation (including many whose poverty had previously been largely invisible to the wider society). Surveys of the time found some individuals who remained too proud to apply for the NAB's means-tested benefits, even when detached from association with the Poor Law; but among those who *did* claim, such surveys recorded widespread satisfaction with this new means-testing, investigative body, and with the help it gave to poor people in claiming their newly destigmatised 'citizen rights' (Zweig, 1962; Thane, 2000, pp 353-63, 370-1).

***

If I am right in suggesting that Poor Law services, particularly at the start of the 20th century, were often less unpopular and more adaptive and user-friendly than their critics allowed, then whence came the drive for total Poor Law abolition, initiated by the Webbs before the First World War, and implemented by a Labour government in the aftermath of the second? Here we must turn for a moment to the much earlier origins of the Poor Law, and to the fact that throughout its history one of its main objectives had been not simply relief of destitution but the buttressing and stabilisation of national economic policy and economic life. The original Tudor laws had been designed to meet the needs of a mass of small, self-contained, largely agrarian communities, deprived of many of the social and economic support functions of the pre-Reformation church. In this the Poor Laws had been relatively successful over several generations, until faced at the end of the 18th century with the population explosion that accompanied the agricultural and industrial revolutions and the boom-and-bust economy of the Napoleonic wars. Historians continue to debate the motivations behind the much more minimalist, slimline, selective and deterrent relief system that emerged from the reformed Poor Law of 1834; but there can, I think, be little doubt that they were closely linked to what would nowadays be seen as the imperatives of modernisation – namely, the freeing up of investment capital by restraint on public expenditure, pursuit of monetary stability and a desire on the part of economists and politicians to generate a much more mobile, productive and market-responsive workforce than had been common in a traditional agrarian economy (Finer, 1970; Hilton, 1977, pp 23-5, 227, 309; Mandler, 1990). Here again, despite the *social* hardships that these policies inflicted, Poor Law *economic* strategy proved highly effective, with public welfare expenditure in Britain halving between 1830 and 1890, real wages doubling, and the exchange value of the pound remaining absolutely stable right down to 1914. Indeed, there were no greater enthusiasts for the New Poor Law than senior officials in the British Treasury, who throughout the Victorian era and well into the 20th century, saw it not primarily as a system of public relief, but as a major building block of a long-term macroeconomic policy that allowed British consumers to enjoy cheap imports from all parts of the globe.[7] Moreover, the minimalist Poor Law was seen in many quarters as part-and-parcel of the fabric of 'English liberties', whereby rational actors freely chose between work and social dependency (as opposed to the much more directive and coercive welfare strategies pursued in Germany and many parts of the continent; Emminghaus, 1870, pp 54, 460, 573; Webb, 1902, pp 169-70).

The Poor Law was therefore much more than just a system of social administration: it was an important tool of public economic management, functionally linked to the gold standard and free trade. Its purpose was to promote 'general welfare' (as opposed to mere 'social welfare'[8]) not through *high* expenditure on extensive social services, but through *low* expenditure on minimal social services, which it was believed would help ward off inflation and unemployment, stabilise demand and maintain Britain's role at the hub of an international trading economy. Within this theory, it is very striking that the client group for whom the services of the New Poor Law were envisaged was not the bulk of the wage-earning classes (who were deemed able normally to lead independent lives) but what was thought to be a small and dwindling minority of those excluded from the modern labour market, such as orphans, widows, disabled persons, and older people left over from a pre-industrial economy. This minimalist conception of social welfare provision, as something needed only for untypical marginal and residual groups, can be found in Treasury responses to proposals for social policy expansion throughout the late-Victorian and Edwardian age, when many reformers were beginning to press for much more extended welfare strategies for the mainstream working class. It can be discerned in the long sequence of unemployment support schemes of the inter-war era, when what looked initially like comprehensive programmes for working people in general, in the end largely boiled down to relabelled and repackaged programmes of means-tested poor relief (Gilbert, 1970, pp 67-97, 162-75, 178-9; Deacon, 1976, pp 21-66). The same was to be apparent in responses to the Beveridge plan in 1942, when – with the notable exception of J.M. Keynes – Treasury officials were horrified by Beveridge's apparent desire *both* to divert scarce resources away from post-war investment *and* to spread those resources 'universally' throughout the whole community (rather than targeting them, as would have happened in the past, on a relatively small, destitute minority; Harris, 1997, pp 398-404).

Given the Treasury's powerful intellectual attachment to the Poor Law as a tool of political economy, how was it that the mid-20th-century shift towards universalism eventually came about? I have already mentioned the impact of mass unemployment, which brought into the ambit of the Poor Law many highly skilled, organised and enfranchised working men who had never previously thought of themselves as clients of public relief. Another factor was that the Treasury theory of welfare spending for the first time for a hundred years seemed to lose its credibility. The welfare and wage cuts of 1931, together with the earlier return to the gold standard, ought in theory to have revived and reflated the 1930s' British economy, whereas instead large parts of it drifted ever deeper into prolonged unemployment and depression. This opened the way for new approaches to macroeconomic policy, advanced by theorists such as J.M. Keynes, James Meade, Evan Durbin and Alvin Hansen, who argued that expansion of welfare spending could be used, along with borrowing, progressive taxes and exchange-rate flexibility, to enable governments to spend their way out of recession. Almost certainly, however, the most crucial factor in precipitating the shift towards universalism was the structural and economic transformation wrought in Britain by the functional imperatives of the Second World War. Not overnight but certainly by the end of 1940, Britain was forcibly converted from being a primarily international trading nation, with a very large financial services sector for whom a strong currency and multilateral trading relations were overriding goals, and it became instead something resembling an economic autarky, where all that mattered was domestic agricultural, manufacturing and above all military production (Hancock and Gowing, 1953; Edgerton, 2006, pp 145-90). Within this scenario, international trade was confined to essential raw materials, cheap imported consumer goods fell to a discount because there were none, Britain's old declining heavy industries sprang to the forefront of the war economy, and maintenance of the health, efficiency and political acquiescence of industrial producers came to take absolute priority. Public investment, financed by compulsory savings together with top tax rates of between 87% and 98%, largely replaced private investment; while the economic model of J.M. Keynes' *General Theory* (1936), where overseas trade played a fairly minimal role and prevention of domestic unemployment took precedence over a strong currency, came to play a persuasive role in discussions of post-war economic reconstruction. The City of London, normally vociferous out of all proportion to its numbers, fell strangely silent throughout the wartime years. Within all of this, Beveridge's rhetoric of social security, universal services and 'fair shares' for all classes, largely financed by contributory insurance (in itself another form of compulsory saving), came to seem not merely morally irresistible, but as functionally suited to the new industrial economy, promised in wartime visions of post-war planning, full employment and domestic reconstruction.

The impact of this was I think clearly seen in many of the social policies of the post-war Labour government. Although National Insurance pensions and benefits were initially introduced at rather lower rates than the subsistence level recommended by Beveridge, social welfare spending appears to have been far less vulnerable to periodic budgetary panics than in the inter-war era. Post-war currency crises were dealt with by American loans and devaluation rather than by a reversion to the targeting, means testing and benefit cuts traditionally urged by the pre-war 'Treasury point of view' (a lone exception being the famous teeth-and-spectacles crisis of 1949, which led to the resignations of Aneurin Bevan and Harold Wilson). Full employment and universal benefits also helped to maintain domestic demand, which Keynesians portrayed as playing an important part in sustaining post-war economic recovery. Post-war surveys suggested that non-means-tested, as-of-right universal services were widely popular, not least with the middle classes, who found themselves for the first time eligible for benefits and services previously available only to the poor.

Nevertheless, there is always a snake in Eden, or in this case two snakes, both of which were to be peculiarly pertinent to the long-term structures and orientation of British social policy. One of these snakes was the spectre of inflation (so tenaciously kept at bay by Treasury economic management for much of the 19th and earlier 20th centuries). Despite the sterling devaluation of 1949, as post-war life gradually returned to normal, the demand for consumer goods rose, and thus prices rose, and throughout the 1950s the pound continually lost ground against the rival currencies of other re-emergent industrial economies. And as prices *rose*, the real value of pensions and benefits of course *fell*; which brings us to the second snake in Eden, namely that innocent-seeming and innocuous-sounding institution, the National Assistance Board, set up by the Act of 1948 to carry over the management of means-tested benefits for a supposedly dwindling residual minority. By the mid-1950s, many Conservative politicians were of course no less formally committed to the general principle of a 'welfare state' than was Labour; but because Conservative ministers gave a much higher priority than Labour to reviving Britain's international financial sector, the policy increasingly adopted in the late-1950s was that of freezing the real value of universalist *insurance* benefits while increasing the level of selective means-related *supplementary* benefits, payable as a top-up to National Insurance through the agency of the NAB. This supplementation policy, designed, not as in 1948 as a temporary expedient to eke out below-subsistence pensions, but by the late-1950s as a long-term strategy for simultaneously addressing both poverty on the one hand and inflation on the other, seems to mark a seminal shift in thinking about the post-war British welfare state (Lowe, 1993; Glennerster, 2000, pp 65-87). And another such turning point came in 1964, when UK public spending on means-tested benefits exceeded spending on National Insurance benefits for the first time since the Second World War. This was of course the year in which a new Labour government came to power under Harold Wilson (a heroic champion of 'universalism' in the teeth-and-spectacles controversy of 15 years before). But the return of Labour brought no reversal of this selectivist trend which, despite much rhetoric to the contrary, has continued ever since (in marked contrast to the opposite trend of a continuous shift towards universalism in such countries as France, Germany and Luxembourg; Flora, 1983, ch 9, 1987, pp 111, 327, 345, 400-1, 517).

★★★

Anticipations of current trends towards selectivism and supplementation in British welfare spending in the first decade of the 21st century are thus not hard to find in policies that were set in train more than 40 years ago, under a government that was then explicitly committed to the opposite philosophy. As I see it, such trends were an inevitable feature of the gradual post-war reversion of the British economy back to the traditional priority given to financial services, free markets and international trade, at the expense of the powerful emphasis on industrial production, full and continuous employment, and 'physical' as well as fiscal management of the domestic economy that prevailed during and immediately after the Second World War. The gradual re-emergence of the earlier Treasury theory of the Poor Law is not difficult to discern in these trends, both as subtly reasserting itself in the fiscal and monetary policies of the later 1950s and 1960s and as much more explicitly apparent in many socio-fiscal welfare strategies of the present day. The essence of that view was and is that *general welfare*, meaning a greater sum of satisfactions for all, is best promoted by concentrating what we think of as *social welfare* upon select disadvantaged minorities, rather than the much more expensive (and inflationary) alternative of providing universalist benefits and services throughout the whole of society. As a return to the industrial and labour market policies of the 1940s and 1950s is nowhere on the agenda of any 'modern' economy, it seems that social policies whose roots lie in the principles (if not in the actual terminology) of ancient Poor Law structures, are likely to be with us for quite a time to come.

However, I shall leave closer analysis of such developments to other contributors to this volume. I want instead to turn in conclusion to certain aspects of the lost legacy of the Poor Law, which were to some extent distorted and obscured by the powerful anti-Poor Law rhetoric of the earlier 20th century, and which are perhaps of more relevance and interest than is often allowed in thinking about social policy problems of the present day. In making this point I should emphasise again that I am in no sense pressing for a return to the 'Victorian' Poor Law, but simply suggesting that overemphasis on the abuses and shortcomings of Poor Law practice may have obscured some of the Poor Law's strengths and advantages, and may also have blamed it for certain difficulties that are in fact latent in any system of public welfare provision. One of the Poor Law's strengths was that, certainly by the early decades of the 20th century, it was a very much more innovatory and evolutionary system than many of its critics allowed. The Royal Commission of 1905-09 found that some at least of the Poor Law's specialist institutions were providing standards of care (for sick people, disabled children and older people, for example) as good as anything available in the voluntary sector; although of course there were also dire and dreadful exceptions that attracted scandalised media attention, as had happened in the early- and mid-Victorian era and continues to happen with similar institutions in the present day.[9]

A second noteworthy feature of the Poor Law was that by the end of the 19th century its governing structures were potentially highly democratic, with many women and working-class people beginning to be elected as Poor Law guardians (Hollis, 1987). Indeed, it was one of the peculiar ironies of social welfare history that popularly elected boards of guardians were to be finally abolished in 1929, just at the very moment when women as well as working men had fully acquired the vote. A third feature worthy of comment is the identity of the Poor Law's client groups. The Poor Law was undoubtedly bad at catering for the needs of normally employed working-class adult males, the majority of whom were very much better provided for by trade union and friendly society social insurance schemes, by the 1911 National Insurance Act, and after 1948 by Beveridgean universal insurance. But, except during the economic crises of the 1920s and 1930s, adult males were never more than a small minority of those who typically applied for various kinds of poor relief. The vast majority of adult paupers were women – widows, deserted wives, lone mothers, women who were simply old, alone and poor. All these categories were only tenuously included in the universalist revolution of the 1940s, and continue to account for the largest client group of post-Poor Law selective social services up to the present day, suggesting perhaps that (not as a matter of conscious discrimination but as a material fact of economic history) National Insurance and universalism are inherently more difficult to apply to the needs and life cycles of women than men (Pedersen, 1993).

A fourth point worth commenting on, and one that has often been the subject of violent distortion, is the question of moral attitudes towards recipients of poor relief. Thousands of books, articles, student essays and exam scripts have been written over the years on pre-welfare-state attitudes to the undeserving poor, and undoubtedly then as now there were many members of the public who believed that recipients of public welfare were by definition mostly idlers and scroungers. What is false, however, is the oft-repeated claim that the Poor Law itself was the main normative and institutional channel for these views and that it practised systematic legal discrimination against the 'undeserving' poor, in the face of public opinion. In fact, in terms of the strict letter of the law almost the exact opposite was true. The New Poor Law had specifically prohibited refusal of relief on grounds of bad behaviour or bad character; and relieving officers, workhouse officers and guardians who denied relief on such grounds were legally liable to prosecution and even imprisonment (Harris, 2002, pp 424-7). Cases of stigmatising and bullying treatment by officials undoubtedly occurred, but evidence to the Edwardian Royal Commission on the Poor Laws suggested that, certainly by the end of the 19th century, it was by no means typical of Poor Law institutional management. On the contrary, the testimony of witnesses to the Commission seemed to indicate that active demand for discrimination against the 'undeserving' came overwhelmingly not from Poor Law administrators but from the poor themselves, who deeply resented both the use of public money on, and their own taint by association with, a small minority of disorderly and 'undeserving' paupers who were seen as making life a misery for other Poor Law clients. Poor Law officials of course shared many of the prejudices of the communities they worked in, but often their attitude appears to have been rather less judgemental than that of many of their clients. Such evidence suggests that this was yet another example of the Poor Law being blamed for problems, not generically peculiar to itself, that were liable to occur within any large-scale system of public relief where resources and privacy were limited (Harris, 2002, pp 431-2).[10]

Finally, I should like to comment on the paradoxical issue of the Poor Law and welfare rights. Once again, the narratives of the 1940s highlighted the transition from a Poor Law regime rooted in selectivity and discretion to one broadly based on universal entitlement and social rights. In this it appeared at the time that the balance of moral righteousness lay heavily on the side of the new institutions of the welfare state; but, seen in the *longue durée*, this judgement is surely open to some degree of revision and qualification. For example, the new rights introduced in the 1940s were with few exceptions largely contractual ones, in that citizens were entitled to unemployment benefit, sick pay, and an old-age pension, not simply *qua* citizens, but if they had paid a certain minimum of insurance contributions into a common fund. The major exception to this rule was the introduction of universal entitlement to healthcare under the new National Health Service; but this exception reinforces my point, because it was rooted, not in National Insurance contributions, but in the universal extension of a right to healthcare long latent within the Poor Law (which since the 1880s had seen numerous piecemeal extensions of Poor Law health provision to people who fell outside the legal category of 'paupers').[11] In fact, despite widespread misconceptions to the contrary, absolute, unconditional rights to assistance from the community in times of need stemmed historically from the ancient legal structures of the English and Scottish Poor Laws (and indeed the same was true of various kinds of Poor Law regime throughout Western Europe; Lamond, 1870; Eastwick, 1873; Horne, 1990, pp 130-1). Attempts to obscure or deny that poor relief was a right had been made by ratepayers, local bigwigs, economisers and public officials throughout the Poor Law's history, but the constant reiteration of such denials did not mean that they were true. Here I refer again to the largely neglected but wonderfully informative volumes of evidence to the Edwardian Royal Commission on the Poor Laws, which found that entitlement to public relief in case of need had been a common law right in England and Scotland since the 14th century (long before the statutory formalisation of the Poor Law under the Tudors). Such rights were in theory enforceable only against one's parish of settlement; but over the centuries common law decisions, formally embodied in the Poor Law Amendment Act of 1834, had given needy persons a right to poor relief throughout the realm in cases of what was known as 'sudden and urgent necessity'. Moreover, such emergency rights were in theory available not just to British subjects, but also to migrants and travellers of whatever origin who found themselves suddenly destitute. Just how far such rights were realisable in practice, in what for centuries remained a highly localised, heavily agrarian, deeply patriarchal and semi-literate society, where conceptions of 'need' were necessarily very Spartan and minimal, is very much open to question. But nevertheless such rights existed in principle both in Poor Law legislation and in the common law (Emminghaus, 1870, pp 53-4, 64, 70, 460-1).[12] If there is such a thing today as a 'human right' to social welfare, then its origins in many countries may be found to lie not in the welfare-state legislation of the 1940s but in the very much more archaic and communitarian roots of the 'law relating to the poor' (Emminghaus, 1870; Graham, 1905; Parry, 1914) [13]

Notes

[1] Interestingly, the dichotomy of selective versus universal provision identified by Beatrice Webb in 1906 appears to have applied at that time only to different gradations of the 'employed' classes. It was only gradually that social theorists, the Webbs among them, came to see 'universalism' as literally applying to the whole community, including not just the 'non-pauper' working class, but the middle and upper classes.

[2] Although not by insurance in the case of the Webbs, who always favoured universalist services funded by direct taxation.

[3] The Ginsberg volume was explicitly designed to demonstrate the shift towards 'social' concerns in national culture, away from the 'constitutional' focus of earlier authorities like A.V. Dicey. For a critique of such trends, see *Unservile State Papers* (Liberal Publications department, 1951-64).

[4] For Hayek's wider views on social welfare policy, see Steele (1993), pp 55, 60-2, 64-9.

[5] Local Government Board, *Poor Laws in Foreign Countries* (P.P. 1875, LX), pp 31-2, 283, 326; Harris, 2002, pp 424-5.

[6] Royal Commission on the Poor Laws, *Minutes of Evidence* (P.P. 1909, XLI) QQ. 46522, 46915; and *Reports on Industrial and Sanitary Conditions* (P.P. 1909, XL).

[7] Monumentally documented in the papers of Sir George Hamilton and Sir Edward Hamilton (National Archives, T168 files).

[8] On the distinction, see Poulett Scrope (1833).

[9] Royal Commission on the Poor Laws, *Majority Report* (P.P. 1909, XXXVII), pp 2647-7; *Minutes of Evidence* (P.P. 1909, vol XL) QQ. 23303, 23327; (P.P. 1910, XLVII), QQ. 76546, 76153, 76728.

[10] Local Government Board, *Poor Laws in Foreign Countries*, pp 33-4; Royal Commission on the Poor Laws (P.P. 1909, XLI), Appendix, CXXV).

[11] For instance, the removal of disfranchisement from clients who claimed only medical relief, the opening of 'pay beds' for better-off clients in Poor Law hospitals and the tendency for Poor Law hospitals to act as general civic infirmaries, all pointed in the same direction.

[12] Local Government Board, *Poor Laws in Foreign Countries* (P.P. 1875, LXV), p 21; Royal Commission on the Poor Laws (P.P. 1909, XXXIX), QQ.74, 939-1.

[13] The great international comparative work on the historic roots of the principles and practices of the Poor Laws throughout Europe, remains Emminghaus's classic study of 1870. On the evolution of the underlying principles of poor relief from a legal perspective, within the wider context of English and Scottish law, see Graham (1905) and Parry (1914).

References

Allen, P. (1982) *Shared Ownership: A stepping Stone to Home Ownership*, London: Department of the Environment.

Baldwin, P. (1990) *The Politics of Social Solidarity: Class Bases of the European Welfare State 1875-1975*, Cambridge: Cambridge University Press.

Balkenhol, B. (ed) (1999) *Credit Unions and the Poverty Challenge: Extending Outreach, Enhancing Sustainability*, Geneva: International Labour Office.

Beveridge, W.H. (1942) *Social Insurance and Allied Services* (the Beveridge Report), Cmd 6404, London: HMSO.

Beveridge, W.H. (1943) 'Freedom from idleness', in G.D.H. Cole (ed) *Plan for Britain: A Collection of Essays Prepared for the Fabian Society*, London: Labour Book Service.

Brand, J.L. (1965) *Doctors and the State: The British Medical Profession and Government Action in Public Health, 1870-1912*, Baltimore, MD: Johns Hopkins Press.

Bruce, M. (1961) *Coming of the Welfare State*, London: Batsford.

Crowther, M.A. (1978) 'The last years of the workhouse', in P. Thane (ed) *The Origins of British Social Policy*, London: Croom Helm.

Crowther, M.A. (1981) *The Workhouse System, 1834-1929: The History of an English Social Institution 1824-1929*, London: Batsford Academic and Educational.

Deacon, A. (1976) *In Search of the Scrounger: The Administration of Unemployment Insurance in Britain 1920-31*, London: Bell.

Eastwick, E.B. (1873) *Poor Relief in Different Parts of Europe*, London: E. Stanford.

Ebenstein, A. (2001) *Friedrich Hayek: A Biography*, New York, NY: Palgrave.

Edgerton, D. (2006) *Warfare State: Britain, 1920-1970*, Cambridge: Cambridge University Press.

Emminghaus, A. (1870) *Das Armenwesen und die Armengesetzgebung in Europäischen Staate*, Berlin: Herbig.

Finer, S.E. (1970) *Life and Times of Sir Edwin Chadwick*, New York, NY: Methuen.

Flora, P. (1983) *State, Economy and Society in Western Europe 1815-1975*, vol 1, Frankfurt: Campus Verlag.

Flora, P. (1987) *Growth to Limits – The Western-European Welfare States since World War II*, Berlin/New York, NY: W. de Gruyter.

Geiger, T. (2004) *Britain and the Economic Problem of the Cold War: The Political Economy and the Economic Impact of the British Defence Effort, 1945-1955*, Aldershot: Ashgate.

Gilbert, B.B. (1966) *The Evolution of National Insurance in Great Britain: The Origins of the Welfare State*, London: Michael Joseph.

Gilbert, B.B. (1970) *British Social Policy 1914-39*, London: Batsford.

Ginsberg, M. (ed) (1959) *Law and Opinion in England in the Twentieth Century*, London: Stevens.

Glennerster, H. (2000) *British Social Policy since 1945* (2nd edition), Oxford: Blackwells.

Gould, A. (1993) *Capitalist Welfare Systems: A Comparison of Japan, Britain and Sweden*, London: Longman.

Graham, J.E. (1905) *The Law Relating to the Poor and Parish Councils*, Edinburgh: William Greene & Sons.

Hancock, W.K. and Gowing, M.M. (1949) *British War Economy*, London: HMSO.

Harris, J. (1997) *William Beveridge: A Biography* (2nd edition), Oxford: Clarendon Press.

Harris, J. (2002) 'From Poor Law to welfare state? A European perspective', in D. Winch and P.K. O'Brien (eds) *The Political Economy of British Historical Experience 1688-1914*, Oxford: Oxford University Press.

Hilton, B. (1977) *Corn, Cash and Commerce: The Economic Policies of the Tory Governments 1815-1830*, Oxford: Oxford University Press.

Hollis, P. (1987) *Ladies Elect: Women in English Local Government, 1865-1914*, Oxford: Oxford University Press.

Horne, T.A. (1990) *Property Rights and Poverty: Political Argument in Britain, 1605-1834*, Chapel Hill, NC: University of North Carolina Press.

Humphreys, R. (1995) *Sin, Organized Charity and the Poor Law in Victorian England*, Basingstoke: Macmillan.

Keynes, J.M. (1936) *General Theory of Employment, Interest and Money*, London: Macmillan.

Lamond, R. (1870) *The Scottish Poor Laws: An Examination of their Policy, History and Practical Action*, Edinburgh: Edmonston and Douglas.

Layet, L. (2005) 'The English branch of the Société de St Vincent de Paul and its influence on the principles of charity organisation', Unpublished M.Stud thesis, Oxford: University of Oxford.

Lees, L. (1998) *The Solidarities of Strangers: The English Poor Laws and the People, 1700-1948*, Cambridge: Cambridge University Press.

Lowe, R. (1993) *The Welfare State in Britain since 1945* (1st edition), Basingstoke: Macmillan.

Mackenzie, N. and Mackenzie, J. (eds) (1984) *The Diary of Beatrice Webb*, vol 3, 1906-24, London: Virago/LSE, pp 44-6.

Mandler, P. (1990) 'Tories and paupers: Christian political economy and the making of the new Poor Law', *Historical Journal*, vol 33, no 1, pp 81-103.

Marshall, T.H. (1950) *Citizenship and Social Class: And Other Essays*, Cambridge: Cambridge University Press.

Moggridge, D. (ed) (1979) *The Collected Writings of John Maynard Keynes*, vol 29, London: Macmillan.

Mommsen, W.J. (ed) (1981) *The Emergence of the Welfare State in Britain and Germany*, London: Croom Helm on behalf of the German Historical Institute.

Parry, E.A. (1914) *The Law and the Poor*, London: Smith, Elder & Co.

Pedersen, S. (1993) *Family, Dependence and the Origins of the Welfare State; Britain and France, 1914-45*, Cambridge: Cambridge University Press.

Poulett Scrope, G. (1833) *Principles of Political Economy: Deduced from the Natural Laws of Social Welfare, and Applied to the Present State of Britain*, London: Longman.

Steele, G.R. (1993) *The Economics of Friedrich Hayek*, New York, NY: St. Martin's Press.

Thane, P. (2000) *Old Age in English History: Past Experiences, Present Issues*, Oxford: Oxford University Press.

Titmuss, R. (1950) *Problems of Social Policy*, London: HMSO.

Tomlinson, J. (1997) *Democratic Socialism and Economic Policy: The Attlee years, 1945-51*, Cambridge: Cambridge University Press.

Trattner, W.I. (1974) *From Poor Law to Welfare State: A History of Social Welfare in America*, London: Macmillan.

Webb, S. (1902) 'The reform of the Poor Law', in S. Webb and B. Webb (eds) *Problems of Modern Industry*, London/New York, NY: Longmans, Green and Co, pp 169-70.

Webb, S. and Webb, B. (1897, 1902) *Industrial Democracy*, London/New York, NY: Longman, Green & Co.

Webb, S. and Webb, B. (1927, 1929) *English Poor Law History*, Part II, vols 1 and 2, London/New York, NY: Longman, Green & Co.

Zweig, F. (1962) *The British Worker*, London: Harmondsworth.

THREE

Welfare: what for?

Tania Burchardt[1]

Introduction

As the title of this volume suggests, much of Howard Glennerster's work has been concerned with exploring the most effective means to achieve the goals of social policy. Glennerster has also made a significant contribution to elucidating the intentions of both historical and contemporary policy makers: their stated objectives and the underlying principles for the programmes of reform they have proposed or implemented. This task of uncovering the range of beliefs among policy makers about the purpose of social policy in general, and the welfare state in particular, is important for making social policy work, I shall argue below, because without clarity over guiding principles, the debate between different normative positions is obscured, and the risk of inadvertently developing contradictory policies is increased.

I begin in the next section by considering whether searching for underlying normative principles in social policy makes sense. I argue that even if different conceptions of what is right and good are necessarily traded against each other and against other values and objectives in the messy business of practical politics, it is nevertheless worthwhile to analyse the theories of social justice that contribute to the overall mix of motivations. Social policy has an important role to play in uncovering and exploring these, as Glennerster's work has demonstrated. An example is given in the following section, examining the rhetoric and practice of the current government and finding evidence of a lack of coherence in values and conceptions of social justice. The following section offers a framework for analysing the different conceptions that may be in play. But is it sufficient to lay out the options and to identify which are applied in different areas of policy? The next section argues that the role of social scientists need not be limited to this descriptive task but can and should go further, to tease out the implications in practice of adopting different normative positions, and to differentiate between those which help to resolve policy dilemmas and those which simply throw up new ones. Particular attention is given to one conception, the capability approach, which I argue has a number of advantages over the others considered. The concluding section returns to the question of whether this is all idealistic nonsense, irrelevant to the real worlds of welfare and policy making.

The search for unifying principles

There are at least three distinct reasons for asserting that the search for an underlying principle of social justice in policy rhetoric or practice is futile: different principles are appropriate for different areas of welfare policy, the values of equity and fairness need to be balanced against considerations of stability and economic efficiency; and in any case politics is a power struggle between competing interests, not a Socratic walk in the park. Each will be considered in turn.

The first, then, is that the reason why we apparently observe different objectives in different areas of welfare policy, is that different distributional principles properly apply to different domains. This view was propounded by Walzer (1983) and has been developed by Miller and Walzer (1995) in the UK context. Walzer argues that the nature of the goods in question – income and employment, or the experience of childhood – determines whether a principle of equality of outcome, equality of opportunity or some other principle should be applied. This seems reasonable, if incomplete: we need to know what it is about the nature of the goods that makes a particular distribution appropriate. This is likely to be derived from some overarching principle or theory, for example about the final objective of welfare. So a meta-principle is still required. In Walzer's case, this is supplied by the communitarian idea that a society is just if life is lived according to the 'shared understandings' of its members – a kind of procedural justice.

The second reason one might have for believing the search for a unifying principle of social justice in practical social policy is mistaken is that considerations of social justice are only one of many concerns that contribute to the formation of policy. Alongside the quest for social justice – granting for the sake of argument that such a quest exists – other commonly cited goals include social stability ('security') and economic efficiency or growth. Stedman-Jones (2004) argues that fear on the part of the ruling class of revolution or social upheaval has been a far more powerful motivation for establishing and expanding welfare systems than any more noble ideals.

Theories of justice handle these other legitimate objectives of government in two ways. One is to incorporate them directly into the theoretical framework. Sen (1999) argues that economic efficiency must itself be defined in terms of promoting human development – the expansion of positive freedom – rather than in terms of increasing Gross Domestic Product (GDP). Economic efficiency is a means to an end rather than an end in itself, and if a strategy of increasing GDP is not contributing optimally to that end, whatever it may be, increasing GDP is not efficient. Rawls (1971) acknowledges a potential trade-off between equity and efficiency but combines them into a single principle of justice: according to the difference principle, the demands of productivity trump equality in the distribution of primary goods, provided the expansion in the economy thereby created is to the benefit of the least well-off group in society. Similarly, the central preoccupation of Rawls' second major book, *Political Liberalism* (1993), is how an 'overlapping consensus' between different ideological perspectives on social and economic institutions can be generated in order to guarantee social stability.

An alternative response is to acknowledge that the value of justice will have to be traded off against other values. Such an acknowledgement does not invalidate analysis of social justice principles and outcomes in their own right, however. On the contrary, if social justice considerations are to be traded off against other considerations, it is all the more important to be clear exactly what the requirements of social justice constitute.

Finally, one might object that the search for a unifying principle of social justice in real-world social policy is mistaken because the role of principles of all kinds – ethical, economic and social – is secondary in the lives of policy makers to the struggle for power and influence, without which they are unable to enact any policies at all. If they use the language of social justice, as the examples in the following section suggest leaders across the political spectrum are prone to do, it is only as a rhetorical device to garner support. Self-interest is the underlying motivation. There is undoubtedly a grain – or more – of truth in this observation. Indeed the difficulty of separating self-interested motives from considerations of justice is the reason Rawls imposes a 'veil of ignorance' on participants in his thought experiment, designed to elicit our moral intuitions about social justice. Only when people are denied knowledge of their own particular role and position in society, their strengths, weaknesses and personal goals, can we be confident that they will think of each and every person as having equal moral weight.[2] But the fact that politicians, and voters for that matter, find it difficult in the real world to separate questions of social justice from self-interest, does not imply that there is nothing to be gained from clarifying what account of social justice is being thrown into the mix.

If the rhetoric of social justice is appealing, it is presumably because it does resonate with some of our deeply held intuitions about fairness, intermingled as these are with other more pragmatic and self-regarding considerations.

New Labour and social justice

If there is, then, a normative component to social policy, what role should social science play? At the very least, academic enquiry can help to progress the debate by uncovering and exploring what values and objectives are being promoted. Glennerster has analysed the motivations and explicit or implicit values of Beveridge (Hills et al, 1994); the series of administrations between 1945 and the present (Glennerster, 2000, 2007); the new Conservative agenda of late 1980s (Glennerster et al, 1991); funding formulae in health, education and housing (Glennerster et al, 2000); and, most recently, in the tensions between the principles applied by the National Institute for Health and Clinical Excellence (NICE) in determining healthcare priorities and those applied at other levels of the system (Glennerster, 2006). In all of these cases, Glennerster has been concerned to identify the ends of policy as well as means.

This is an important task because in its absence, the debate between different normative positions is obscured. The Labour Party put the language of social justice at the forefront of its social policy while still in opposition with the Commission on Social Justice under John Smith, which reported just after his death in 1994. Although rather few of the Commission's specific proposals were carried through into government (Pearce and Paxton, 2005), the rhetoric certainly was, and it has survived the vicissitudes of 10 years in power. This very fact may be taken to indicate the elasticity of the term 'social justice' rather than as evidence of an enduring philosophy.

The latest incarnation of the unit charged with tackling social exclusion, the Social Exclusion Task Force (SETF), opened its first policy document with the statement: 'We live in a society that aspires to be fair and just' (SETF, 2006, p 9), which corresponds quite closely to the view of the Commission on Social Justice that 'The values of social justice are for us essential' (Commission on Social Justice, 1994, p 1), but the proposals that follow each statement could hardly have been more different. While the Commission advocated an 'Investors' Britain', with enhanced lifelong learning, increased labour demand, redistribution and hypothecated taxation to prevent poverty among young and old, the SETF's concern is with 'high-harm, high-cost' individuals and the damage they do to the rest of society. This has more in common with the Hobbesian conception of the state as necessary to keep in check the vicious tendencies of those with nothing to lose, than it has to do with the liberal egalitarianism that informed the original Commission.

On the other hand, the Commission's perspective may find a champion in Prime Minister Gordon Brown. In a speech to the Fabian Society in 2006, he argued that 'Britishness' resided in our shared values, which he identified as liberty, responsibility and fairness. So far this could equally well have been a speech by Tony Blair, but in the Chancellor's explanation of the nature of fairness as 'evolving into the exciting idea of empowering citizens to control their own lives', and 'an empowering equality of opportunity for all', he seems to be emphasising the idea of substantive or positive freedom associated with Marshall's fully fledged citizenship, rather than the narrower version espoused by the SETF.[3]

Given this breadth of interpretation it should come as no surprise that the Conservatives have also found it within themselves to embrace social justice as a goal. Iain Duncan Smith established a Centre for Social Justice on his departure from the leadership, and the Party's statement of its aims and values launched by David Cameron lists as its second aim: 'To fight social injustice and help the most disadvantaged by building a strong society' (The Conservative Party, 2006, p 5). They have clearly come a long way since Margaret Thatcher's observation that there is no such thing as society.[4] It seems as if social justice has become less controversial even than motherhood and apple pie (both of which have been the subject of public debate in recent years).

Any position across the political spectrum can adopt the language of social justice, but of course the policies that follow are entirely different. It is only by scratching beneath the surface of the rhetoric to uncover the underlying values that the differences between them become apparent.

Furthermore, without clarity over the fundamental objectives of welfare, the risk that contradictory policies are developed within a single administration is increased. Hills and Stewart (2005) characterise the overall approach to social security and fiscal welfare since 1997 as one of progressive universalism, that is, retaining a broad base of entitlement but ensuring that additional resources go to the worst off. The expansion of tax credits, particularly for parents who work, is the clearest example. The Child Trust Fund (universal for every child, but more for those at the bottom) is another. The progressive universalist strategy could be characterised as an application of Rawls' maxim in principle: ensuring that the standard of living of the least well-off group or groups in society is as high as possible.[5] The universalist element is intended to ensure that those on 'middle incomes' perceive some benefit from the policy, which in turn enhances their willingness to pay higher taxes, thus permitting the more progressive elements of the programme, at least in theory.

In other areas of policy, however, a stronger version of substantive equality seems to be in operation. The reorganisation of services for children, joining together aspects of social services, youth justice, health, education, careers advice, and sport and leisure, has as its aim: 'for every child, whatever their background or their circumstances, to have the support they need to: Be healthy, Stay safe, Enjoy and achieve, Make a positive contribution, and Achieve economic well-being' (*Every Child Matters*, 2006). This seems closer in inspiration to the capability approach developed by Amartya Sen, with its focus on valued 'beings and doings', and the endeavour to promote the well-being of all children, not just those who are worst off.

One of the drawbacks for the government of the absence of a detailed, explicit, normative framework for welfare policy is that policies drawing on different underlying conceptions can be in tension with each other. So, for example, the tax credit regime, which I have characterised as Rawlsian in origin, entails encouraging parents of young children to take paid employment, while the balance of research evidence now suggests that the expansion of children's capabilities, such as those listed by *Every Child Matters*, is in most cases best achieved by parental or one-to-one care up to the age of at least two (Waldfogel, 2006). Although the government has stopped short of making jobseeking compulsory for lone parents of children under five, the financial incentives of child and childcare tax credits are heavily stacked in favour of paid work. Indeed it is economically rational for two lone parents to swap children, thereby each receiving tax credits and a childcare subsidy, rather than to look after their own children, a situation that is clearly not designed with support for children's ability to 'enjoy and achieve' in mind.

Dimensions of social justice

If social justice is, then, an independent motivation for social policy, albeit often confused and mixed with other values and a dose of self-interest, how are we to analyse the social justice content of different social policies? This section outlines a framework for analysis and offers some illustrations of the way in which different versions of social justice could, or do, influence particular policies.

The first important distinction is between *distributional* concerns and concerns about *process* (see Figure 3.1). Both usually enter into a theory of social justice but different theorists accord them different priority. Libertarians, represented for example by Nozick (1974), argue that any outcome that is the result of a process that respects individuals' liberties is just. Assuming the initial allocation is fair, and provided all subsequent exchanges are entered into voluntarily and do not infringe anyone's civil and political liberties, the resulting distribution, however unequal, is also fair. Moreover, state interference with this distribution, for example through taxation, is unjust because it is tantamount to forced labour: for a percentage of their working time, the worker is required to work for no financial gain to themselves. This is one of those cases where the principles derived from an idealised scenario give rather little guidance as to the correct policy in the world as we in fact find it, since neither the premise about the initial distribution (at whatever point in historical time one would wish to choose), nor the premise about the process by which we have got from there to here, in fact holds. The balance of global wealth and power today are the result, at least in part, of a history of violence and slavery.

Concerns about process are not limited to libertarians, however. Feminist philosophers have emphasised the value of equality of respect (Fraser and Honneth, 2003): the manner in which the cake is offered rather than the size of each slice. This leads to some interesting implications for both the process of policy making and its content. Policy makers have already tumbled to the fact that involving the

Figure 3.1: Theories of social justice

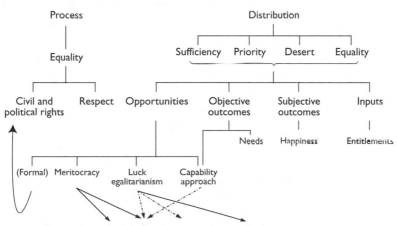

Opportunity = talents + effort + resources + conversion factors

'beneficiaries' of a policy, say area regeneration, in devising the strategy is likely to make it a more successful programme. Emphasising equality of respect adds an ethical dimension to this pragmatic justification for promoting participation in policy formation, ensuring that people are 'doing' rather than 'done to'. In terms of the content of policy, Wolff (1998, pp 121-2) argues, for example, that means testing is inconsistent with equality of respect, due to 'the disrespect communicated by subjecting the poor to a level of scrutiny and control not experienced by the better off'. He concludes that unconditional benefits may be preferred to means-tested benefits even where the price to be paid is a somewhat greater degree of distributional inequality.

Turning to questions of distribution, there are broadly speaking four principles: sufficiency, priority, desert and equality (see Arneson, 2002). 'Meeting basic needs' is one application of a principle of sufficiency, for example: 'Social policy is concerned with the way societies meet the basic needs of their populations over an individual's life cycle' (Glennerster, 2003, p 1), and, 'How are we to ensure that all citizens are able to have access to a standard of life compatible with their identity as fellow human beings and citizens of the same nation?' (Glennerster et al, 2000, p 9). It is clear that in Glennerster's view, social policy should aim to ensure that everyone's basic needs are fulfilled, including at least a minimum standard of material well-being. Basic needs have of course been defined in a number of different ways (for example, Maslow, 1943; Doyal and Gough, 1991). Glennerster's own formulation draws on T.H. Marshall's (1950) account of the nature of the relationship between welfare and citizenship. Marshall argued that the basic requirements of citizenship extended beyond the legal, civil and political rights established over the centuries from the Magna Carta onwards, to the social and economic security envisaged – or, as Marshall rather optimistically thought, implemented – by the founding fathers of the modern welfare state. Moreover, Marshall saw these entitlements as jointly necessary to establish full and equal citizenship. To be able to benefit from personal liberty and participation in a democracy, one also needs to be free from Beveridge's five giants – Want, Disease, Ignorance, Squalor and Idleness. As Glennerster (1991) puts it, 'These negative and positive freedoms were ... interdependent. One was useless without the others' (p 47).

The distributional principle of 'priority' refers to giving extra weight to the position of a particular group, usually the worst off, as in Rawls''maximin' principle. As the condition of the worst-off group is improved, another group may fall into that relative position, thus becoming the new priority. This is arguably the case with the changes in the income distribution since 1997: as extra resources have been directed to pensioners and families with children (especially lone parents), these groups have moved up from the bottom of the income distribution, leaving single or couple households without children to occupy that position (Glennerster et al, 2004).

A principle of 'desert' requires that goods are distributed according to how well or badly individuals have performed according to some measure of merit, for example the extent to which they have fulfilled their social obligations. The current government's mantra, 'rewarding hard-working families', seems to reflect this conception. The definition of 'hard-working' is left vague, no doubt intentionally. Since most people would like to think of themselves as hard-working, everyone can understand the policy as especially designed to benefit them, with a warm sense of satisfaction that the lazy, undeserving 'others' are rightfully put in their place. In the actual policies implemented, of course, such as tax credits, 'work' is equated with paid work, and effort is measured in hours rather than in sweat and tears.

Finally, the principle of equality, self-evidently, concerns itself with the shape of the overall distribution. It is important to note that the other three principles – sufficiency, priority and desert – each require equality of some kind   equality of treatment with respect to whatever characteristic that particular conception has identified as significant – but none of them are concerned with overall equality and may be consistent with a wide range of distributions of income and other public and private goods.

Whichever principle of distribution is applied, the consequences depend greatly on what is regarded as the relevant 'space' for distributive justice: inputs, outcomes, or opportunities of some kind (3rd row of Figure 3.1). Atkinson (1989) has observed that concerns about poverty can be motivated by the belief that individuals have an entitlement to a minimum level of resources. In this case it does not matter what they can or do in fact do with their income, what matters is that a minimum input is guaranteed. In practice this seems to be the basis for much social security provision, although it is an open question whether this is because income is a useful proxy for a range of desirable outcomes and opportunities, or whether it is because minimum entitlement is valued for its own sake.

The proposal that social policy should concern itself with subjective outcomes, specifically happiness, has regained prominence recently (Layard, 2005), and the kingdom of Bhutan has gone as far as supplementing traditional measures of GDP with an index of Gross Domestic Happiness in its official statistics. The idea dates back to

Bentham's objective of securing the 'greatest happiness of the greatest number' and has resurfaced as a result of dissatisfaction with narrowly materialistic conceptions of well-being. Unfortunately both the original utilitarian philosophy and its modern-day descendants run the risk of producing some fairly unpalatable distributional consequences and policy implications (Burchardt, 2006). If it turns out that some people are better at translating resources into happiness, then the maximising rule requires that a larger share of resources should be directed towards them, at the expense of those whose happiness is resource-intensive (for example because their physical impairment means that they require assistance to participate in leisure activities).[6]

Objective outcomes can be characterised as need fulfilment, as in Doyal and Gough's (1991) framework, or as achieving a certain level of functioning, in Sen's (1987) terminology. Both needs and functionings potentially cover a broad range of a person's life, so further specification is necessary before a framework of this kind can be operationalised and a number of lists have been proposed (Alkire, 2002). The belief that social policy should facilitate a minimum level of functioning in important areas of life seems to underpin the provision of social services, at least in their traditional form. Social care assessments consider whether the client needs help to perform a number of specific tasks – eating, dressing and so on – and then puts together a package of services to enable them to do so. In recent years, direct payments to clients with which to purchase their own support have increasingly replaced provision of services by local authorities (see Chapter Eight). This perhaps represents a move away from a functionings-based policy, towards something less prescriptive of the outcomes that are desirable, and closer to a goal of positive freedom or substantive opportunity.

This leads us to the final category of responses to the question, 'distribution of what?', namely, opportunities. Equality of opportunity conceptions can be placed on a spectrum from weak to strong, with the positions determined by which factors are assumed to be legitimate sources of variation in outcome and which factors are not. Before considering these, we can dispose of a purely formal version of equal opportunities, which is better thought of as a process-based conception of justice. This is the kind usually espoused by organisations in their recruitment procedures, for example. It simply means treating everyone the same, regardless of their background, which of course results in significant *in*equality of opportunity for people with disadvantaged backgrounds or characteristics.

Meaningful equality of opportunity is secured when the effects of illegitimate sources of variation have been compensated for or eliminated. But what constitutes a legitimate source of variation varies between conceptions. A meritocratic interpretation, for example, regards inequalities arising from talent and effort as desirable (as indicated by the solid arrows in Figure 3.1), but is usually silent on the role played by resources or the way in which individuals are able to convert resources into outcomes. By contrast, approaches sometimes referred to as luck egalitarianism (such as Le Grand, 1991, and Dworkin, 2000) regard talents as unjust sources of variation, because they are beyond an individual's control. Redistribution is required to equalise what people can reasonably expect given the characteristics they are born with and circumstances they are born into. On the other hand, inequality arising from choices made by the individual in accordance with their preferences, for example about the amount of effort they will exert, or for one kind of activity rather than another, are not unjust according to this approach. Hence the links to effort and resources are shown with dashed arrows in Figure 3.1, to indicate that only that part of these which is beyond individual control is to be regarded as legitimate sources of variation. Crucially, this is a resource-based conception of justice; what someone is or is not able to do with those resources is beyond the scope of its consideration. Differences in the rate at which people can convert resources into well-being are, by default, legitimate sources of variation in opportunities and the connection is therefore shown with a solid arrow in Figure 3.1.

A yet stronger interpretation of equality of opportunity is provided by the capability approach. No amount of redistribution may be sufficient to achieve substantive equality of opportunity according to this conception, because what matters is what people are able to be and do, not just what resources (financial or otherwise) they have at their disposal. Financial compensation might make a wheelchair user feel better about being unable to attend a public event, but altering the physical environment to enable them to participate widens their capability set (and, incidentally, that of many others). The implications of the capability approach for social policies are considered in more detail below.

Conceptions based on equality of opportunity differ significantly on the characteristics and circumstances for which an individual is held responsible. This too is a crucial dimension for analysing and understanding the differences between social policies. Alesina and colleagues (2001) use survey data on social attitudes to individual responsibility to explain differences in generosity between North American and European welfare states. They report that a large majority (71%) of Americans think that the poor could become rich if they just tried hard enough, while that is a minority view (40%) in Europe. Similarly, the British Social Attitudes survey showed that in 2000, 23% of people believed that people in Britain were living in need mainly 'because of laziness or lack of willpower', while 21% thought it was mainly 'because of injustice in our society' (Hills, 2001). Which of these constituencies policy makers wish to woo – in addition to their own beliefs on this subject – is likely to influence the shape and generosity of the policies they adopt.

The capability approach

The previous section offered a framework for analysing a range of conceptions of social justice that might underlie different aspects of social policy. The conventional view is that the limit of the role of the social scientist should be to describe, elucidate and identify alternatives. The tricky task of determining which is the better theory, inevitably involving normative judgements, should be left to the political philosophers. Such arguments are, after all, their bread and butter. But is that conventional view correct? I want to suggest here that social scientists, and those with an interest in social policy in particular, can and should be bolder. In the first place, many political philosophers, with some honourable exceptions, appear not to inhabit the same world as the rest of us: John Rawls would have us imagine ourselves with no personal identity or experience when determining policy choices; Ronald Dworkin, and others following him, have spent considerable effort on the implications of there being people with an incurable taste for plovers' eggs and pre-phylloxera claret in the context of an auction with cowrie shells on a desert island; while Robert Nozick has discussed brains in vats wired up to virtual reality machines. Illuminating as these examples may be at a theoretical level, they are not the stuff of real-life social policy.

Moreover, if we examine the kinds of criteria that are used in political philosophy to establish the advantages of one theory over another, they are not so alien to social sciences as one might think. A theory that can be shown to be internally inconsistent, to be significantly incomplete, or to have unpalatable implications, is generally considered weaker than one without these defects. An assessment applying these same criteria from a social policy perspective could shed new light on the comparison between theories, complementing the more abstract comparison carried out by political philosophers. Scrutiny from a social policy standpoint could reveal whether the approach under consideration is coherent not just theoretically but also when applied to the world as we find it – trading one's labour in a job centre rather than cowrie shells on a desert island. A relevant test would become whether the theory helps to resolve current policy dilemmas rather than whether it is theoretically complete – agonising choices between secondary schools rather than between different vintages of wine – and the implications of the theory that would need to be assessed would be those which would result from its application in the here and now, rather than in some hypothetical society with no history of inequality or injustice.

Using these kind of criteria, the capability approach shows some promise. A full comparative assessment is beyond the scope of this essay, but some indications of the key advantages of the approach can be given. One implication of the approach is that social policy should be concerned with more than just the distribution of material resources. It is doubtful that material resources can be translated into all valuable outcomes even in principle (and certainly not with a conversion factor invariant across people, as some theories appear to assume), but there is no doubt at all that in the actual world, imperfect markets prevent some people from using their resources as they would choose, public goods and negative externalities have significant and unequal impacts for better and worse, and large aspects of life that are critical to human well-being, such as intimate relationships, are largely independent of material resources. The capability approach, in both its Sen and Nussbaum variants, recognises that human flourishing consists of more than material comfort and that resources are only one part of what makes life go well or badly. Individuals have many different goals in life and the opportunity to achieve these goals cannot be straightforwardly proxied by income. This is in one sense the same intuition as that which has motivated renewed interest in the economics of happiness, but instead of replacing the single dimension of 'income' with the single dimension of 'happiness', the capability approach suggests that outcomes ('objects of value') are inherently multidimensional. If social policy is to promote well-being, it will need to be directed towards a range of outcomes, and correspondingly, indicators of the success or failure of social policies will need to be multidimensional.

This feature has been increasingly acknowledged in policy evaluation and a range of multidimensional indices of social inclusion has been developed (for example, Burchardt et al, 1999; Pantazis et al, 2006). Which particular dimensions, or capabilities, should be evaluated is the subject of ongoing debate. Nussbaum (2000) has proposed a list of 10 central human capabilities, derived from a combination of a priori reasoning, and an assessment of the aspirations expressed by peoples over time and across cultures (using sources as diverse as state constitutions and poetry). In contrast, Sen (1997) argues that there can be no universal list of important capabilities, first, because the content of an evaluation is always context-specific, and second, because there is reasonable disagreement between people about the relative value of different capabilities. Instead, Sen proposes that a democratic, and ideally participatory, procedure be adopted to determine the list of capabilities relevant for the particular evaluation or policy in question. This has the attraction of furthering the objective of equality of respect, as discussed above, in the policy process, while at the same time enhancing the legitimacy of the policies developed. The disadvantages of time and cost, and the risk of the process being dominated by those groups and individuals already in positions of power, are familiar critiques of participatory research in general and can be mitigated by careful design and skilful facilitation (Narayan et al, 2000). Recently, these approaches have been combined in an exercise to develop a list of central and valuable capabilities for the Equalities Review in Britain. An initial core list was derived from the international human rights framework (including social and economic rights alongside civil and political), and this was then supplemented and refined by deliberative consultation with members of the general public and groups and individuals at high risk of disadvantage (Vizard and Burchardt, 2007).

A second attractive feature of the capability approach is its focus on outcomes that are valuable in themselves, rather than being simply a means to an end. This lends it a coherence when applied to developing policies that is often lacking in theories which concentrate on the means, since the means–ends relationship is often not as tight in practice as it is in theory. The most well-known application where the importance of this distinction can be seen is in the United Nations Development Programme's (UNDP's) Human Development Index (HDI). The HDI includes literacy, education and life expectancy alongside a traditional measure of GDP per capita. A comparison of the ranking of countries according to the HDI and according to GDP per capita, reveals a number of countries which have succeeded in securing better health and education outcomes for their population than their resources would lead one to expect.[7] Economic growth is necessary but not sufficient for development, and an index that encourages countries to consider their performance on other dimensions which are intrinsically important is more likely to produce the desired outcomes.

A similar argument can be made with respect to domestic policy in more developed countries. Indicators of success and failure all too often focus on outputs rather than outcomes, meaning that too much attention is devoted to the existing range of services at the expense of considering what would actually make a difference to the lives of the disadvantaged (Piachaud, 2005). Moreover, within a given service, targets or funding based on 'means' rather than 'ends' can create perverse incentives for service providers (Glennerster et al, 2000). Although indicators for valuable outcomes may be harder to devise than measures based on administrative processes, the cost of failing to do so is a damaging kind of 'service-fetishism' in social policy.

Finally, the capability approach helps to resolve a dilemma that arises in a number of areas of policy, especially welfare, of devising systems that will work to incentivise those who need sticks without penalising those who are 'genuinely' in need of assistance. Since Dworkin, the theoretical significance of the division between what individuals should properly be held responsible for and what they should not ('Dworkin's cut') has been the centre of attention, and in real-life social policy, the attempt to distinguish between the deserving and undeserving poor is as old as the Poor Law itself (as are the varying interpretations of the distinction; see Chapter Two). Recent advances in understanding the interplay between our genes and the environment we grow up in are likely to make this question even more vexed. Despairing of the possibility of making a defensible distinction between choice and constraint, Fleurbaey (1995) advocates retreating to a framework based on actual outcomes (functionings) but this compromises the principle of respecting individuals' own conceptions of the good, which may not coincide with that of the policy maker. An alternative is to focus on the expansion of capabilities. Even if it is difficult to determine in a particular case whether someone has or has not freely chosen to do something (for example to become unemployed), we can have a good idea about the kinds of intervention that are likely to expand employment capabilities in general, and for this individual in particular: a strong economy, redressing regional inequalities, tackling discrimination, opportunities for education and retraining before and throughout working life, high-quality affordable childcare and so on. Expansion of capabilities in turn results in the expansion of people's capacity for responsibility. To paraphrase Sen (2002), if someone's capability set includes only options that are 'bad, awful and terrible', then their responsibility for selecting an option that is 'bad', even if it is detrimental to others, is limited. On the other hand, if their capability set is expanded to include 'good, great and terrific' in addition, then it is not unreasonable to hold them to account if they choose an option that is 'bad' not only for themselves but also for others.

Policies based on a capability approach have as their aim promoting well-being, conceived as an expansion of capabilities across a range of domains of life, with the exact specification determined a priori, or by a participatory process, or both. I have argued that a conception of this kind has advantages when considered in the light of its application to actual policy problems. It highlights ways in which material resources are converted by different people at different rates into valuable outcomes, and that there are many other determinants of what people are able to be and do, and hence provides a rationale for a broader range of possible interventions than those concerned exclusively with the distribution of incomes. It concentrates on expanding people's capacity for responsibility in general, rather than getting drawn into the blind alley of devising policies to separate responsible sheep from irresponsible goats. It also has theoretical attractions, respecting the diversity of human ends and recognising the importance of individual liberty, but at the same time – and consistent with the insight that Glennerster emphasises in Marshall's framework based on citizenship – acknowledging the interdependence of civil and political liberties on the one hand, with positive social and economic freedoms on the other.

Concluding remarks

The capability approach is open to charges of vagueness and idealism, and much remains to be done both in terms of refining the theoretical framework and in translating it into operational forms. That incompleteness has not, however, prevented it from becoming mainstream as far as global development is concerned, following on from the UNDP's Human Development Index. Truly 'human' development should not of course come to an end with industrialisation and there are signs that the approach is being adopted in the global north as well. The European Union has formulated a set of multidimensional indicators to evaluate progress on its social agenda (Atkinson et al, 2002), which bear more than a passing resemblance to capability-based indicators, including for example education and health outcomes alongside income and employment. Individual nation states including Germany and the Netherlands are developing evaluations of domestic social programmes explicitly within the capability framework. In the UK, the capability approach has found its way into ministerial speeches (Brown, 2005), and the final report of the Equalities Review (2007), the body overseeing the formation of the combined Commission for Equality and Human Rights, recommends that inequality in Britain could in future be monitored in terms of the 'substantive freedoms' enjoyed by different subgroups of the population.

Whether the emergence of a new terminology will significantly change the policies implemented in any of these contexts remains to be seen. But the history of social policy suggests that the beliefs held by policy makers about the objectives of welfare do indeed make a difference to the policies they devise, albeit subject to political compromise and more self-interested considerations. The connection between policy intent and what happens on the ground is another crucial link in the chain, since that is what determines whether the eventual outcome for the people concerned is beneficial or otherwise. Social scientists have an important role to play in exploring each of these links, identifying and clarifying the normative assumptions behind policy proposals and examining the effectiveness (or otherwise) of their translation into practice. Few have made such a significant contribution to these tasks as Howard Glennerster.

Notes

[1] I am very grateful to David Piachaud and Polly Vizard for helpful discussions in the process of writing this chapter, and to Tony Atkinson, Julian Le Grand and participants at a one-day conference on 'Making Social Policy Work' at the London School of Economics and Political Science (LSE) in October 2006 for useful comments. Above all, I am grateful to Howard Glennerster. I have benefited immeasurably from his encouragement, lively intellectual engagement and wise counsel over many years.

[2] Doubts have been raised about the feasibility and usefulness of Rawls' Original Position, even as a thought experiment (for example, Daniels, 1975; Le Grand, 1991), but the intention is clear: by stripping participants of knowledge of their particular circumstances, they are obliged to consider each person's interests as having equal potential importance. For Rawls, considering others as you would wish to be considered if you were in their circumstances is fundamental to the idea of justice.

[3] Speech at the Fabian New Year Conference, London, 14 January 2006, www. hm-treasury.gov.uk/newsroom_and_speeches/press/2006/press_03_06.cfm (accessed 18 September 2006).

[4] In an interview with Douglas Keay for *Woman's Own* magazine, published 31 October 1987.

[5] Rawls' principle is expressed in terms of the distribution of primary goods, rather than standard of living, but the 'maximin' formula is the same.

[6] Lionel Robbins (1938) recounts the story of a high-caste Brahmin responding to the explanation of the Benthamite system by saying, 'That cannot possibly be right. I am ten times more capable of happiness as that untouchable over there'. Robbins acknowledged that in the face of such beliefs, it is necessary to introduce an additional assumption of equal capacity for satisfaction, which he regarded as an ethical rather than an empirical claim.

[7] Among the top 50 ranked by the HDI, the HDI ranking of Argentina, Australia, Barbados, Chile, Costa Rica, Cuba, Japan, Poland, Sweden and Uruguay is in each case 10 or more places higher than their GDP per capita ranking. In the case of Cuba, the difference is 43 places (UNDP, 2006).

References

Alesina, A., Glaeser, E. and Sacerdote, B. (2001) 'Why doesn't the US have a European-style welfare state?', *Brookings Papers on Economic Activity*, no 2, pp 187-277.

Alkire, S. (2002) 'Dimensions of human development', *World Development*, vol 30, no 2, pp 181-205.

Arneson, R. (2002) 'Egalitarianism', in E. Zalta (ed) *The Stanford Encyclopedia of Philosophy (fall 2002 edition)*, http://plato.stanford.edu/archives/fall2002/entries/egalitarianism/ (accessed 09 January 2006).

Atkinson, A.B. (1989) *Poverty and Social Security*, Hemel Hempstead: Harvester Wheatsheaf.

Atkinson, A.B., Cantillon, B., Marlier, E. and Nolan, B. (2002) *Social Indicators: The EU and Social Inclusion*, Oxford: Oxford University Press.

Brown, G. (2005) 'From debt relief to empowerment', Annual UNICEF lecture, 29 June, www.hm-treasury.gov.uk/newsroom_and_speeches/press/2005/press_60_05.cfm (accessed 09 January 2006).

Burchardt, T. (2006) 'Happiness and social policy: barking up the right tree in the wrong neck of the woods', in L. Bauld, K. Clarke and T. Maltby (eds) *Social Policy Review 18: Analysis and Debate in Social Policy*, Bristol: The Policy Press.

Burchardt, T., Le Grand, J. and Piachaud, D. (1999) 'Social exclusion in Britain 1991-1995', *Social Policy and Administration*, vol 33, no 3, pp 227-44.

Commission on Social Justice (1994) *Social Justice: Strategies for National Renewal*, London: Vintage.

Conservative Party, The (2006) *Built to Last: The Aims and Values of the Conservative Party*, London: The Conservative Party, www.conservatives.com/pdf/BuiltToLast-AimsandValues.pdf (accessed 20 September 2006).

Daniels, N. (ed) (1975) *Reading Rawls*, Oxford: Blackwell.

Doyal, L. and Gough, I. (1991) *A Theory of Human Need*, London: Macmillan.

Dworkin, R. (2000) *Sovereign Virtue: The Theory and Practice of Equality*, Cambridge, MA: Harvard University Press.

Equalities Review, The (2007) *Fairness and Freedom. Final Report of The Equalities Review*, London: The Equalities Review, www.theequalitiesreview.org.uk/upload/assets/www.theequalitiesreview.org.uk/equality_review.pdf (accessed 12 March 2007).

Every Child Matters (2006) *Aims and Outcomes*, www.everychildmatters.gov.uk/aims/ (accessed 21 September 2006).

Fleurbaey, M. (1995) 'Equal opportunity or equal social outcome?', *Economics and Philosophy*, vol 11, pp 25-55.

Fraser, N. and Honneth, A. (2003) *Redistribution or Recognition? A Political–Philosophical Exchange*, London: Verso.

Glennerster, H. (1991) 'The radical right and the future of the welfare state', in H. Glennerster and J. Midgley (eds) *The Radical Right and the Welfare State*, Hemel Hempstead: Harvester Wheatsheaf.

Glennerster, H. (2000) *British Social Policy since 1945* (2nd edition), Oxford: Blackwell.

Glennerster, H. (2003) *Understanding the Finance of Welfare: What Welfare Costs and How to Pay for It*, Bristol: The Policy Press.

Glennerster, H. (2006) 'The UK system of health funding and resource allocation', Paper presented at the University of St Andrews, Unpublished.

Glennerster, H. (2007) *British Social Policy since 1945* (3rd edition), Oxford: Blackwell.

Glennerster, H., Power, A. and Travers, T. (1991) 'A new era for social policy: a new enlightenment or a new leviathan?', *Journal of Social Policy*, vol 20, no 3, pp 389-414.

Glennerster, H., Hills, J., Piachaud, D. and Webb, J. (2004) *One Hundred Years of Poverty and Policy*, York: Joseph Rowntree Foundation.

Glennerster, H., Hills, J. and Travers, T. with Hendry, R. (2000) *Paying for Health, Education and Housing: How does the Centre Pull the Purse Strings*, Oxford: Oxford University Press.

Hills, J. (2001) 'Poverty and social security: what rights? Whose responsibilities?', in J. Park, J. Curtice, K. Thomson, L. Jarvis and C. Bromley (eds) *British Social Attitudes: The 18th Report*, London: Sage Publications.

Hills, J. and Stewart, K. (2005) 'A tide turned but mountains yet to climb?', in J. Hills and K. Stewart (eds) *A More Equal Society? New Labour, Poverty, Inequality and Exclusion*, Bristol: The Policy Press.

Hills, J., Ditch, J. and Glennerster, H. (1994) 'Introduction', in J. Hills, J. Ditch and H. Glennerster (eds) *Beveridge and Social Security: An International Retrospective*, Oxford: Clarendon Press.

Layard, R. (2005) *Happiness: Lessons from a New Science*, London: Allen Lane.

Le Grand, J. (1991) *Equity and Choice*, London: Harper Collins.

Marshall, T.H. (1950) *Citizenship and Social Class, and Other Essays*, Cambridge: Cambridge University Press.

Maslow, A.H. (1943) 'A theory of human motivation', *Psychological Review*, no 50, pp 370-96.

Miller, D. and Walzer, M. (eds) (1995) *Pluralism, Justice, and Equality*, Oxford: Oxford University Press.

Narayan, D., Chambers, R., Shah, M. and Petesch, P. (2000) *Voices of the Poor: Crying out for Change*, New York: Oxford University Press (for the World Bank).

Nozick, R. (1974) *Anarchy, State and Utopia*, Oxford: Blackwell.

Nussbaum, M. (2000) *Women and Human Development: The Capabilities Approach*, Cambridge: Cambridge University Press.

Pantazis, C., Gordon, D. and Levitas, R. (eds) (2006) *Poverty and Social Exclusion in Britain: The Millennium Survey*, Bristol: The Policy Press.

Pearce, N. and Paxton, W. (eds) (2005) *Social Justice: Building a Fairer Britain*, London: Institute for Public Policy Research.

Piachaud, D. (2005) 'Social policy and politics', *Political Quarterly*, vol 76, no 3, pp 350-6.

Rawls, J. (1971) *A Theory of Justice*, Oxford: Oxford University Press.

Rawls, J. (1993) *Political Liberalism*, New York, NY: Columbia University Press.

Robbins, L. (1938) 'Interpersonal comparisons of utility: a comment', *The Economic Journal*, vol 48, no 192, pp: 635-41.

Sen, A. (1987) *The Standard of Living*, Cambridge: Cambridge University Press.

Sen, A. (1997) *On Economic Inequality* (2nd edition), Oxford: Clarendon Press.

Sen, A. (1999) *Development as Freedom*, Oxford: Oxford University Press.

Sen, A. (2002) *Rationality and Freedom*, Cambridge, MA: Harvard University Press.

SETF (Social Exclusion Task Force) (2006) *Reaching Out: An Action Plan on Social Exclusion*, London: Cabinet Office, www.cabinetoffice.gov. uk/social_exclusion_task_force/documents/reaching_out/reaching_ out_full.pdf (accessed 18 September 2006).

Stedman-Jones, G. (2004) *An End to Poverty? A Historical Debate*, London: Profile Books.

UNDP (United Nations Development Programme) (2006) *Human Development Report 2006*, New York, NY: UNDP.

Vizard, P. and Burchardt, T. (2007) *Developing a Capability List: Final Recommendations of the Equalities Review Steering Group on Measurement, Paper 2*, www.theequalitiesreview.org.uk/upload/assets/www. theequalitiesreview.org.uk/paper2capability.pdf (accessed 13 March 2007).

Waldfogel, J. (2006) *What Children Need*, Cambridge, MA: Harvard University Press.

Walzer, M. (1983) *Spheres of Justice: A Defence of Pluralism and Equality*, New York, NY: Basic Books.

Wolff, J. (1998) 'Fairness, respect and the egalitarian ethos', *Philosophy and Public Affairs*, vol 27, no 2, pp 97–122.

Part Two
Delivering social policy

FOUR

Families, individuals and the state

Jane Lewis

'The family' is difficult territory for policy makers. There is little consensus on what it should look like these days and politicians in particular often find themselves on dangerous ground if they make judgements about sexual morality or particular forms of intimate relationships. Yet families have always been the most important provider of welfare for young and old dependants and governments have long been concerned about, or have taken for granted, what they are able and willing to do. Family policy issues have reached the top of the policy agenda over the last decade in most western European Union (EU) member states: how can fertility be increased, the welfare of children best be secured, the old looked after, and the labour market participation rates of adults increased? These are all pressing social issues, but they represent policy aims that are not necessarily easy to reconcile with each other – for example, increasing participation rates, particularly of women, may help to address child poverty as much as economic growth, but carework for children and older dependants may require an adult to be present in the home. Furthermore, family and personal life are still very much a private matter in the sense that there remains a boundary between state and family, even if changing cultural practices, including the use of mobile telephones and watching 'reality' television, have made much that was considered private public. The interests of different types and groups of families, and of individual family members, differ, and the choices they make may not be compatible. Thus the scope and nature of intervention by liberal democratic states is a delicate matter and subject to fierce debate.

The first two parts of this chapter tease out these tensions and examine why family issues are so difficult for policy to tackle, by outlining changes in the normative understandings of family which underpin policies, in terms of changes in family form and how men and women contribute to families. The assumptions made by policy makers about the contributions that adult family members should make have changed dramatically, in large part in response to behavioural change, especially women's increased employment rates, but also in line with government's economic priorities. However, changed assumptions about the extent to which adult family members will be in the labour market are not necessarily any more in line with people's behaviour and beliefs than the older assumptions about gendered roles and responsibilities, not least because of the wide variation in behaviour, belief and interests that now exists in an increasingly pluralist society.

State intervention in respect of the family has changed dramatically in the UK since 1997, with more explicit interventions affecting all families with children and not just those 'at risk'. This in turn has required a new accommodation between the longstanding commitment to a firm boundary between state and family. The third part of the chapter examines a relatively successful[1] policy example from the years of the Labour government: the development of work/family balance policies, which nevertheless demonstrates the difficulty of negotiating conflicting policy aims and the different interests of family members. Labour has done so by stressing its regard for the importance of 'parental choice', while developing policies on childcare services, leaves and working hours that inevitably provide certain kinds of incentives and disincentives to work and care. The final section of the chapter suggests the need to develop a framework for thinking about state intervention and the family that is more firmly centred on supporting the relationships and commitments that are central to family welfare, going beyond a simple model of enabling parental choice.

From 'the family' to 'families'

Governments did not always have to tread warily in making assumptions about what families looked like and how they operated. In the emerging liberal democratic state, the voter and the *paterfamilias*, the 'head of the household', were as one and other family members were for the most part invisible in the public sphere in any formal sense. The conjugal family was the place in which obligations to care and support were fulfilled and the weak protected, and as such was deemed to be necessarily and properly separate from the competitive public world of politics, business and employment (Spencer, 1876). It was assumed that the family would consist of two married parents who would look after dependent members, the husband by earning and the wife by caring and performing domestic labour.

The male breadwinner family remained the ideal family form in most western countries until well after the Second World War. In the post-war decades, sociologists argued that this traditional family model provided the best way of socialising children and was the most efficient family form for modern industrialised societies (Parsons and Bales, 1955). Economists maintained that at the household level it allowed men and women to maximise the gains that followed from an economically rational gendered division of labour (Becker, 1981); however, it should be noted there was in fact nothing in this model that required the adult relationship to be based on marriage.

This traditional conceptualisation of the family lasted a long time, surviving the advance of individual rights and freedoms – political, social and, increasingly, economic and sexual – on the part of women, chiefly because, as per Becker's arguments, it was assumed that it was biological difference that made it economically rational, which in turn made it possible to argue that the traditional family form was freely chosen (Burgess and Locke, 1953). For the most part this picture of the family conveniently ignored tensions between the interests of family members[2] and thus allowed evidence of increasing individualism, freedom and autonomy to coexist with a commitment to the traditional family. Beveridge's blueprint for the post-war welfare state gave enthusiastic support to the equal-but-different ideas inherent in this view of marriage and the family when he insisted on using the term 'partnership' and drew attention to the importance of recognising women's role in reproduction (at a time when the low birth rate gave rise to concern; Beveridge, 1942).

Normative ideas about family form and how the family worked were inscribed in all the major social policy reforms of the early and mid-20th century. As Strohmeier (2002, p 346) has commented: 'Family policy to a considerable extent is nothing less than the incorporation of social values into political institutions and social services'. In addition, until the 1960s, the traditional family model was internalised as an ideal even by those who could not hope to achieve it (that is, in families where women had often to engage in casual labour), as well as by (male) working-class leaders in the shape of politicians and trades unionists anxious to make a case for a 'family wage' for male workers. As the use of birth control increased and the burden of frequent pregnancy diminished, and as the demand for female labour in a much wider variety of jobs also increased, signing up to the traditional family model was no longer so necessary for women. Second wave feminism encouraged them further to rethink their position. Nor, by the late 20th century, in face of rising house prices and falling male manual workers' wages relative to average incomes, was the traditional family model feasible for most men. Their attitudes towards women's work underwent major change, albeit that they are still more traditional than those of women. Between 1989 and 2002 the percentage of men agreeing with the statement that 'a man's job is to earn money; a woman's job is to look after the home and family' fell from 32 to 20, and the percentage agreeing with the statement 'women should stay at home when there is a child under school age' fell from 67 to 51 (Crompton et al, 2003).[3]

Changes in reproductive technology, in labour markets, in the nature of social provision made by modern welfare states, and in attitudes due to the decline of stigma and the declining hold of organised Christian religion in Western Europe[4] have resulted in people's lives becoming more 'individualised' (Beck and Beck-Gernsheim, 1995; Kohli, 1986; Buchmann, 1989). Adult family members are no longer so closely bound by need. In the UK, considerable freedom in choosing a partner has been long lived,[5] but 'elective relationships' or 'families of choice' (Silva and Smart, 1999) involving most notably homosexual partners have proliferated, and fluidity in family forms involving marriage, divorce, cohabitation and living-apart-together has rendered the individual's lifecourse increasingly complicated. Freedom to choose intimate relationships is fundamental in western societies, but commentators have not been slow to portray the changes in family form over the lifecourse in terms of selfish individualism – thus reading off motivation from the aggregate statistics of family change and deriving cause from effect – and to raise fears about the extent to which people will fulfil their 'family obligations'.[6]

Nevertheless, at the macro level, the fear is that that increasingly atomised individuals, with the capacity to choose unfettered by shared values, are unlikely to engage fully with either family or community is not without foundation. From the 1960s, it has increasingly been expected by religious as well as political elites that morality must come from within rather than be imposed from without. Reflecting on the politics of Thatcherism, Marilyn Strathern (1992, p 159) questioned the effects of fetishising individual choice on the person, arguing that the individual's identity becomes fragmented in the face of consumerist ideology, such that 'the interior has itself no structure'. Increasing pluralism, whether in terms of family form, the way adult family members organise their contributions to family life, or the 'family values' that people hold in western societies that are increasingly diverse in terms of behaviour and belief, makes it more difficult for the state to prescribe or enable behaviour for the common good. Thus Lawrence Mead's (1997) argument in favour of a new paternalism, other than in cases of neglect of legally established commitments (for example between parent and child), seems increasingly difficult to implement. Indeed, Alesina and Glaeser (2004) have suggested that it is the 'cultural variable' and the issue of diversity and pluralist values that pose the greatest challenge to modern welfare states. Certainly, it is not surprising that the debate occasioned by the demise of the traditional family form is fiercest in the US, or that the policy response is the most confused (as discussed below).

At the micro level of the household, the interests of individual family members have become more obviously hard to reconcile. The traditional family model made provision for carework, albeit at the expense of female economic dependence. The changing nature of women's contribution to families above all in the form of earnings, which has been much greater than that of men in respect of care (Gershuny, 2000), has meant that the part played by adult men and women in families is no longer so obviously complementary. Indeed, there are likely to be problems in meshing the labour market biographies of two adults with family life and the work of care (Beck and Beck-Gernsheim, 1995). Thus at both the societal and household levels, policy makers face grave difficulties in devising policies 'to support families'. Not even the use of the word 'families' rather than 'family' (HO, 1998) can obscure these difficulties. In short, there is no longer any neat fit between the normative assumptions about family form and functioning that policy makers make or may wish to make on the one hand, and people's behaviour, ideals and preferences on the other. What then are the implications of this for the relationship between state and family?

State intervention and the public/private boundary

Pluralism of family form and function poses challenges for state intervention, both 'directly', in terms of the entry of government officials into the household, and 'indirectly', in terms of the assumptions informing policies. In many respects, the fundamental trigger for direct intervention by the state – some form of 'family failure' – has not undergone major change, but family change has made it more difficult for frontline workers to know what they are trying to achieve. In the English-speaking countries, there has historically been relatively little attempt to devise family policies to try to manipulate or support certain kinds of behaviours.[7] But policies have nevertheless carried strong assumptions about what the family should look like and what family members should contribute, which have been inscribed implicitly or explicitly in policies to deliver cash and services. In what follows, I focus mainly on the implications of family change and changing assumptions about the family in terms of what is considered possible and/or desirable for the state to do.

Notwithstanding the degree of general support enjoyed by the traditional family model until relatively recently, political and social elites were never without anxiety about the family and whether it would carry out its responsibilities to socialise children and care for its dependent members. The family was bedrock, but somewhat paradoxically was also perceived as fragile. At the turn of the 19th century, a small army of voluntary, middle-class, female 'visitors' went from house to house to try to promote good standards of domestic management and economic self-sufficiency, in other words to try to effect a change in individual behaviour (which was believed by many to be the only way of securing social change) in line with the traditional family model. Much direct social provision of this sort, from marriage guidance to birth control advice, was delivered by the voluntary sector until well into the post-war period, often because governments felt such issues were too delicate to permit state intervention. But, increasingly, health visitors and social workers employed by local government – 'agents of the state' (Mount, 1983) – entered homes, particularly when there was some conspicuous 'failure' in respect of child welfare to be addressed. Direct intervention by the state in the family thus tended to be largely confined to picking up the pieces and was not infrequently harsh, culminating in the swift removal of a child from a family deemed to have failed for reasons that were likely to include destitution as abuse (Hendrick, 1994).

In many respects, direct intervention in the family has continued to be confined to cases of family failure, primarily situations where children are deemed to be at risk of abuse. But the problems of addressing even such gross examples of 'failure' have become legion, and have proved increasingly difficult in families with non-western childrearing practices and belief systems.

In fact, in the English-speaking countries, family policy has been for the most part implicit rather than explicit (Land and Parker, 1978), based on normative understandings of how families should look and work. Access to social welfare, particularly cash benefits, was shot through with assumptions about women's economic dependency on their husbands and hence with assumptions about the prevalence of the traditional family form, regardless of the fact that in terms of the contributions that adults make to families it was the majority experience for only a very short time in the mid-20th century. In continental Europe, there was much more explicit use of family policy – in France, for example, social security policy was built around families with or without children – and much more effort to use policy incentives in the form of cash benefits to promote or support particular kinds of behaviour, especially in respect of policies to encourage or discourage fertility (in face of which, behaviour has proved remarkably unresponsive; Gauthier, 1996).

Since the 1970s the pace of family change – defined in terms both of changes in family form and as changes in the nature of the contributions that men and women make to families – has been rapid and dramatic, especially in North America and in Northern and Western Europe. There is much debate among academics as to the nature of the relationship between law and behaviour in regard to these changes and the possibility of intended as well as unintended consequences. For example, while it is unlikely that changes in family law or in social policies have caused the rise in the divorce rate or in the proportion of lone-mother families (Phillips, 1988; Bane and Ellwood, 1994), it is perfectly possible for legal changes to have facilitated family change. Once something like divorce becomes easier in law and part of the climate within which marriages exist, it loses its stigma and becomes more common, notwithstanding that all divorce law reform has been promoted with the explicit aim of strengthening marriage. Untangling the precise nature of the relationship between law and behaviour is difficult, but for policy makers, family change in all its dimensions has made it well nigh impossible to hang on to the assumptions about the form and functions of the traditional male breadwinner family. This has been important for family law, as policy makers have resorted to a new form of regulation 'at a distance',[8] allowing adults to make their own arrangements, but requiring them do so in respect of children. It has also been of major significance for welfare states, which were founded on two key settlements: that between capital and labour, and that between men and women at the household level (Lewis, 2001a; Supiot, 2001).

In respect of family policy, increasing individualisation has legitimated and to some extent required the shift that all western governments have made over the last two decades away from the traditional family model and towards assuming the existence of an 'adult worker model family' (Lewis, 2001b, 2002). Changes in family form, which, for example, have made it increasingly difficult to administer policy on the basis of relationships between 'husbands and wives', together with growing – but certainly not equal – economic independence on the part of women have made it positively tempting for governments to treat family members as if they were indeed fully individualised. The shift to an adult worker model family has been prompted by at least three factors. First, by the pursuit of economic competitiveness and growth, which at both the UK and EU levels has been recognised to require higher rates of female labour participation (HM Treasury, 2002; Council of the European Union, 2000); second, by family changes that have made it difficult to assume or enforce traditional patterns of support and care between adults and a consequent desire to reduce the cost of an increasing proportion of lone-mother families to the Exchequer; and third, by the determination to increase and enforce the individual's responsibility for self-provisioning and for parenting (via, for example, individual parenting contracts). In retrospect, it becomes apparent that the 1974 Finer Commission report on one-parent families, which concluded that there was 'no method consistent with the basic tenets of a free society of discharging the community from this responsibility [to maintain]' (Finer Commission, 1974, para 2.22), represented the last historical moment when it was assumed that the state would have to bear the brunt of responsibility for meeting the costs of family change. Since the 1980s, there has been much more attention paid to the behaviour of the individual (Deacon, 2002).

Modern social provision was built around the work–welfare relationship and the incentive and disincentive effects of social provision on the worker's inclination to search for employment and to support *him*self; it was conditional (see Harris, Chapter Two, this volume). However, the work–welfare relationship has been substantially recast. Gilbert (2002) has characterised the new trends in terms of a series of shifts from social support to social inclusion via employment, from measures of decommodification (that enable people to leave the labour market for due cause) to ways of securing commodification, and from unconditional benefits to benefits that are heavily conditional on work or training. Crucially, for the first time, this recast work–welfare relationship has been extended to women as well as men (Lewis, 2002). Increasingly it is assumed that individuals, male and female, will be able to be more self-provisioning, particularly in respect of pensions. But there is a real danger that the change in assumptions will outrun the behavioural reality. The gender pay gap and the very high rates of female part-time employment in the UK (and also the Netherlands and Germany) mean that it is as misguided (and potentially damaging to women's welfare in particular) to assume individualisation in the sense of economic autonomy as it was to assume the existence (as opposed to the ideal) of the traditional male breadwinner model family.

This broad shift in assumptions about how the family works and the contributions that adults make to it has been common to all western countries, nevertheless the changes in family form and function have elicited very different responses in terms of the degree to which they are combined with a determination to preserve a strict dividing line between public and private.

Broadly speaking, three types of reactions on the part of governments have been evident in respect of adult family members: (i) a strong desire, particularly in the US, to 'put the clock back', at least in respect of family form and to promote marriage, but not in terms of pushing women back into the home; (ii) to endorse and even to promote the changes, but to leave family members to make their own adjustments – the US approach to the implications of women's employment for family carework; and (iii) to recognise the changes and to work with the grain of change, for example by introducing 'partnership' legislation for cohabiting couples, or policies to help adult family members to reconcile or balance work and family responsibilities, which are more characteristic of European approaches.

Family privacy is important as American writers in particular have long insisted (Elshtain, 1981). The historical experience of forced abortion and forced reproduction in Nazi Germany, or the one-child policy in China, bears testimony to this. However, oddly, it is in the US that there has been seemingly least hesitation in intervening to promote marriage, via family policy rather than family law, and most strikingly in regard to welfare reform. This relates to the 'culture wars' involving the moral right, but also has to do with the state's determination to preserve the public/private split and to have the family perform its duties of support and care without state intervention, something that is perceived to be particularly threatened by family fluidity. The third response – government working with the grain of social change – has long been the approach of northern and western continental European countries, and has been adopted in the UK since 1997. Continental European countries have tended to accept state finance and provision in making their family policies, but lack of a tradition in terms of state intervention in this field and the strongly established feeling among employers that family issues should be sorted out privately has posed problems for New Labour in developing policy in the UK.

The focus of much proactive family policy has fallen more squarely on children. In the face of a lack of consensus as to what the family is and how it should work, focusing on the needs of children makes good policy sense. Western European countries have long recognised a collective obligation to address the problem of the wage as a reward for individual effort by implementing family allowance or child benefit programmes. However, recent social expenditure on children has tended to be justified in terms of 'social investment' (Lister, 2003). Welfare state restructuring over the past two decades, with the importance it has attached to 'active welfare' and 'social policy as a productive factor' (Commission of the European Communities, 2000), has encouraged both the adult worker model family and expenditure on the next generation in terms of both cash benefits and social services, including early years learning. However, the interests of young children or older children in trouble in respect of care, may not wholly accord with shifting assumptions regarding an adult worker model family.[9]

In the comparative literature on welfare states, it has increasingly been recognised that family change in all its dimensions is an independent variable (Esping-Andersen, 1999; Esping-Andersen et al, 2002), something that family sociologists have long argued, with huge implications for social and economic policies. Low fertility rates are key to population ageing and the perceived crisis in pensions. Women's employment is a crucial part of economic policy. It follows that care may be one of the few genuine examples of a 'new social risk' (Bonoli, 2005).[10] Under some conditions (especially in Southern Europe, but also among highly educated women in Germany) it is seemingly difficult to persuade women to both work and have children. It may be, as Bianchi and Casper (2004) have argued, that it is impossible for women to choose to do more paid work unless men do more unpaid work in the family. In which case, can men be 'forced' to care? And should women of all ethnicities and cultural backgrounds be expected to work? Unsurprisingly, policy makers shy away from such hard questions and problems, hiding behind a gender- and ethnicity-neutral language.

In performing a 180-degree turn in making its approach to family policy explicit rather than implicit, the Labour government in the UK has had a particularly difficult balancing act to perform in terms of guarding against the charge that it is undermining family privacy and becoming a 'nanny state'. Thus, while taking active steps to intervene to support all family members, and particularly to invest in children, Labour has insisted on the importance of 'parental choice' in respect of family practices. However, choice tends to be used synonymously with preferences, which are in turn, notwithstanding the arguments of Hakim (2000), rooted in previous experience and social, cultural and economic context.[11] Choice is also problematic when people make the 'wrong' choices. For example, mothers may choose to stay at home to care for children without realising that this will cost them dear in terms of their pension entitlements. Should government merely applaud such altruism, seek to inform the choice, or compensate mothers for it? It is surely dishonourable to do the first without attempting either the second or third of these. In addition, given the diversity of interests, at the group and household levels, there are inevitably tensions that are hard to reconcile; for example, men's choice not to care constrains women's choice to work; and parents' choices in respect of children do not always put the welfare of children first. Thus the resort to promoting parental choice in face of diverse behaviours, beliefs and interests is unlikely to provide an adequate basis for family policy, something that I return to in the last section of this chapter.

At the policy-making level, motivation is often instrumental, designed, for example, to increase fertility or get women into work – in order to increase the tax base, address the cost of pensions and so on – as much or more than they are centred on promoting the welfare of family members. And, because welfare provision by families has as much to do with care as money, policies are often residual, just as social care as a policy field tends to be residual to healthcare. Policies that expand genuine or real choices for families and family members are difficult to achieve. There remains the issue as to what norms, values and responsibilities government can reasonably expect all families to sign up to. The next section seeks to illustrate these points in relation to the package of explicit family policies introduced to help parents to reconcile work and family responsibilities in the UK.

The development of work/family balance policies in the UK[12]

The rapid development of work/family balance policies in the UK since 1997 represents a shift in ideas about the role of the state and serves to demonstrate the extent to which shifting normative assumptions away from the traditional family model, together with a potent mix of economic and social aims, drove policy. The policy aims were not necessarily easy to reconcile and the development of the new policies risked outrunning behavioural change, especially in respect of women. While the importance of parental choice was emphasised from the outset in acknowledgement of the family as a private sphere, in some important respects this served only to mask the existence of tensions between different kinds of family groups and family members at the household level.

The UK long occupied a place towards the bottom of the EU 'league tables' on work/family balance policies, particularly regarding different kinds of leaves for mothers and fathers (hereafter care leaves) and care services for children. In common with other English–speaking counties, the care of dependants was treated as a private, family responsibility. Successive governments in the post-war period eschewed the development of explicit family policies (Hantrais, 2004). Thus, until recently, the UK offered only very limited childcare services, largely aimed at 'children at risk' (Randall, 2000), and statutory maternity leave that was neither very long nor well remunerated.

Since its election in 1997, the Labour government has developed a range of policies encompassing money, time and services to promote a better 'balance' between work and family life by: (i) introducing new forms of leave and extending existing ones; (ii) investing in childcare; and (iii) addressing working hours in the form of a statutory 'right to request' a flexible working pattern, plus a campaign to get employers to adopt best practice.[13]

In terms of what the policies actually provided: part-time free nursery care was offered to three- and four-year-olds in 1998, parental leave was introduced in 1999, and paid adoption and (a two-week) paid paternity leave in 2003.[14] The 2006 Work and Families Act provides for fathers to be able to take over the hugely extended maternity leave from 20 weeks after the birth if the mother returns to work (DTI, 2006). However, as with parental leave, the low level of compensation will likely mean that take-up among fathers is low. Finally, in 2001, Labour departed from the strong voluntarist tradition in British industrial relations (Fagan and Lallement, 2000) and introduced 'light touch' legislation to establish a right to *request* flexible working patterns for the parents of children under the age of six, to be extended to carers of adults under the 2006 Work and Families Act. While the measure is weak compared to legislation in many continental European countries, take-up levels have been high, for example in comparison with Germany (Hegewisch, 2005). Taken together, these policies not only represent a new departure in terms of the role of the state, but by 2004 had achieved coherence as a package.

Work/family balance policies have thus been developed rapidly since 1997 and have been based on explicit assumptions regarding the erosion of the traditional family model and the desirability of an adult worker model family. In its 1997 *Pre-Budget Report*, the Treasury commented that 'important social changes have left the single male breadwinner the exception rather than the rule' (HM Treasury, 1997: para 4.13). The importance of the erosion of the male breadwinner model family was taken up by the Department of Trade and Industry in 2000 in its Green Paper on work and family policies (DTI, 2000, p 10), and further elaborated by the Chancellor in his 2001, 2002 and 2003 Budget speeches:

This Budget applies the Beveridge principles to the realities and needs of modern family life. Today many families rely on two incomes and most women work. Some of the greatest pressures parents face were almost unknown to Beveridge's time; the loss of income because one parent ceases employment and is at home or works part-time after the birth of a child, and the costs of child care when the mother goes out to work. (HC, 2002: col 586)

The dual-earner family is certainly the dominant form in the UK: the proportion of couples with dependent children where both partners worked stood at 68% in spring 2004 (Walling, 2005). However, the figure for couples with pre-school children dropped to 56%. In addition, there are very high rates of part-time work for women. In March–May 2006, Labour Force Survey data showed 11.3% of women working between 6 and 15 hours and 29.3% between 16 and 30 hours. Hours for men in the UK are on the other hand long relative to other EU member states, although there has been a slight fall in the proportion of men working more than 45 hours by almost two percentage points to 30% between 2004 and 2006 (LFS, 2006, Table 08).[15]

A high proportion of mothers work very short hours and the precise extent to which, and the manner in which, the male breadwinner family form has been eroded varies according to age of the child, and also region (employment rates for married and cohabiting mothers and lone mothers are lowest in London (Walling, 2005). Employment rates of mothers also vary by social class and ethnicity (a variable that helps to account for the low rates of mothers' employment in London). Smeaton's (2006) recent survey of 920 new fathers in two-parent families has shown big differences between different ethnic groups: only 32% of White families were 'traditional' in outlook, compared with 79% of Black and 83% of Asian families.

Thus, to assume, as Labour did initially, that work/life balance policies should be slanted heavily towards providing incentives to work rather than time to care (in line with shifting normative assumptions towards an adult worker model family) did not necessarily accord with behaviour or values, albeit that the amount of time to be devoted to employment by mothers in particular was never specified.

Policies to enable adults to achieve a better balance between work and family responsibilities have been presented as being 'good for everyone': for business, the wider society, children and parents (DfEE, 2000). As Dex (2003) has remarked, many things are hoped for from such policies: they can be seen as the means of doing something about the challenges of an ageing society (by enabling women to earn and thereby improving the dependency ratio), falling fertility rates (thought to be exacerbated by lack of support for women workers), tackling child poverty (by encouraging and enabling mothers – especially lone mothers – to work), and children's development (particularly by promoting high-quality early learning) (see also OECD, 2005). The objectives have been economic as well as social: these have encompassed both the desire to increase employment as a means to greater growth and competitiveness (stressed particularly by the Treasury) and the narrower interests of business in managing an increasingly 'diverse' workforce – avoiding high turnover and absenteeism, and improving recruitment, retention, loyalty and productivity (stressed particularly by the Department of Trade and Industry in a strategic effort to win over employers, especially between 2000 and 2001). The social objective has sought to put 'family first', which has also meant increasing employment – as a means to social inclusion and tackling child poverty – but which has increasingly led to proposals regarding working time and time to care that are more difficult to square with the business case (CBI, 2005).

In addition there have been tensions at the level of the household inherent in the aim of promoting 'family welfare'. Two dimensions of family welfare were clearly identified in the policy documents: the importance of securing the welfare of children and of supporting the choices that 'parents' (the policy documents tend to be gender-neutral) make about work and care. In respect of the first of these, the policy goals initially emphasised the importance of investing in children, which as Lister (2003) has argued, has tended to be as much or more about children as future 'citizen workers' as about children's well-being in the present. Thus the promotion of formal childcare provision and early years learning, targeted to the poorest areas, was justified by Margaret Hodge (then a Department for Education and Employment minister) as an investment in the poorest children (HC, 2001, Q 474). Similarly, Baroness Ashton told the Department of Work and Pensions Select Committee that the provision of childcare was part of the government's anti-poverty strategy (HC, 2003, Q 31). However, by 2003, the policy documents began to take a perspective that was more centred on children *qua* children, and to cite research evidence on the different kinds of care that might be best for pre-school children, acknowledging in particular the importance of high-quality formal provision for children over the age of three and the value of one-to-one care during the first year (HM Treasury et al, 2004, para 2.15).[16] But this raised potential difficulties in squaring the best interests of the very young child with support for parents' choices, let alone with the interests of the broader economy and of business for maximising female labour market participation. In 2001, Margaret Hodge told the Select Committee on Education and Employment:

> We are not about in any way forcing mothers into work. What we are about is ensuring that those mothers who need to or choose to work ... are given appropriate support in the childcare infrastructure ... it is all about providing choice, it is not about forcing anyone into work. (HC, 2001, Q 499)

While the policy documents on balancing work and family always acknowledged the importance of the choices parents wished to make, by 2004 it was additionally recognised that they needed to be able to make '*real* choices between attractive and viable alternatives' (HM Treasury et al, 2004, para 2.51; emphasis added) in terms of the quality and affordability of childcare services, the compensation offered to those wanting to take leaves, and the willingness of employers to consider flexible ways of working. Thus the constraints on individual family members were to be addressed more seriously by introducing a wider range of policies. Whether the combination of a legislative floor that has often proved to be minimalist with enabling individual choice in respect of working patterns (rather than via collective bargaining) is sufficient to guarantee real or genuine choice for adult worker citizens remains an issue. Nevertheless, the strength of the early link between childcare services in particular and employment was substantially modified. If family welfare is to be prioritised, and if a 'real choice' to balance work and care is to be possible for men and for women, it has been demonstrated philosophically (Fraser, 1997; Lewis and Giullari, 2005) and empirically (Gornick and Meyers, 2003) that a wide range of policies are necessary in terms of time, money and services. These have been developed incrementally in the UK since 1997. However, much more has been targeted at mothers than at fathers; the UK now has the longest maternity leave in Europe, but little by way of the flexible and well-compensated parental or paternity leave that would encourage men to do carework. Such a strategy, relying on the deepening of existing policies, was more likely to succeed with employers, but sidelined the problem of gender inequality and of securing genuine choice for mothers, although how far the state can lead in such matters is, of course, inherently problematic. There is also the deeper issue as to whether reliance on parental choice is an adequate and sufficient basis for the development of family policies. While it is an obvious way of accommodating increasing pluralism in behaviour and beliefs, it does not necessarily recognise the importance of the way in which the choices of adult family members are embedded in commitments and relationships.

Conclusion

Individualisation and pluralism make it difficult to insist on particular modes of behaviour in families. Many commentators have bemoaned the effects of changes in family form ('family breakdown') and changes in how families organise themselves ('working mothers') on children. However, no government has sought to curb the freedoms of the individual to partner, un-partner, and re-partner, or to try and encourage women back into the home. It is difficult if not impossible to put the clock back in respect of adult behaviour in families.

In many ways, the major success of the development of work/family balance policies in the UK lies in the decision to work with the grain of social change. This reverses the long-established approach in the English-speaking countries, which still prevails in the US and has reasserted itself in Australia (thus demonstrating that change in the UK may be fragile), of treating the family as private and expecting adult family members to work out their own salvation in the face of rapid change. It is perhaps significant in this regard that most of the academic literature on family crisis and in particular the crisis of care is American (Heyman, 2000; Skocpol, 2000; Schor, 2001). Beyond that, through a series of incremental changes that had to accommodate many interests and in particular to mediate the relationship between employers and the family (which historically in the UK has not been perceived as government's role), and that also had multiple policy goals emanating from different government departments, the Labour government 'muddled through' to a policy framework that provides a not dissimilar policy package – in terms of incentives for mothers to stay at home for the first year after the birth and then to enter the labour market – as other continental European countries. Albeit that different policy instruments have been used – in particular long maternity leaves rather than parental leaves – that are arguably more in tune with the historical experience in the UK and are therefore more likely to prove acceptable to more interest groups, especially business, but also parents. Indeed, Labour made a point of citing the 'evidence base' on what flexible working patterns could deliver for business and on what children need in the first year of their life. Research evidence was important, given the charged nature of the debate. Nevertheless, the evidence base is often conflicting and always hard to disentangle, and the comparative evidence is difficult to interpret without extensive knowledge of the context. Furthermore, the evidence regarding what is 'good for', say, mothers might not accord with what is 'good for' children. In the end, it is not possible to avoid the politics of the family, which are increasingly complicated.

There is much to be said for caution in approaching policies affecting families and some degree of muddling through in the absence of agreement on family forms and functions and in the presence of a variety of well-entrenched positions is also inevitable. Pragmatically, family policy is a particularly difficult area for governments to lead public opinion. It is also likely that government will be prioritising a particular policy aim – as was perhaps the case early in Labour's first term with the focus on getting more women, especially lone mothers, into the workforce, and focusing more on the provision of childcare services than on supported leaves during the child's first year. Notwithstanding that this may well be in the best financial interests of mothers, and therefore of children, such an approach was at risk of being seriously out of step with what significant numbers of people regarded as the 'proper thing to do' (Finch and Mason, 1993) by apparently failing to appreciate care needs and carework.

The problems for the development of family policies are therefore twofold:

- State intervention cannot be based on assumptions about family form and function that are too far from the reality of people's own ideas and behaviours. The major shift to an adult worker family model has posed problems in this regard.
- People's ideas about family and family practices are increasingly diverse, which makes it plausible for government to stress 'parental choice'. However, the idea of a freely choosing citizen ignores both the conflict of interests that may often exist between family members and between different types of family, and the efforts that people may make to maintain their commitments.

Family policies need careful focus and, more fundamentally, rethinking in relation to the nature of the relationship between state and family. Too much is often hoped for from family policies. Work/family balance policies cannot serve as a 'magic bullet' to solve problems as various as low fertility rates, child poverty and encouraging women into employment, as has all too often been suggested. It is important at least to prioritise 'family welfare' (even though this is not easy to define) and care-centred policies, which Labour did in the case of work/family balance policies by the early 2000s, rather than treat it as a residual. As Bettio and Plantenga (2004, p 107) state, 'care regimes function as "social joins", ensuring complementarity between economic and demographic institutions and processes' (see also Lewis and Giullari, 2005). It *is* tempting for government to abandon the territory of the family to voluntary organisations, as largely happened in the past, or to follow the time-honoured course of leaving decisions to the 'private choice' of 'families'. But this is surely dangerous at a time of profound social change, when there is increasingly little by way of common ground on how to live in families.

The public/private boundary will always be difficult to negotiate. In developing its new, interventionist approach in respect of all families, rather than confining direct intervention to those at risk, Labour has respected family privacy by insisting on 'parental choice', which has been conceptualised as the agreed expression of the couple's preferences. It is legitimate for social policies to aim to increase the real or genuine choices that people have, which means tackling the constraints they face. Furthermore, policies that stand in contradiction to people's notions of the 'ought' in family matters – for example privileging one form of childcare or childcare services over leaves – are likely to be difficult to implement. However, providing real choice is something that the work/family balance example shows to be particularly difficult given the interrelated choice-sets and dynamic of inequality between men and women in families. Thus a single policy such as providing cash for care in the form of care accounts may be attractive in that it allows people 'choice' in meeting their care needs, but fails to address the problem of securing real choice for women and men to work and to care.

Indeed, the promotion of parental choice requires more investigation. Choices that promote social solidarity and cohesion must have regard for the other, they are shaped fundamentally by commitments and relationships, and this is something that goes beyond the simple model of the choosing citizen. The notion of an ethic of care developed over more than two decades (Gilligan, 1982; Tronto, 1993; Sevenhuijsen, 1998; Nussbaum, 1999) has demonstrated the centrality of relationship, connection, interdependence and the importance of a more care-centred approach to policy. This does not mean a return to the kind of policies that reinforced involuntary dependency in the male breadwinner family model (as per Morgan, 1996). But choices that add to the complement of the 'good society' cannot be made in the policy values vacuum that individualisation and pluralism increasingly threaten to create, where there is no commonly recognised and prescribed basis for making choice other than individual preference and at worst personal gain.

Government intervention has a responsibility to recognise the importance of choices made with reference to the needs of others, on the part of men, women and children in families, schools and workplaces. What happens when government fails to do this is exemplified in the disastrous history of the UK Child Support Agency, which provided no recognition of, or incentives for, absent fathers or mothers-with-care to cooperate either with each other, or with the state. Individualised policy responses in the form of a parenting contract in respect of a truanting child employ a market rationality in the attempt to recognise and enforce responsibilities, which is justified in the absence of commitments that are legally enforceable, such as those between parent and child. But other commitments and relationships must also be recognised and enabled. The concern to encourage the reciprocity between the individual's real rights and freedoms (whereby the state takes seriously the work of enabling; White, 2003) and duties is crucial, but cannot succeed if there is no wider appreciation of the extent to which connection and relationship play a part in the choices that adult family members make; it cannot succeed in what amounts to a wider relational vacuum.[17] Family welfare and the promotion of the 'web of connection' require a more care-centred policy approach, which would represent a major departure from the historically central relationship between paid work and welfare, and which also requires attention to the politics of time as well as money, and to the individual in the context of his or her social commitments. Such an approach would provide a value base for policy making in the face of increasing diversity and competing interests between market, state and family, and between individual family members.

Notes

[1] I am not attempting to define 'successful' rigorously. There is evidence of political success and relatively high take-up levels for some policies.

[2] Although in fact Parsons' (1949, p 243) early work had acknowledged that the asymmetric roles of men and women, while functional, were 'at the same time an important source of strain'.

[3] As Oppenheimer (1994) has commented, this serves fundamentally to undermine the assumptions that Becker made about marriage and signals a real change in the meaning of marriage.

[4] This part of the argument does not hold for the US.

[5] Davidoff and Hall (1987) have shown the extent to which suitable matches were dictated by the considerations of family businesses in the early 19th century.

[6] This has been particularly true in the US (Popenoe, 1993), but has also been the view of UK commentators on the political Left and Right (see Lewis, 2001a, for a review).

[7] Although early 20th-century eugenic policies made considerably more headway in the US than in the UK.

[8] It is not too fanciful to see this as mirroring patterns of new governance more generally (Newman, 2001).

[9] A sample 'parenting contract' for parents of truanting children makes reference to meetings between parents and teachers between 16.00 and 16.30 hours, which may not be compatible with employment (Teachernet, 2006: 'Sample Parenting Contract', www.teachernet.gov.uk/wholeschool/behaviour/exclusion/parentingorders/, accessed 2 August 2006).

[10] 'New social risks' (as opposed to the old ones of poverty, illness, unemployment and the like) are hard to identify, although new social risk groups are not.

[11] A European Foundation for the Improvement of Living and Working Conditions survey of parents with children under six years old in 1998 found considerable differences in preferences for part-time work between member states (with relatively low levels in both Sweden and Southern Europe) (OECD, 2001, Table 4.3). Kangas and Rostgaard (2005), using International Social Survey Programme (ISSP) data for seven countries including England, have argued that care leaves and childcare services – the 'constraining' lack thereof – play a part in determining preferences. On the problem of preference theory in relation to work and family issues see also Crompton (2006).

[12] This part draws on work financed by the Economic and Social Research Council (ESRC) (grant no. RES 225 25 2001) and on (Lewis and Campbell, 2007a, 2007b).

[13] Measured in terms of the increase in annual government spending between 1997 and 2005, the initiatives are significant: amounting to about £2.4 billion on the supply side for childcare for the under-fives (HC, 2005a, Annex A) and

about £650 million on the demand side (HM Treasury et al, 2004; Brewer et al, 2005); over £800 million for maternity pay (DWP annual Departmental Reports); and about £60 million and £5 million respectively for paternity pay and adoption pay (introduced in 2003) (DTI, 2000, 2001a, 2001b). The initiatives are also significant when measured in terms of increased annual costs to employers (HC, 2005b, Appendix 6): maternity leave and pay – over £100 million; parental leave – £45 million; and the right to request flexible working – £290 million. Much of the benefit of the UK's adoption of the EU's working-time and part-time work Directives also went to those with care responsibilities – these cost employers £2.9 billion and £27 million annually (HC, 2005b, Appendix 6).

[14] Twelve-and-a-half hours of nursery care were offered in 1998, to be extended to 15 hours by 2010, with longer hours of opening for children aged 3-14 promised in the 10-year childcare strategy announced in 2004 (HM Treasury et al, 2004). The 13 weeks of parental leave are unpaid and inflexible.

[15] But almost a quarter of men with dependent children worked more than 48 hours a week in 1998 (Kodz et al, 2003) and the asymmetry between men's and women's working hours is greatest when children are young. 'Shift parenting' is also relatively common in the UK with 53% of employed mothers and 79% of employed fathers working non-standard hours (Lavalle et al, 2002; OECD, 2005).

[16] The results of the Effective Provision of Pre-School Education (EPPE) and National Institute of Child Health and Human Development (NICHD) studies were cited (HM Treasury et al, 2004, Appendix on Child Development, Annex A, pp 65-71).

[17] This is not necessarily an argument against welfare conditionality; as Deacon (2007) has pointed out, some forms of conditionality can be grounded more effectively in an ethic of care than in contractual ethics.

References

Alesina, A. and Glaeser, E.L. (2004) *Fighting Poverty in the US and Europe*, Oxford: Oxford University Press.

Bane, M.J. and Ellwood, D.T. (1994) *Welfare Realities from Rhetoric to Reform*, Cambridge, MA: Harvard University Press.

Beck, U. and Beck-Gernsheim, E. (1995) *The Normal Chaos of Love*, Cambridge: Polity Press.

Becker, G. (1981) *A Treatise on the Family*, Cambridge, MA: Harvard University Press.

Bettio, F. and Plantenga, J. (2004) 'Comparing care regimes in Europe', *Feminist Economics*, vol 10, no 1, pp 85-113.

Beveridge, W.H. (1942) *Social Insurance and Allied Services*, Cmd 6404, London: HMSO.

Bianchi, S.M. and Casper, L.M. (2004) 'The stalled revolution: gender and time allocation in the US', Paper presented at the International Conference on Work and Family, CRFR, University of Edinburgh, 30 June-2 July.

Bonoli, G. (2005) 'The politics of the new social policies: providing coverage against new social risks in mature welfare states', *Policy & Politics*, vol 33, no 3, pp 431-49.

Brewer, M., Crawford, C. and Dearden, L. (2005) 'Reforms to childcare policy', *Green Budget*, London: Institute for Fiscal Studies.

Buchmann, M. (1989) *The Script of Life in Modern Society: Entry into Adulthood in a Changing World*, Chicago, IL: University of Chicago Press.

Burgess, E.W. and Locke, H.J. (1953) *The Family from Institution to Companionship* (2nd edition), New York, NY: American Book Co (1st edition 1945).

CBI (Confederation of British Industry) (2005) *Second Reading Briefing on Work and Families Bill*, December, London: CBI.

Commission of the European Communities (2000) *Social Policy Agenda*. Communication, COM (2000) 379 final of 28/6/00.

Council of the European Union (2000) Lisbon European Council of 23 and 24 March 2000: *Conclusions of the Presidency*.

Crompton, R. (2006) *Employment and the Family*, Cambridge: Cambridge University Press.

Crompton, R., Brockmann, M. and Wiggins, R.D. (2003) 'A woman's place ... employment and family life for men and women', in A. Park, J. Curtice, K. Thomson, L. Jarvis and C. Bromley (eds) *British Social Attitudes: The 20th Report*, London: Sage Publications.

Davidoff, L. and Hall, C. (1987) *Family Fortunes: Men and Women of the English Middle Class*, London: Hutchinson.

Deacon, A. (2002) *Perspective on Welfare: Ideas, Ideologies and Policy*, Buckingham: Open University Press.

Deacon, A. (2007) 'Civic labour or Doulia? Care, reciprocity and welfare', *Social Policy and Society*, vol 6, no 4.

Dex, S. (2003) *Work and Family in the Twenty-First Century*, York: Joseph Rowntree Foundation.

DfEE (Department for Education and Employment) (2000) *Work Life Balance: Changing Patterns in a Changing World*, Discussion Document, London: DfEE.

DTI (Department of Trade and Industry) (2000) *Work and Parents: Competitiveness and Choice*, Cm 5005, Norwich: The Stationery Office.

DTI (2001a) *Work and Parents: Competitiveness and Choice, A Framework for Adoption Leave*, London: DTI.

DTI (2001b) *Work and Parents: Competitiveness and Choice: A Framework for Paternity Leave*, London: DTI.

DTI (2006) *Draft Regulations on Maternity and Adoption Leave and Flexible Working*, London: DTI.

Elshtain, J.B. (1981) *Public Man, Private Woman: Women in Social and Political Thought*, Princeton, NJ: Princeton University Press.

Esping-Andersen, G. (1999) *Social Foundations of Post-Industrial Economies*, Oxford: Oxford University Press.

Esping-Andersen, G., Gallie, D., Hemerijck, A. and Myles, J. (2002) *Why we Need a New Welfare State*, Oxford: Oxford University Press.

Fagan, C. and Lallement, M. (2000) 'Working time, social integration and transitional labour markets', in J. O'Reilly, I. Cebriean, M. Lallement (eds) *Working-Time Changes: Social Integration through Transitional Labour Markets*, Cheltenham: Edward Elgar.

Finch, J. and Mason, J. (1993) *Negotiating Family Responsibilities*, London: Tavistock/Routledge.

Finer Commission (1974) *Report of the Committee on One-Parent Families*, Cmnd 5629, London: HMSO.

Fraser, N. (1997) *Justice Interruptus: Critical Reflections on The 'Post-Socialist' Condition*, London: Routledge.

Gauthier, A.H. (1996) *The State and the Family: A Comparative Analysis of Family Policies in Industrialized Countries*, Oxford: Clarendon Press.

Gershuny, J. (2000) *Changing Times: Work and Leisure in Post-Industrial Society*, Oxford: Oxford University Press.

Gilbert, N. (2002) *The Transformation of the Welfare State: The Silent Surrender of Public Responsibility*, Oxford: Oxford University Press.

Gilligan, C. (1982) *In a Different Voice: Psychological Theory and Women's Development*, Cambridge, MA: Harvard University Press.

Gornick, J. and Meyers, M. (2003) *Families that Work: Policies for Reconciling Parenthood and Employment*, New York, NY: Russell Sage.

Hakim, C. (2000) *Work-Lifestyle Choices in the Twenty-First Century: Preference Theory*, Oxford: Oxford University Press.

Hantrais, L. (2004) *Family Policy Matters: Responding to Family Change in Europe*, Bristol: The Policy Press.

HC (House of Commons) (2001) Oral evidence from Margaret Hodge, *Early Years Follow-Up*, Select Committee on Education and Employment, 2000-2001 Session, HC 438, Hansard.

HC (2002) *Budget Statement*, 17 April, Hansard.

HC (2003) *Fifth Report*, Work and Pensions Select Committee, 2002-03 Session, HC 564, Hansard.

HC (2005a) *Ninth Report*, Education and Skills Select Committee, 2004-05 Session, HC 40, Hansard.

HC (2005b) *Seventh Report*, Trade and Industry Select Committee, 2004-05 Session, HC 90, Hansard.

Hegewisch, A. (2005) 'Individual working time rights in Germany and the UK: how a little law can go a long way', in A. Hegewisch (ed) *Working Time for Working Families: Europe and the United States*, Washington, DC: Friedrich-Ebert-Stiftung.

Hendrick, H. (1994) *Child Welfare: England, 1872-1989*, London: Routledge.

Heyman, J. (2000) *The Widening Gap: Why America's Working Families are in Jeopardy and What Can be Done about it*, New York, NY: Basic Books.

HM Treasury (1997) *Pre-Budget Report*, London: HM Treasury.

HM Treasury (2002) *Realising Europe's Potential: Economic Reform in Europe*, Cm 5318, Norwich: The Stationery Office.

HM Treasury, DfES (Department for Education and Skills), DWP (Department for Work and Pensions) and DTI (Department of Trade and Industry) (2004) *Choice for Parents, the Best Start for Children: A Ten-Year Strategy for Childcare*, London: HM Treasury.

HO (Home Office) (1998) *Supporting Families*, London: The Stationery Office.

Kangas, O. and Rostgaard, T. (2005) 'Preferences of care context: opinions on family and employment in seven European countries', Paper presented at the ESPAnet meeting, Freiburg, 22-24 September.

Kodz, J., Davis, S., Lain, D., Strebler, M., Rick, J., Bates, P., Cummings, J. and Meager, N. (2003) *Working Long Hours: A Review of the Evidence*, London: Department of Trade and Industry.

Kohli, M. (1986) 'The world we forgot: a historical review of the life-course', in V.W. Marshall (ed) *Later Life: The Social Psychology of Ageing*, London: Sage Publications.

Land, H. and Parker, R. (1978) 'Family policy in Britain: the hidden dimensions', in A. Kahn and S. Kamerman (eds) *Family Policy in Fourteen Countries*, New York, NY: Columbia University Press.

Lavalle, I., Arthur, S., Millward, C., Scott, J. and Clayden, M. (2002) *Happy Families? Atypical Work and its Influence on Family Life*, Bristol: The Policy Press.

LFS (Labour Force Survey) (2006) www.statistics.gov.uk/downloads/theme_labour/LMS_Fr_Hs/webtable08, accessed 31 July 2006.

Lewis, J. (2001a) *The End of Marriage? Individualism and Intimate Relations*, Cheltenham: Edward Elgar.

Lewis, J. (2001b) 'The decline of the male breadwinner model: the implications for work and care', *Social Politics*, vol 8, no (2) pp 152-70.

Lewis, J. (2002) 'Gender and welfare state change', *European Societies*, vol 4, no 4, pp 331-57.

Lewis, J. and Campbell, M. (2007a) 'UK work/family balance policies and gender equality, 1997-2005', *Social Politics*, vol 14, no 1, pp 4-30.

Lewis, J. and Campbell, M. (2007b) 'Work/family balance policies in the UK since 1997: a new departure?', *Journal of Social Policy*, vol 36, no 3, pp 365-81.

Lewis, J. and Giullari, S. (2005) 'The adult worker model family, gender equality and care: the search for new policy principles and the possibilities and problems of a capabilities approach', *Economy and Society*, vol 34, no 1, pp 76-104.

Lister, R.. (2003) 'Investing in the citizen-workers of the future: transformations in citizenship and the state under New Labour', *Social Policy and Administration*, vol 37, no 5, pp 427-43.

Mead, L. (1997) *The New Paternalism*, Washington, DC: Brookings Institution.

Morgan, P. (1996) *Are Families Affordable?*, London: Centre for Policy Studies.

Mount, F. (1983) *The Subversive Family*, London: Allen and Unwin.

Newman, J. (2001) *Modernising Governance: New Labour, Policy and Society*, London: Sage Publications.

Nussbaum, M. (1999) *Sex and Social Justice*, Oxford: Oxford University Press.

OECD (Organisation for Economic Co-operation and Development) (2001) *Employment Outlook*, June, Paris: OECD.

OECD (2005) *Babies and Bosses: Reconciling Work and Family Life*, vol 4, Paris: OECD.

Oppenheimer, V.K. (1994) 'Women's rising employment and the future of the family in industrialised societies', *Population and Development Review*, vol 20, no 2, pp 293-342.

Parsons, T. (1949) *Essays in Sociological Theory Pure and Applied*, Glencoe, Ill: Free Press.

Parsons, T. and Bales, R.F. (1955) *Family Socialization and Interaction Process*, Glencoe, Ill: Free Press.

Phillips, R. (1988) *Putting Asunder: A History of Divorce in Western Society*, Cambridge: Cambridge University Press.

Popenoe, D. (1993) 'American family decline, 1960-1900: a review and appraisal', *Journal of Marriage and the Family*, vol 55 (August), pp 527-55.

Randall, V. (2000) *The Politics of Child Daycare in Britain*, Oxford: Oxford University Press.

Schor, J. (2001) *The Overworked American*, New York, NY: Basic Books.

Silva, B. and Smart, C. (eds) (1999) *The New Family*, London: Sage Publications.

Sevenhuijsen, S. (1998) *Citizenship and the Ethics of Care*, London: Routledge.

Skocpol, T. (2000) *The Missing Middle: Working Families and the Future of American Social Policy*, New York, NY: W.W. Norton & Company.

Smeaton, D. (2006) *Dads and their Babies: A Household Analysis*, Working Paper Series, no 44, London: PSI.

Spencer, H. (1876) *The Principles of Sociology*, vol 1, London: Williams and Norgate.

Strathern, M. (1992) *After Nature: English Kinship in the Late Twentieth Century*, Cambridge: Cambridge University Press.

Strohmeier, K.P. (2002) 'Family policy – how does it work?', in F.X. Kaufmann, A. Kuijsten, H.J. Schulze and K.P. Strohmeier (eds) *Family Life and Family Policies in Europe*, vol 2, Oxford: Oxford University Press.

Supiot, A. (2001) *Beyond Employment*, Oxford: Oxford University Press.

Tronto, J. (1993) *Moral Boundaries: A Political Argument for and Ethic of Care*, London: Routledge.

Walling, A. (2005) 'Families and work', *Labour Market Trends* (July), pp 275-83.

White, S. (2003) *The Civic Minimum: On the Rights and Obligations of Economic Citizenship*, Oxford: Oxford University Press.

FIVE

Schools, financing and educational standards

Anne West[1]

Introduction

Howard Glennerster has carried out research on almost all the social services, but above all, he has worked on financing systems and the state of welfare (for example, Glennerster and Hills, 1998; Glennerster, 2003). His work on the financing of education is unsurpassed. This chapter takes as its starting point a seminal paper, 'United Kingdom education 1997-2001' (Glennerster, 2002), which reviews the achievements of the Labour government's education policy and in so doing addresses education funding and school performance. In this chapter, these two themes are re-examined in light of the objectives of Labour administrations since 1997.

Education policy has had a high political profile since the Labour government was elected into office in 1997. In three manifestos – 1997, 2001 and 2005 – education has been the government's 'number one priority' (Labour Party, 2001, 2005). The objectives of the government have been far-reaching. In relation to schools, these have included increasing resources, improving educational standards and tackling disadvantage.

This chapter argues that, although some objectives are clearly being met, tensions exist and some policies need to be re-evaluated if the overall aim is to ensure that the school system in England offers the highest-quality education to all children. The longstanding achievement gaps between children from different social groups remain significant (DfES, 2005a). It is further argued that some of the policies need to be re-evaluated in light of their potential to increase segregation and reduce social cohesion.

More specifically, the chapter examines the extent to which key aspects of the Labour Party's manifesto have been realised and what still needs to be done to ensure that the educational needs of those who are disadvantaged are met. The focus is on two main issues about which Labour made commitments: levels of resourcing and improving educational standards. The focus in both cases will be on examining the extent to which policies are meeting the needs of all children including those who are disadvantaged. The final section concludes, reviewing the extent to which the Labour government has succeeded in meeting its objectives and highlighting the challenges that remain.

Resourcing

Prior to each election, the Labour Party in its manifesto made commitments to increase the proportion of national income spent on education. In 2005, a more radical proposal was also made:

> We will continue to raise the share of national income devoted to education. And we will continue to recognise the needs of disadvantaged pupils.... There will be a dedicated national schools budget set by central government, with a guaranteed per pupil increase for every school. (Labour Party, 2005, p 33)

Labour's commitment to increase expenditure on education was not immediately apparent after the 1997 election. Total expenditure in real terms was higher than that under the previous Conservative government by 1998-99 and it has continued to increase. However, it did not increase noticeably as a percentage of Gross Domestic Product (GDP). In 1996-97 this stood at 4.7%. It then fell and did not reach 1996-97 levels until 2001-02; by 2003-04 it had reached 5.3% (see Table 5.1).

In relation to England – the main focus in this chapter – current expenditure on schools by central and local government increased in real terms year on year, from £20,910 million in 1996-97 to £30,630 million in 2003-04, an increase of 46% (DfES, 2004b) (see Table 5.2).

Although additional money is 'no guarantee of better results' (Glennerster, 2002, p 122), the view held by the government is that there is an association (HM Treasury, 2004). Moreover, there is now evidence that in England higher expenditure is associated with higher national test and/or public examination results (West et al, 2001; Noden et al, 2002; Levačić et al, 2005; Jenkins et al, 2006). Two studies that used high-quality pupil-level data are particularly relevant in this context. Levačić et al (2005) found a statistically significant association between expenditure and attainment in science and mathematics,

Table 5.1: Public expenditure on education as a percentage of GDP, UK

	Total education expenditure in real terms (£ million)[a]	Education expenditure as a percentage of GDP in real terms[a]
1996-97	42,803	4.7
1997-98	42,753	4.5
1998-99	43,728	4.5
1999-00	44,988	4.4
2000-01	48,117	4.6
2001-02	52,762	4.9
2002-03	54,730	5.0
2003-04	59,323	5.3

Note: [a] At 2003-04 prices (author's calculations, see HM Treasury, 2005).
Source for raw data: DfES (2001a, 2002, 2004a, 2005b)

Table 5.2: Education expenditure by central and local government on schools in real terms, England

	Current expenditure on schools in real terms (£ million)[a]	Index 1996-97=100
1996-97	20,910	100
1997-98	21,129	101
1998-99	21,501	103
1999-00	23,034	110
2000-01	25,088	120
2001-02	27,462	131
2002-03	28,337	136
2003-04 (estimated)	30,630	146

Note: [a] At 2003-04 prices (author's calculations, see HM Treasury, 2005).
Source: DfES (2004b)

but not English, in terms of national test results at the age of 14 and the gain appeared to be greater for pupils from poorer backgrounds. Jenkins et al (2006) also found that higher levels of expenditure were associated with higher attainment as measured by General Certificate of Secondary Education (GCSE)[2] point score and GCSE science; for GCSE mathematics, there was a statistically significant relationship between expenditure and attainment for the 40% of pupils with the lowest prior attainment in the national tests at the age of 11. This is a particularly significant finding in light of the concerns about inequalities in educational achievement in England (Glennerster, 2002; West and Pennell, 2003; DfES, 2005a).

The question arises as to whether the resources for education are going where needs are greatest. The changes in the allocation of resources to local authorities and in the distribution from local authorities to schools are now examined and an analysis of the adequacy of the extent of the redistribution follows.

Allocation of resources to local authorities

The systems for allocating resources from central to local government have changed since 1997. However, all have been redistributive, with more disadvantaged areas benefiting from an element for 'additional educational needs' (AEN) in both the Education Standard Spending Assessment (SSA), which was in place until the end of 2002-03, and in the Education Formula Spending Share (EFSS), which was introduced from 2003-04 (for further discussion of area-based funding, see Chapter Twelve). However, the overall amount of funding allocated for AEN was broadly similar. In the allocations under the last year of the SSA system (2002-03) and the first year of the FSS system (2003-04) according to Department for Education and Skills (DfES) calculations, around 19% of funding was allocated across the country on the basis of AEN, with around 75% of the funding being allocated on a per pupil basis, 1-2% for population sparsity and 4% for additional costs associated with the south east of England (DfES, 2003a).

From 2006-07 an earmarked or 'ring-fenced' grant for most school-based education was introduced, as promised in the 2005 Labour Party manifesto. The Dedicated Schools Grant (DSG), as it is known, is distributed by the DfES to local authorities. This provides for the same items as had been funded via the Schools FSS.[3] The method used to distribute the funds to local authorities for the two-year period 2006-07 and 2007-08 reflects the previous allocation through the Schools FSS and preceding Education SSA formulae (DfES, 2006a). Moreover, the DfES estimated the funding for disadvantage delivered by the DSG 'using the proportion of deprivation funding delivered through each authority's 2005-06 Schools FSS allocation' (DfES, 2006a, para 46). On this basis, in 2006-07, approximately 11% of the funding was allocated on the basis of deprivation.[4] Thus, while the system for distributing resources changed, the basic underlying principles underpinning the allocation of resources from central to local government – in terms of providing resources to meet the educational needs associated with disadvantage – remained unchanged.

Allocation of resources to schools

Although local authorities set their own budgets for education, they must spend the DSG on school-based education. The local authority schools budget is divided into different parts. The part delegated to schools is the 'individual schools budget' and is distributed via a formula and managed by school governing bodies.

Originally, following the 1988 Education Reform Act, 80% of the budget allocated to schools was 'pupil-led', carrying the same value 'for all pupils of a certain age whatever school they attend' (DfES/HM Treasury, 2005, p 22). This percentage was reduced to 75% in 2002-03 (OPSI, 2002). The requirement for a certain percentage of funding to be pupil-led was removed from 2006 (DfES/HM Treasury, 2005; see also OPSI, 2006).

However, funding formulae must take into account pupil numbers (OPSI, 2006). Other factors that are permitted include pupils with special educational needs, pupils for whom English is not their first language, pupil mobility, characteristics of the school buildings and site, use of energy by schools, salaries at a school, incidence of pupils from minority ethnic groups having below average levels of academic achievement in relation to other pupils in the local authority area, and prior attainment of pupils entering a school.

Adequacy of redistribution

Since 2002-03, local authorities have also been obliged to include a factor in their formulae based on the incidence of social deprivation in their schools (OPSI, 2002, 2006). However, there is no requirement as to the minimum amount to be distributed by such a factor. In fact, according to the findings from a survey of local authorities carried out by the DfES/HM Treasury, where such a factor had been introduced in response to the new legal requirements, the amounts were low (DfES/HM Treasury, 2005): 'At least one authority ... [gives] all its schools £1 each through the social deprivation factor' (p 22).

Although funding is designed to meet the educational needs associated with disadvantage, there are concerns about whether redistribution is sufficient to meet the needs that exist. Ruth Lupton, who worked in the Centre for Analysis of Social Exclusion at the London School of Economics and Political Science, focused on four secondary schools in highly disadvantaged areas of England in her research. She identified a variety of challenges for schools: staff recruitment, pressures on teacher performance, pressures on management and inadequate resources for complex problems. She argues that the complex nature of the difficulties faced by these schools means that 'standard resources for teaching and standard resources for pastoral care are insufficient in themselves....' (Lupton, 2005, p 600) and stresses that resources are needed for 'smaller teaching groups, more teachers in the classroom, more non-contact time for front-line staff, a higher ratio of managers to staff, and substantially more investment in learning support, language teaching, pupil welfare or parental liaison roles' (p 602).

Some of the schools in Lupton's study were located in local authorities that benefited from the government's AEN funding. However, she argues that certain areas with high proportions of children, known to be eligible for free school meals and from minority ethnic groups may 'offer more favourable environments for schooling than white, lower poverty areas' (Lupton, 2004, p 19) and stresses the need for 'better measures of context' and 'funding mechanisms based on an assessment of the roles and activities needed, rather than on crude measures of intake' (p 19).

What is not clear is whether the concerns with funding levels are a function of the central to local government allocation mechanism or because of the funding formulae adopted by the local authorities to distribute funds to schools. A recent report by the DfES/HM Treasury (2005) argues that the real problem is to do with the way local authorities allocate funds to schools. A particular concern is that the amount of resource for disadvantage in the national distribution mechanism from central to local government is not always reflected locally (see, also, West, 2008: forthcoming). Following a survey of the 150 local authorities in England with responsibility for education, it was found that there was a lack of an objective basis for social deprivation factors; that the amount of funding allocated to schools tended to bear little relationship to funding received by local authorities from central government to meet AEN; and that in many cases, local authorities 'allocated funding for deprivation simply on a historic basis' (p 31).

Raising educational standards

Major commitments were made by the Labour Party, in each manifesto, to improve the overall quality of education and raise standards:

> There are excellent schools in Britain's state education system. But far too many children are denied the opportunity to succeed. Our task is to raise the standards of every school. (Labour Party, 1997, p 7)

In 2001, a target 'for an 85% success rate for 11-year-olds in English and maths' was set (Labour Party, 2001, p 18). This was reiterated in 2005 (Labour Party, 2005).

The national test result scores for 11-year-olds show an increase in the percentage of pupils reaching the expected levels in English and mathematics (DfEE, 1999a; DfES, 2006b). However, the government has not reached its target of an 85% success rate. In English, 79% reached this level in 2006, an increase of 16 percentage points since 1997 (63%); and in mathematics 76% reached this level in 2006, an increase of 14 percentage points since 1997 (62%).[5] There have also been improvements in GCSE results taken at the end of compulsory education. The percentage of pupils aged 15 at the beginning of the academic year, who achieved five or more GCSE examination passes at grades A★ to C, increased from 45% in 1997 to 56% in 2005, an increase of 11 percentage points in absolute terms (DfES, 2001b, 2006c).[6]

Several approaches have been used by the Labour government in its efforts to improve school standards, as measured by national test and examination results. First, there are national policies, some of which have been universally targeted on all schools and some of which have been targeted on particular local areas. Second, the quasi-market reforms emanating from the 1988 Education Reform Act 1988 have continued under Labour; it is argued that these have been driving up standards, but with some untoward if not unexpected consequences. These two approaches are now explored.

National and targeted policies to improve standards

National strategies focusing on literacy and numeracy have been introduced into the primary school curriculum in England by Labour. The literacy strategy was introduced in 1998/99 and includes an hour of literacy teaching a day. Prior to the introduction of the national strategy, the national literacy project was introduced into approximately 400 schools in 1996/97 and 1997/98. Using a treatment and control group approach, Machin and McNally (2004) analysed what had happened to reading attainment in schools that were part of the project compared with those that were not. They found that reading at the age of 11 years rose by more in schools that were part of the project between 1996 and 1998. The improvements in national test results are thus likely to be associated, at least in part, with the introduction of the literacy strategy.

In terms of specific policies targeted on disadvantaged areas, a high-profile development in the early days of the Labour government was the setting up of statutory Education Action Zones (EAZs). These were designed to target resources on disadvantaged areas (see NAO, 2001). However, the initiative was short-lived and in 2005 all statutory EAZs ended. As noted by Halpin et al (2004, p 77): 'the indifferent and mixed success of many EAZs ... provide the backdrop to the Government's ... decision to phase out their funding and not to create any new ones'.

In 1999, another policy targeting disadvantaged areas, Excellence in Cities (EiC), was launched. This benefited 58 of the 150 local education authorities in England (Kendall et al, 2005), 50 of which were the most deprived in England.[7] EiC was focused on areas, not on either disadvantaged schools or disadvantaged pupils. One of the three core strands focused on 'gifted and talented' pupils; a second, 'learning mentors', provided support to pupils who had particular obstacles to learning; and a third, 'learning support units', was designed to tackle disruption in schools (Simkins, 2004; Kendall et al, 2005).[8] Another initiative focusing on disadvantaged schools was the Pupil Learning Credits (PLC) pilot scheme (see Braun et al, 2005), which operated from 2001 to 2003. This provided additional resources to secondary schools with high proportions of pupils known to be eligible for free school meals in some EiC areas; the aim of the scheme was for schools to provide additional learning opportunities to pupils whose social circumstances were especially difficult.

The national evaluation of EiC revealed that the greatest impact of the policy was in terms of attainment in mathematics at the age of 14 for pupils in the most disadvantaged schools. Overall, pupils who attended schools in receipt of EiC funding had higher levels of attainment in mathematics at 14 than those who attended other schools, having taken into account a range of school and pupil factors including prior attainment (Kendall et al, 2005). Interestingly, higher attainment was observed in schools that became part of EiC in the first year of the programme, many of which were also part of the PLC pilot scheme (see McNally, 2005).

The most recent policy initiative that seeks to improve the achievement levels of children in disadvantaged areas is that of 'personalised learning', for which the DfES provides funding:

> Personalisation is the key to tackling the persistent achievement gaps between different social and ethnic groups. It means a tailored education for every child and young person, that gives them strength in the basics, stretches their aspirations, and builds their life chances. It will create

> opportunity for every child, regardless of their background.
> (DfES, 2005c, p 50)

Personalisation is intended to provide intensive support for pupils who are not making expected progress and is focused on local authorities with the highest numbers of underachieving and deprived children. The aim is for personalisation of learning to help reduce the attainment gap. Some of this funding goes directly to schools via the School Standards Grant (HM Treasury, 2006).

Choice, diversity and competition

The quasi-market reforms introduced by the Conservative government following the 1988 Education Reform Act, have been maintained and indeed extended under Labour (Glennerster, 2002). Testing and the publication of results have continued and school diversity, particularly at secondary level, is higher on the agenda than it was under the Conservatives. A key aim of the quasi-market reforms was to encourage competition between schools and in so doing to raise standards. Has this happened? And to the extent that it has, what have the consequences been?

In this section, the related issues of choice and diversity, competition and cream-skimming are explored. The focus is on secondary schools, where the quasi-market is most developed, although reference is also made to primary schools.

Choice and diversity

The Labour Party manifestos for both 2001 and 2005 addressed the issue of school diversity. In the 2001 manifesto there was a pledge to expand the numbers of specialist schools 'to at least 1,500 by 2006.... We will encourage more church and other faith-sponsored schools, where parents wish it. We will establish more City Academies....' (Labour Party, 2001, p 19).

In 2005, the manifesto reiterated the desire for all schools to become specialist. It also highlighted the role that new education providers could play:

> Britain has a positive tradition of independent providers within the state system, including church and other faith schools. Where new educational providers can help boost standards and opportunities in a locality we will welcome

> them into the state system, subject to parental demand, fair
> funding and fair admissions. (Labour Party, 2005, p 37)

The number of specialist schools has increased markedly, with 82%
(DfES, 2006d) of maintained secondary schools having this status and
specialising in one or more of a prescribed set of subjects as well as
offering the national curriculum (see Noden and Schagen, 2006).

Academies have been introduced by the Labour government, and
there is a target to establish 200 by 2010 (DfES 2005c). These are similar
to the city technology colleges that were introduced by the previous
Conservative government. Like city technology colleges, academies are
classified as independent, but are in receipt of public revenue funding.
Unlike city technology college sponsors, academy sponsors have
only been expected to contribute a very small share of capital costs
– a 'charitable donation of 10% of the building costs' (DfES, 2006e,
p 3). In September 2006, there were 46 academies (DfES, 2006f). The
increasing role of religious bodies is highlighted with this new type of
school. *The Independent* reported in September 2006 that 42 of the first
100 academies have Christian sponsors; this is important as academies
do not have to follow the national curriculum, unlike other publicly
funded schools, and concerns have been expressed about the religious
education offered in some academies.

The vast majority of voluntary-aided faith schools are Christian.
Since Labour came into office, five Muslim and two Sikh schools have
become part of the maintained sector as voluntary-aided schools (DfES,
2005d). Religious schools, almost invariably, select pupils on the basis
of their religion or religious denomination in the event of there being
more applicants than places (West et al, 2004). One of the outcomes of
this is that religious schools are likely to increase segregation.

As most religious schools are Christian, children of Bangladeshi
or Pakistani origin who are more likely to be Muslim, are less likely
to attend them (see West and Hind, 2007). As noted in the Cantle
Report produced following riots in 2001 in Oldham, Burnley and
Bradford: 'many schools (including the existing faith schools – mainly
Christian) can appear to foster separation' (Cantle, 2001, p 28). The
report also expressed concern that 'some existing faith schools appear
to be operating discriminatory policies where religious affiliations
protect cultural and ethnic divisions' (p 33).

The Labour government has retained fully academically selective
grammar schools, but has not extended the 11-plus (in line with
its manifesto commitments). There are still 164 grammar schools in
England – accounting for 5% of secondary schools. Very few pupils

from disadvantaged families attend them. According to research by the Sutton Trust (2005), the percentage of pupils known to be eligible for free school meals in grammar schools was found to be 2% compared with the national secondary school average of 14%. In London the percentage in grammar schools was also found to be 2% compared with 16% in comprehensive schools in those local authorities with grammar schools (West and Hind, 2007). Gorard et al (2003) found that certain types of schools, such as those that are selective or responsible for their own admissions, 'tend to increase the socio-economic segregation of school intakes' (p 136).

Competition

The question arises as to whether or not schools see themselves as being in competition with one another. And to the extent that there is competition, how is this impacting on standards? A number of qualitative research studies suggest that schools do see themselves as being in competition with others. Yeomans et al (2000) found that local competitive pressures hampered cooperative links between specialist schools and other secondary schools in the neighbourhood. They found evidence of hostility from both specialist and non-specialist schools to the idea of working together.

Adnett and Davies (2001) and Bell and West (2003) focused on cooperation between schools, and in so doing found that competitive pressures appeared to hamper cooperation. Noden et al (2004) found that there were difficulties with specialist secondary schools establishing links with other secondary schools. As noted by one interviewee: 'There's a problem about the ownership of results. What if their results go up? Or ours? Who takes the credit?' (p 12). There is, then, some qualitative evidence to suggest that secondary schools do see themselves to be in competition.

The second question concerns the extent to which competition is affecting standards. Two large-scale quantitative studies shed light on this. Bradley and Taylor (2002) investigated the effects of the quasi-market on efficiency and equity in secondary schools in the 1990s. They found strong evidence that the quasi-market has led to a substantial improvement in schools' examination results.

Levačić (2004) also examined the relationship between competition and performance. She found that competition, as measured in terms of five or more perceived competitors, had a positive and statistically significant impact on examination results. At the GCSE level, the key indicator is five or more high-grade passes (grades A*, A, B and C).

Levačić found no impact in terms of the pupils obtaining five or more GCSE passes at grades A★ to G, but a positive impact in terms of the proportion of pupils obtaining five or more GCSE passes at grades A★ to C:

> Schools do respond to competitive pressures to improve a particularly well publicized and widely used performance indicator. This supports the view that competitive pressures do stimulate managers and teachers in schools to improve a measure of performance accorded a high public profile. This only serves to emphasize the importance for the policy of choosing the right indicators in the first place.' (Levačić, 2004, p 188)

This raises a fundamental question. If competition is an effective means of raising performance, is the current focus on the percentage of pupils achieving five GCSE passes at grades A★ to C the most appropriate indicator if one of the aims of government policy is to raise the standards of all pupils? And what are the consequences of focusing on the higher achievers as opposed to those who are low attainers or have more difficulty with school work?

The evidence suggests that pupils who are perceived to be on the borderline between grade C and grade D are targeted for additional teaching support with a view to increasing their grades from five GCSE D grades to five C grades (West and Pennell, 2000; Golden et al, 2002; Wilson et al, 2006). While such 'performance-maximising behaviour' is designed to improve the school's league table position and indeed the qualifications of the pupil concerned, the incentive structure is likely to benefit certain pupils only. The major losers are likely to be those performing well below the target levels; they are, moreover, the group most in need of additional help in order to increase their personal opportunities and to minimise the risk of failure, disaffection and the consequent costs to society (see West and Pennell, 2003).

Another concern with the current high-profile indicator is that schools will seek to maximise league table performance by entering pupils for examinations that they judge are easier to pass, at the expense of focusing on, for example, English and mathematics. This is particularly worrying. Competence in English is necessary for employment and is a vital life skill. And American research suggests that numeracy skills have a strong relationship with lower income in later life (Glennerster, 2002; Sparkes and Glennerster, 2002). The evidence indicates that this is a cause for concern as although the percentage of pupils obtaining five or more GCSE examination passes at grades A* to C at the end of compulsory schooling in 2005 was 56%, the percentage obtaining this number of passes including mathematics and English was only 44% (DfES, 2006c).

Cream-skimming

One of Howard Glennerster's worries was that 'competition would merely induce cream-skimming or competition for better pupils, rather than improved efficiency' (2002, p 130). Increasingly, the evidence suggests that there is likely to be cream-skimming by certain types of schools.

Bradley and Taylor (2002) found that schools with 'good' examination results, by comparison with schools in the same district, had experienced a reduction in the proportion of children from poor families and vice versa. While it is not possible, from their analysis, to explain the processes by which this might have occurred, one possibility is that this is a result of cream-skimming, which relates to school admissions.

In its 1997 manifesto, the Labour Party responded to concerns being made at that time about the impact of what was then a largely unregulated schools' quasi-market, by expressing support for 'guidelines for open and fair admissions' (Labour Party, 1997, p 9). The 1998 School Standards and Framework Act set a new legal framework for admissions with an associated Code of Practice (DfEE, 1999b; DfES, 2003b). According to the Code of Practice, admissions criteria should be objective, clear and fair.

At this stage it is necessary to outline how the process for secondary school admissions works in practice. Parents or carers of children who are in their final year of primary school (age 11) express 'preferences' for the secondary schools they wish their child to attend. If there are more applicants than places, the decision as to whether or not a pupil is offered a place is taken by either the local authority (in the case of community and voluntary-controlled schools), or the school in the case of schools that control their own admissions – voluntary-aided (in the main faith) and foundation (former grant-maintained) schools, city technology colleges and academies.[9] In the case of community and voluntary-controlled schools, the local authority makes an 'administrative' decision allocating pupils to a school on the basis of the parents' preferences and schools' published admissions criteria. In the case of faith and foundation schools, the school decides or 'chooses' which pupils should be admitted; this too should be a purely 'administrative' decision based on parents' preferences and the school's admissions criteria (see also West, 2006).

A major study of secondary school admissions criteria and practices in England for 2001 (West et al, 2004), found that the majority of criteria were objective, clear and fair. However, a significant minority of 'comprehensive' schools used a variety of admissions criteria or practices that could be used to select certain pupils over others.[10] Nearly half of secondary schools that controlled their own admissions used these or overtly selective criteria (such as selecting a proportion of children with an aptitude in a specified subject area; this is permitted for schools with a specialism) compared with only one in ten schools whose admissions were the responsibility of the local authority (West et al, 2006). In addition, voluntary-aided faith schools select on the basis of religious commitment or denomination.

In light of this, it is perhaps unsurprising to find that school composition varies according to school type. West and Hind (2007) found that secondary schools in London that controlled their own admissions admitted higher-performing children as measured by the results in the national tests taken at the age of 11, prior to admission to secondary school, than schools where the local authority controlled admissions. In addition, schools with selective/potentially selective criteria admitted even higher-performing pupils. The percentage of pupils known to be eligible for free school meals was lower in schools that controlled their own admissions as was the percentage of students with 'statements' of special educational needs (which carry additional resources to help meet pupils' needs) and without.

In relation to voluntary-aided schools, Chamberlain et al (2006) found that the proportion of pupils known to be eligible for free school meals was lower in both primary and secondary schools compared with the proportion in the local communities. And Gibbons and Silva (2006) found that faith primary schools had a very small impact on pupils' progress, noting that:

> There is clear positive selection into Faith schools (and into schools that have autonomous admissions and governance arrangements) on the basis of observable characteristics that are favourable to education – even when we compare pupils that originate in the same block of residential housing. (p 32)

They suggest that 'any performance impact from "Faith" schools in England seems to be linked to autonomous governance and admissions arrangements, and not to religious affiliation' (p 29).

There are no national data on the characteristics of parents who apply to different types of school for their children, and which are offered places. However, on the basis of previous research, there are likely to be differences. Parents have different preferences and those from different social groups engage with the choice process in different ways (see David et al, 1994; West et al, 1995; Ball et al, 1996; Ball and Gewirtz, 1997; Woods et al, 1998; Gorard, 1999). In a major DfES-funded research project, Flatley et al (2001) found that where the mother was in a manual social class, parents were less likely to cite academic factors as among the reasons for wanting a place at their favourite school. Noden et al (1998) in a smaller study in London found that parents of children from working-class families were less likely to apply to, and their children less likely to go on to attend, higher-performing secondary schools. This may arise from self-selection by parents/carers, differences in resources to pay for transport, and differences between the capacities of different parents/carers to successfully negotiate school admissions' administrative systems, as well as schools' admissions criteria and practices.

However, even with consistently different patterns of application, this would not be sufficient to argue against school selectivity, as parents would be acting in an irrational way if they applied to a particular school in the knowledge that their child did not meet the school's admissions criteria.

There are also barriers imposed by some schools responsible for their own admissions. In particular, parents may be required to complete a supplementary form in addition to the application form they submit to the local authority (Pennell et al, 2006). These forms may ask parents to provide information quite unrelated to the school's admissions criteria – for example, their occupations, marital status, whether they live in hostel or bed and breakfast accommodation or whether they have refugee status. The fact that schools are seeking out personal information, irrelevant to the school's oversubscription admissions criteria, suggests that they may well be cream-skimming.

Notwithstanding ongoing concerns about school admissions, the Labour government's second Code of Practice on School Admissions, which was more stringent than the first version (DfEE, 1999b; DfES, 2003b) has resulted in an increase in the use of criteria that could be said to enhance social justice and inclusion, in particular prioritising children in care (Pennell et al, 2006). The 2006 Education and Inspections Act and associated School Admissions Code is also likely to enhance social justice further, although whether it will be sufficient remains to be seen, given that the administrative allocation to schools will still rest with individual schools that are responsible for admissions, as opposed to an independent body with no vested interest in the outcome of the admissions process.

Conclusion

This chapter has focused on financing schools and educational standards, and examined the extent to which the Labour government has succeeded in meeting its objectives through its various policies and initiatives. In terms of resourcing, while expenditure did not rise in the early years of the Labour government from 1997, it has, since then, increased as a proportion of GDP. The system of distributing resources to local authorities has changed although the allocation to meet AEN has not changed. There have been changes in the way in which local authorities allocate funds to schools and there is now a requirement to include a factor to take account of disadvantage; significantly, there is no longer a requirement for 75% of the funding to be pupil-led. One of the major concerns is that the allocation of resources by local authorities to schools does not take sufficient account of pupils who are from disadvantaged backgrounds; this is clearly an area where further government action is needed.

Educational standards at the end of primary school and at the end of compulsory school have improved; the literacy and numeracy strategies, together with other targeted policy initiatives, such as EiC, appear to have had a positive effect on standards. The research evidence suggests that the market-oriented reforms have also had a positive impact on standards, especially with respect to the proportion of pupils obtaining five or more GCSE passes at grades A* to C. However, this is unlikely to benefit pupils who are low attainers or from disadvantaged backgrounds. If schools are to focus more attention on disadvantaged and/or low-achieving pupils, the incentives need to change. Given that there is a need for everyone to be literate and numerate, it may be that there should be indicators to address functional literacy and numeracy.

The evidence suggests that some schools that have autonomy over admissions are cream-skimming. A stronger School Admissions Code of Practice accompanies the 2006 Education and Inspections Act. This should have some impact in terms of equity of access to different types of school, although without close monitoring, it is unlikely to eliminate school selectivity, as the admissions process is not open to public scrutiny. A more radical way forward would be for the allocation of school places to be taken away from schools and given to another body, which would be responsible for matching parental preferences with schools admissions criteria. As Howard Glennerster (2002, p 133) commented: 'We have done far too little to offset the incentives for schools to cream-skim the most able or the least difficult to teach'.

Although not new, concerns about the extent to which schools with a religious character can segregate communities, serve to highlight the major tensions that exist between school diversity and social cohesion. Voluntary-aided schools receive their revenue funding and 90% of capital funding from the state. Given that the state is a major stakeholder, the question arises as to whether a certain – relatively high – proportion of places should be open to all children in a given community. Giving priority to children from one faith, as is currently the case for the majority of faith schools, is potentially divisive, and does not foster greater cohesion. Education is not just about increasing human capital, it is about socialisation, tolerance and fostering a cohesive society. A cause for concern is that for many ethnic groups, children are more segregated in their schools than in the areas where they live (Burgess et al, 2005). If children from different social, religious and ethnic backgrounds are educated in the same school, a more cohesive society is likely to be created and sustained. Incentives to create such a system need to be in place. By providing differential resourcing based on school intakes – with higher amounts going to schools with intakes that are socially and ethnically mixed to incentivise greater pupil diversity in schools – there is an opportunity for greater social cohesion to be fostered. The government has a responsibility to the wider society and not merely to parents making individualised choices for their children's schooling.

Notes

[1] I would like to thank Julian Le Grand and Hazel Pennell for comments on an earlier version of this chapter and Peter Currie for help with the preparation of the chapter.

[2] GCSE examinations are taken in separate subjects, normally at the age of 16, the end of compulsory education. They are graded A* to G. Five GCSE passes at grades A*, A, B and C are normally required to progress to General Certificate of Education Advanced Subsidiary and Advanced (GCE AS and A) level. Two A levels are the normal minimum requirement for progression to university.

[3] The functions of local authorities with responsibility for education continue to be funded through the local education authority block in the Revenue Support Grant.

[4] These are the author's own calculations. The DSG only relates to part of the previous Education FSS and so the proportions allocated to AEN are not directly comparable.

[5] As these tests are 'high stakes' they provide incentives for teachers to teach test technique and 'teach to the test'. There has been a debate about the extent of the improvement (see Tymms, 2004; Statistics Commission, 2005). However, while national test scores might not be a perfect way to measure educational standards over time: 'There is no real alternative at present to using statutory test scores for setting targets for aggregate standards' (Statistics Commission, 2005, para 25).

[6] This improvement continues an upward trajectory of examination results, although there has been much discussion as to whether or not the increase reflects a genuine improvement in standards (see West and Pennell, 2003).

[7] DfES expenditure on EiC (excluding specialist and beacon schools that were part of EiC) rose from about £24 million in 1999-2000 to £139 million in 2000-01 (the first full year) and to about £386 million in 2005-06 (House of Commons Hansard, 2004). While representing a significant use of resources, this needs to be seen in the context of overall local authority recurrent expenditure on secondary schools of over £9,000 million in 2000-01 (Kendall et al, 2005).

[8] After statutory EAZs ended, they continued under a different guise as EiC Action Zones (see Kendall et al, 2005).

[9] Voluntary-aided schools have always had autonomy over admissions (see West et al, 2006). Following the 1988 Education Reform Act, schools were able to opt out of local authority control and become grant-maintained and take over control of school admissions from the local authority. Under the Labour government's 1998 School Standards and Framework Act, they became foundation schools (or reverted to voluntary status), but still retained control over admissions. State-maintained secondary schools in England (N=3,385) comprise 64.8% community schools, 3.5% voluntary-controlled schools, 16.5% voluntary-aided (mostly religious) schools and 15.1% foundation schools (DfES, 2005d).

---

[10] These included interviews with pupils/parents; giving priority to a child of an employee/a governor/a former pupil; giving priority to a child with a family connection to the school; pastoral or compassionate factors; primary school report; headteacher's recommendation; and the academic record of a sibling (see West et al, 2006).

References

Adnett, N. and Davies, P. (2001) 'Schooling reforms in England: from quasi-markets to co-opetition?', *Journal of Education Policy*, vol 18, no 4, pp 393-406.

Ball, S. and Gewirtz, S. (1997) 'Is research possible? A rejoinder to Tooley's "On school choice and social class"', *British Journal of Sociology of Education*, vol 18, no 4, pp 575-86.

Ball, S., Bowe, R. and Gewirtz, S. (1996) 'School choice, social class and distinction: the realization of social advantage in education', *Journal of Education Policy*, vol 11, no 1, pp 89-112.

Bell, K. and West, A. (2003) 'Specialist schools: an exploration of competition and co-operation', *Educational Studies*, vol 29, no 2/3, pp 273-89.

Bradley, S. and Taylor, J. (2002) 'The effect of the quasi-market on the efficiency-equity trade-off in the secondary school sector', *Bulletin of Economic Research*, vol 54, no 3, pp 295-314.

Braun, A., Noden, P., Hind, A., McNally, S. and West, A. (2005) *Final Report of the Evaluation of the Pupil Learning Credits Pilot Scheme*, Research Report 687, London: Department for Education and Skills, www.dfes.gov.uk/research/data/uploadfiles/RR687.pdf

Burgess, S., Wilson, D. and Lupton, R. (2005) 'Parallel lives? Ethnic segregation in schools and neighbourhoods', *Urban Studies*, vol 42, no 7, pp 1027-56.

Cantle, T. (2001) *Community Cohesion: A Report of Independent Review Team*, Chaired by Ted Cantle, London: Home Office.

Chamberlain, T., Rutt, S. and Fletcher-Campbell, F. (2006) *Admissions: Who goes Where? Messages from Statistics*, Slough: National Foundation for Educational Research.

David, M., West, A. and Ribbens, J. (1994) *Mother's Intuition? Choosing Secondary Schools*, London: The Falmer Press.

DfEE (Department for Education and Employment) (1999a) *Statistics of Education: National Curriculum Assessments of 7, 11 and 14 year olds in England 1998*, London: The Stationery Office, www.dfes.gov.uk/rsgateway/DB/SBU/b000053/nca.pdf

DfEE (1999b) *Code of Practice on School Admissions*, London: DfEE.

DfES (Department for Education and Skills) (2001a) *Statistics of Education: Education and Training Statistics for the United Kingdom 2001*, London: The Stationery Office.

DfES (2001b) *Statistics of Education: Public Examinations GCSE/GNVQ and GCE/AGNVQ in England 2000*, London: DfES, www.dfes.gov. uk/rsgateway/DB/VOL/v000279/vol02-2001.pdf

DfES (2002) *Statistics of Education: Education and Training Statistics for the United Kingdom 2002*, London: The Stationery Office.

DfES (2003a) *Technical Note on the New Education Funding System*, London: DfES.

DfES (2003b) *School Admissions Code of Practice*, London: DfES.

DfES (2004a) *Statistics of Education: Education and Training Statistics for the United Kingdom 2004*, London: The Stationery Office.

DfES (2004b) *Statistics of Education: Education and Training Expenditure since 1994/95*, London: The Stationery Office.

DfES (2005a) *Has the Social Class Gap Narrowed in Primary Schools?*, London: DfES.

DfES (2005b) *Statistics of Education: Education and Training Statistics for the United Kingdom 2005*, London: The Stationery Office.

DfES (2005c) *Higher Standards, Better Schools for All*, Cm 6677, London: The Stationery Office, www.dfes.gov.uk/publications/ schoolswhitepaper/

DfES (2005d) *Schools and Pupils in England, January 2005 (Final)*, London: DfES.

DfES (2006a) *Dedicated Schools Grant 2005-06 and 2007-08*, London: DfES, www.teachernet.gov.uk/docbank/index.cfm?id=9405

DfES (2006b) *National Curriculum Assessments at Key Stage 2 in England, 2006 (Provisional)*, London: DfES, www.dfes.gov.uk/rsgateway/DB/ SFR/s000673/SFR31-2006.pdf

DfES (2006c) *GCSE and equivalent results and associated value added measures in England, 2004/05 (Final)*, London: DfES, www.dfes.gov. uk/rsgateway/DB/SFR/s000664/index.shtml

DfES (2006d) *100 More Specialist Schools – Knight*, Press Notice, 4 July 2006, www.dfes.gov.uk/pns/DisplayPN.cgi?pn_id=2006_0097

DfES (2006e) *Academies Sponsor Prospectus 2005*, London: DfES.

DfES (2006f) *Academies that are Open*, 25 September, www.standards. dfes.gov.uk/academies/projects/openacademies/?version=1

DfES/HM Treasury (2005) *Child Poverty: Fair Funding for Schools*, London: DfES/HM Treasury, www.teachernet.gov.uk/docbank/ index.cfm?id=9404

Flatley, J., Connolly, H., Higgins, V., Williams, J., Coldron, J., Stephenson, K., Logie, A. and Smith, N. (2001) *Parents' Experiences of the Process of Choosing a Secondary School Research Report 278*, London: DfES, www.dfes.gov.uk/research/data/uploadfiles/RR278.pdf

Gibbons, S. and Silva, O. (2006) *Faith Primary Schools: Better Schools or Better Pupils?*, London: Centre for Economic Performance, London School of Economics and Political Science.

Glennerster, H. (2002) 'United Kingdom education 1997-2001', *Oxford Review of Economic Policy*, vol 18, no 2, pp 120-35.

Glennerster, H. (2003) *Understanding the Finance of Welfare: What Welfare Costs and How to Pay for It*, Bristol: The Policy Press.

Glennerster, H. and Hills, J. (eds) (1998) *The State of Welfare: The Economics of Social Spending*, Oxford: Oxford University Press.

Golden, S., Knight, S., O'Donnell, L., Smith, P. and Sims, D. (2002) *Learning Mentors' Strand Study, Excellence in Cities Report 16/2002*, Slough: National Foundation for Educational Research.

Gorard, S. (1999) '"Well. That about wraps it up for school choice research": a state of the art review', *School Leadership and Management*, vol 19, no 1, pp 25-47.

Gorard, S., Taylor, C. and Fitz, J. (2003) *Schools, Markets and Choice Policies*, London: RoutledgeFalmer.

Halpin, D., Dickson, M., Power, S., Whitty, G. and Gewirtz, S. (2004) 'Area-based approaches to educational regeneration', *Policy Studies*, vol 25, no 2, pp 75-85.

HM Treasury (2004) *Child Poverty Review*, London: HM Treasury.

HM Treasury (2005) *GDP Deflators at Market Prices, and Money GDP*, updated 23 December 2005, www.hm-treasury.gov.uk/economic_data_and_tools/gdp_deflators/data_gdp_fig.cfm

HM Treasury (2006) *Budget 2006*, HC968, London: The Stationery Office.

House of Commons Hansard (2004) *Parliamentary Answer*, 1 March, www.publications.parliament.uk/pa/cm200304/cmhansrd/vo040301/text/40301w10.htm

Independent, The (2006) *Special Report: State and Religion*, 10 September.

Jenkins, A., Levačić, R. and Vignoles, A. (2006) *Estimating the Relationship between School Resources and Pupil Attainment at GCSE*, London: DfES, www.dfes.gov.uk/research/data/uploadfiles/RR727.pdf

Kendall, L., O'Donnell, L., Golden, S., Ridley, K., Machin, S., Rutt, S., McNally, S., Schagen, I., Meghir, C., Stoney, S., Morris, M., West, A. and Noden, P. (2005) *Excellence in Cities: The National Evaluation of a Policy to Raise Standards in Urban Schools 2000-2003*, Research Report 675a, London: DfES, www.dfes.gov.uk/research/programmeofresearch/index.cfm?type=5&keywordlist1=0&keywordlist2=0&keywordlist3=0&andor=or&keyword=excellence+in+cities%3A+the+&x=48&y=12

Labour Party (1997) *The Labour Party Manifesto 1997*, London: The Labour Party.

Labour Party (2001) *The Labour Party Manifesto 2001*, London: The Labour Party.

Labour Party (2005) *The Labour Party Manifesto 2005*, London: The Labour Party.

Levačić, R. (2004) 'Competition and the performance of English secondary schools: further evidence', *Education Economics*, vol 12, no 2, pp 177-93.

Levačić, R., Jenkins, A., Vignoles, A., Steele, F. and Allen, R. (2005) *Estimating the Relationship between School Resources and Pupil Attainment at key stage 3*, London: DfES, www.dfes.gov.uk/research/data/uploadfiles/RR679.pdf

Lupton, R. (2004) 'Do poor neighbourhoods mean poor schools?', Education and the Neighbourhood Conference, 9 January, www.bristol.ac.uk/sps/cnrpapersword/edu/lupton.doc

Lupton, R. (2005) 'Social justice and school improvement: improving the quality of schooling in the poorest neighbourhoods', *British Educational Research Journal*, vol 31, no 5, pp 589-604.

Machin, S. and McNally, S. (2004) *The Literacy Hour*, London: Centre for the Economics of Education, London School of Economics and Political Science.

McNally, S. (2005) *Economic Evaluation of the Pupil Learning Credits Pilot Scheme*, London: DfES, www.standards.dfes.gov.uk/studysupport/816987/817959/econeval.pdf

NAO (National Audit Office) (2001) *Education Action Zones*, London: The Stationery Office.

Noden, P. and Schagen, I. (2006) 'The specialist schools programme: golden goose or conjuring trick?', Oxford Review of Education, vol 32, no 4, pp 431-48.

Noden, P., Braun, A., Pennell, H. and West, A. (2004) *A Qualitative Study of Specialist Schools in Excellence in Cities Areas: Excellence in Cities Evaluation*, Slough: National Foundation for Educational Research.

Noden, P., West, A., David, M. and Edge, A. (1998) 'Choices and destinations at transfer to secondary schools in London', *Journal of Education Policy*, vol 13, no 2, pp 221-36.

Noden, P., West, A. and West, R. (2002) *Mapping Resources, Assessing Effects*, London: National Foundation for Educational Research.

OPSI (Office of Public Sector Information) (2002) *The Financing of Maintained Schools (England) Regulations 2002*, www.opsi.gov.uk/si/si2002/20020377.htm

OPSI (2006) *The School Finance (England) Regulations 2006*, www.opsi.gov.uk/si/si2006/20060468.htm

Pennell, H., West, A. and Hind, A. (2006) *Secondary School Admissions in London*, Clare Market Papers 19, London: Centre for Educational Research, London School of Economics and Political Science, www.lse.ac.uk/collections/ERG/pdf/cmp19.pdf

Simkins, T. (2004) 'School finance and equity in England', *Educational Management, Administration and Leadership*, vol 32, no 4, pp 369-86.

Sparkes, J. and Glennerster, H. (2002) 'Preventing social exclusion: education's contribution', in J. Hills, J. Le Grand and D. Piachaud (eds) *Understanding Social Exclusion*, Oxford: Oxford University Press.

Statistics Commission (2005) *Measuring Standards in English Primary Schools*, Report Number 23, London: Statistics Commission.

Sutton Trust (2005) *Rates of Eligibility for Free School Meals at the Top State Schools*, London: The Sutton Trust.

Tymms, P. (2004) 'Are standards rising in English primary schools?', *British Educational Research Journal*, vol 30, no 4, pp 477-94.

West, A. (2006) 'School choice, equity and social justice: the case for more control', *British Journal of Educational Studies*, vol 54, no 1, pp 15-33.

West, A. (2008: forthcoming) 'Redistribution and financing schools in England under Labour: are resources going where needs are greatest?', *Educational Management, Administration and Leadership*.

West, A. and Hind, A. (2007) 'School choice in London, England: characteristics of students in different types of schools', *Peabody Journal of Education*, vol 82, no 2-3, pp 498-529.

West, A. and Pennell, H. (2000) 'Publishing school examination results in England: incentives and consequences', *Educational Studies*, vol 26, no 4, pp 423-36.

West, A. and Pennell, H. (2003) *Underachievement in Schools*, London: RoutledgeFalmer.

West, A., David, M., Hailes, J. and Ribbens, J. (1995) 'Parents and the process of choosing secondary schools: implications for schools', *Educational Management and Administration*, vol 23, no 1, pp 28-38.

West, A., Hind, A. and Pennell, H. (2004) 'School admissions and "selection" in comprehensive schools: policy and practice', *Oxford Review of Education*, vol 30, no 3, pp 347-69.

West, A., Ingram, D. and Hind, A. (2006) 'Skimming the cream? Admissions to charter schools in the US and autonomous schools in England', *Educational Policy*, vol 20, no 4, pp 615-39.

West, A., West, R., Pennell, H. and Travers, T. (2001) 'Financing school-based education in England: poverty, examination results and expenditure', *Environment and Planning C: Government and Policy*, vol 19, no 3, pp 461-71.

Wilson, D., Croxson, B. and Atkinson, A. (2006) '"What gets measured gets done": headteachers' responses to the English secondary school performance management system', *Policy Studies*, vol 27, no 2, pp 153-71.

Woods, P.A., Bagley, C. and Glatter, R. (1998) *School Choice and Competition: Markets in the Public Interest?*, London: Routledge.

Yeomans, D., Higham, J. and Sharp, P. (2000) *The Impact of the Specialist Schools Programme: Case Studies*, London: Department for Education and Employment.

SIX

Financing higher education: tax, graduate tax or loans?

Nicholas Barr[1]

One of life's battles is between analytical rigour and political feasibility. Politicians claim both, but when the chips are down mostly give greater weight to politics. Academics should follow logic wherever it leads, and the most distinguished do so even in a hostile political environment. Scholars were overrepresented among the active opponents of the communist regimes in Central and Eastern Europe. In the UK, examples of counter-cultural social policy proposals include support in the late 1980s for judicious experiments with competition in the delivery of healthcare within the National Health Service (Barr, Glennerster and Le Grand, 1988), and agreement with the Conservative policy of GP fundholding in the 1990s (Glennerster and Matsaganis, 1993), to which Chapter Seven refers.

Another example, the focus of this chapter, is an early proposal for financing higher education in part via a graduate tax (Glennerster et al, 1968) – a policy originally proposed by Milton Friedman (1955). At the time, the idea of a graduate contribution was simultaneously an anathema and visionary. Since then, the question of how to pay for universities has become central, with widespread agreement about widening access, but debate about how best to do so. To many, it is obvious that higher education should continue to be 'free' (that is, paid for by taxpayers) because, they argue, the introduction of fees will deter demand. That view informed Labour Party policy in the UK until the 1990s (and for many Labour supporters to this day), and the policy of the Conservative and Liberal Democratic parties into the 2000s.

This chapter discusses controversial reforms of higher education finance in England in 2006, arguing that – contrary to popular belief – they are strongly progressive. It explains why those reforms have the shape they do, looking through the twin lenses of the economics of information and the major changes in higher education over time, notably sharp increases in size and diversity. A central conclusion is that a regulated market is a more suitable model for higher education than central planning. This line of argument does not deny that higher education matters also for other reasons: to promote cultural values, to protect the freedom of ideas and to pursue new knowledge for its own sake.

The opening discussion sets out the 2006 system. The following two sections explore the historical confluence of ideas between Friedman's work and that of Glennerster and colleagues, and then the analytical principles that should underpin policy. The most elegant policy, however, will fail unless properly implemented (the easy part is to disburse the money; collecting loan repayments is harder); the next section briefly discusses this aspect of making social policy work. A further section considers the choice between a graduate tax (where a person's repayments continue permanently or until some date such as retirement) and a loan with income-contingent repayments (where a person's repayments are a fraction of earnings, but, in contrast with a graduate tax, stop once the borrower has repaid what he or she has borrowed, plus interest), and concludes that the general case that brings the two together is social insurance. The final section considers the unfinished agenda.

The current state of play: the 2006 reforms in England

The finance of higher education in England can be divided into four phases:

*   until 1990, tuition fees were paid from taxation and students' living expenses by a mixture of a tax-funded grant and, for better-off families, a parental contribution;
*   between 1990 and 1998, tax finance of tuition fees continued, but a student loan, with mortgage-type repayments, covered part of living costs, alongside a smaller system of grants and parental contributions;
*   in 1998, a fixed charge for tuition fees was introduced, with poor people exempt. There was no loan to cover fees. The grant was abolished, with living costs financed in part by parental contributions and in part by an income-contingent loan. The great gain was the introduction of income-contingency; for a critique, see Barr (2004b);
*   the 2006 reforms brought in variable tuition fees, and extended income-contingent loans to cover both living costs *and* fees.

The 2006 reforms can be presented as a strategy with three elements: variable fees (that is, prices) assist the efficient allocation of resources within higher education; well-designed loans allow people to borrow against their future earnings to pay those fees and living costs; and wide-ranging measures to promote access seek to tackle exclusion at source.

Element 1: deferred variable fees

In place of the previous upfront flat fee, from 2006 each university can set the fee for each of its courses up to a maximum of £3,000 per year. Students can pay upfront or can take out a loan, in which case the Student Loans Company pays the fee directly to the university. Thus the strategy is one of deferred variable fees.

The strategy is rooted in the economics of information, as discussed in the third part of the chapter, which explains the potential efficiency and equity gains. The strategy also draws on international experience by liberalising fees, but not completely. The fees cap (that is, the ceiling of £3,000) is important in this context. It should be high enough (a) to bring in significant additional resources and (b) to create competition, but low enough (c) to ensure that the new regime is politically sustainable by giving students and parents time to adjust, and (d) to give universities time to put in place management suitable for a competitive environment.

Variable fees alone, however, would impede access – hence the other two legs of the strategy.

Element 2: a well-designed loan scheme

The discussion in a subsequent section argues that loans should have income-contingent repayments, should charge an interest rate broadly equal to the government's cost of borrowing, and should be large enough to make higher education free at the point of use. Until 2006, although loans had income-contingent repayments, they were too small to cover realistic living costs and did not cover tuition fees at all.

The 2006 reforms extended loans to cover fees and increased the element for living costs. The change is important. From the student's viewpoint the situation is little different from the days of 'free' higher education: their fees are paid on their behalf by the Student Loans Company, and money is paid into their bank account to cover living costs. From the graduate's viewpoint the arrangements are like a system financed out of Income Tax, except that the repayments (a) are only by people who have been to university and benefited financially and (b) do not go on forever. Three points are noteworthy: higher education is free at the point of use; lower-earning graduates do not repay in full, and perhaps not at all; and graduates who do well repay their loan in full. In one respect, the new loan arrangements are deficient: they perpetuate the interest subsidy.

Element 3: action to promote access

If all students are well informed and with a good school education, the first two elements of the strategy are sufficient.

However, not all students are well informed, most particularly the group for whom we want to promote access. If such students underestimate the benefits of higher education and/or overestimate the costs, it might be rational for them, *given what they know*, to be unwilling to take out a loan. This is the origin of so-called debt aversion.[2] Addressing the problem requires measures to tackle exclusion, which, it can be argued, has three roots: financial poverty, information poverty and poor school education.

To address financial poverty, grants to cover part of living costs – mistakenly abolished in 1998 – were restored, supported by other policies already in place, such as Education Maintenance Allowances, which offer income-tested support to schoolchildren post-16. Both policies are supported by financial and other measures to universities to widen participation. People with low incomes after graduation are helped by income-contingent repayments, and because any loan that has not been repaid after 25 years is forgiven.

Information poverty, the second strategic impediment to access, is starting to receive more attention, although still not enough. Relevant policies include AimHigher, to raise the aspirations of schoolchildren and improve their knowledge of what going to university involves, and its benefits. The 2006 reforms bring in an Access Regulator to ensure that institutions have satisfactory plans to widen access. As well as scholarships, such plans also include outreach to schools by universities to improve the information available to schoolchildren. In all this, raising aspirations is fundamental.

Finally, problems of access cannot be solved entirely within higher education. More resources are needed earlier in the system, not least because of the growing evidence (Feinstein, 2003) that the roots of exclusion lie in early childhood. Policies of this sort include Sure Start.

The history of ideas

The 2006 strategy has important roots in the history of ideas. The starting point is to ask why student loans are important and why government needs to get involved.

Student loans: what is the problem?[3]

A person who wants to buy a house normally borrows from a building society or similar lender, a private solution with limited government involvement. Similar loans exist for cars. Why has the private market not provided analogous loans for borrowing to finance investment in human capital?

Home loans are a relatively low-risk activity both for buyer and lender:

(a) the person who buys a house generally knows what he is buying, having lived in a house all his life;
(b) the house is unlikely to fall down and is, in any case, insurable;
(c) the real value of the house will generally (although not always) increase, and certainly has done so in the UK over the medium term;
(d) the existence of a physical asset reduces risk for the borrower: if their income falls, making repayments impossible, he or she can sell the house and repay the outstanding loan;
(e) the house acts as physical security, reducing risk for the lender, who can if necessary repossess the asset; thus loans are available with only a small risk premium.

Thus it is not surprising that an efficient market solution exists. The contrast with human capital is clear. As argued below, although the generality of applicants to university are well-informed, this is not the case in families where nobody has been to university, violating (a). A qualification can 'fall down', violating (b), since students may fail exams, facing them with repayments but without the qualification that would have generated the increased earnings from which to make those repayments. Although the real rate of return to a degree continues to be high, there is a variance around the average so that the same is not necessarily true for all students, violating (c).

Finally, because there is no collateral, someone who has borrowed to finance a degree but then experiences low earnings does not have the option to sell the qualification, violating (d), and can therefore borrow, if at all, only at a substantial risk premium, violating (e). One solution is to introduce collateral in the form of a guarantee, say from a parent, but this runs counter to the drive to widen access.

Thus borrowing to finance a degree has technical characteristics that differ substantially from borrowing to buy a house. Conventional loans are the wrong model for investment in human capital. They lead to inefficiently low borrowing and lending. They are also inequitable. The various efficiency problems impact most on people from poor backgrounds, women and minority ethnic groups, who may be less well informed about the benefits of a qualification and therefore less prepared to risk a loan. In addition, these groups are likely to be on the wrong end of cherry picking by lenders.

Friedman and the benefit principle

As befits a libertarian writer, Milton Friedman began from the benefit principle – that he/she who benefits should pay. His work with Simon Kuznets (1954) on the incomes of professionals showed a higher return to human capital than to physical capital, creating a prima facie argument that investment in human capital was inefficiently low. In an article in 1955,[4] Friedman considered the proper role of government in education and, for higher education, what could be done to address underinvestment. His starting point was the capital market imperfections just discussed, in particular the riskiness for lender and borrower.

> [I]n a non-slave state, the individual embodying the investment cannot be bought and sold. But even if he could, the security would not be comparable. The productivity of ... physical capital does not ... depend on the cooperativeness of the original borrower. The productivity of the human capital quite obviously does.... A loan to finance the training of an individual who has no security to offer other than his future earnings is therefore a much less attractive proposition than a loan to finance, say, the erection of a building....
>
> A further complication is ... the inappropriateness of fixed money loans to finance investment in training. Such an investment necessarily involves much risk. The average expected return may be high, but there is wide variation about the average. (Friedman, 1955, p 137)

In accepting the problem he also proposed a solution:

> The device adopted to meet the corresponding problem
> for other risky investments is equity investment plus limited
> liability on the part of shareholders. The counterpart for
> education would be to 'buy' a share in an individual's earning
> prospects: to advance him [sic] the funds needed to finance
> his training on condition that he agree to pay the lender a
> specified fraction of his future earnings. (Friedman, 1955,
> p 138)

On that basis he advocated loans from government, in return for
which,

> [T]he individual would agree in return to pay to the
> government in each future year x% of his earnings in excess
> of y dollars for each \$1,000 that he gets in this way. This
> payment could easily be combined with payment of income
> tax and so involve a minimum of additional administrative
> expense. (Friedman, 1955, p 140)

It is important to be clear that Friedman was not advocating loan
finance but equity finance. If a company sells corporate bonds, what
it is selling is an IOU – an agreement to repay the sum on the face
of the bond at a future date and, in the meantime, to make interest
payments to the bond holder. With equities, in contrast, there is no debt
to the shareholder and no promise to repay; instead, the shareholder
owns a slice of the firm's action, and is thereby entitled to a fraction
of the firm's profits into the indefinite future. If the firm prospers,
the value of the shares will increase, offering a potential capital gain
as well as a flow of dividends. Friedman's proposal is that the lender
should own a slice of the graduate's action, that is, should be entitled
to a flow of dividends in the form of a fraction of the person's income
for the life of the individual (just as dividends are payable for the life
of the corporation). Analytically, the proposal introduces an element of
slavery, but with two differences: it relates not to the person's freedom
but to his or her income; and it relates only to a fraction of his or her
income – partial slavery.

Glennerster and the ability-to-pay principle

The Friedman proposals, with their apparent application of capitalist principles to the lives of individuals, sound about as far as it is possible to get from socialist policies rooted in the idea of high-quality public services available freely to all. Glennerster et al (1968) started from this latter ideological stance, and specifically from the ability-to-pay principle. Thus their predisposition was towards free, tax-financed education, abandoning that model only because of its regressiveness when applied to higher education. They argued that:

> [I]n the United Kingdom, higher education is now financed as a social service. Nearly all the costs are borne out of general taxation.... But it differs radically from other social services. It is reserved for a small and highly selected group.... It is exceptionally expensive.... [And] education confers benefits which reveal themselves in the form of higher earnings. A graduate tax would enable the community to recover the value of the resources devoted to higher education from those who have themselves derived such substantial benefit from it. (Glennerster et al, 1968, p 26)

Thus recipients of higher education should pay a tax in addition to Income Tax, that is, should pay a higher rate of Income Tax for life. The argument is twofold: the amount a graduate thus repays is strictly related to subsequent earnings; and the government, as recipient of the funds, is able to use them for redistributive purposes, for example to widen access. Both aspects are entirely compatible with the ability-to-pay principle.

The conclusion is that the benefit principle and the ability-to-pay approach, despite their very different starting points, lead to identical policy prescriptions. Specifically, both lead to a graduate tax, that is, equity participation, rather than loan participation. The discussion that follows is mostly about the loans approach, returning in a later section to the choice between equity participation and loan finance.

Designing policy: analytical principles

How do proposals for a graduate tax fit into today's analysis, given advances in economic theory and changes in higher education? A number of questions stand out: why mass higher education; why fees (and what type of fees); why loans; and what type of repayments?[5]

Why mass higher education?

Higher education has expanded in all countries in the UK in a spurt after the Robbins Report (UK Committee on Higher Education, 1963) and another spurt in the 1990s. Was such a move desirable?

In times past, notwithstanding its importance for other reasons, higher education was not fundamental to national economic performance nor to individual life chances. Today it is essential for both. A key driver is technological advance, which increases the demand for skilled workers. Furthermore, skills date more quickly. The 'information age' can be taken to mean a need for education and training that is larger, more diverse and more frequent, given the need for periodic retraining.

Demographic change offers a second economic reason why higher education is essential. The rising proportion of older people foreshadows increased spending on pensions, medical care and long-term care. Part of the solution is to increase output sufficiently to meet the combined expectations of workers and pensioners.[6] If workers are becoming relatively more scarce, the efficient response is to increase labour productivity. Demographic change is thus an argument for additional spending on investment in both physical and human capital.

Why fees?

Higher education creates benefits to society above those to the individual — benefits in terms of growth, social cohesion, the transmission of values and the development of knowledge for its own sake. Those arguments suggest that taxpayer subsidies to higher education should be a permanent part of the landscape. Equally (and on sounder quantitative footing), higher education creates substantial private benefits (Blundell et al, 2000). Those estimates are based on data for an earlier, smaller cohort of graduates, suggesting that increased numbers may drive down those returns. But Blundell et al rightly point out that the demand for graduates is also increasing. To the extent that demand and supply increase broadly in line, there is no reason why private returns should fall. Thus it is efficient that graduates bear some of the costs of their degree, in principle the fraction that reflects their private benefits.

That economic argument for fees is reinforced by brute politics. It was possible (albeit regressive, as Glennerster et al [1968] pointed out) to finance higher education from taxation when it was an elite system with a 5% participation rate. But the need to finance a large, high-quality system of higher education collides with other imperatives for public spending, notably population ageing, medical advances and the needs of other parts of the education system, all of which are politically more salient than universities.

Why variable fees?

Given the case for fees, the next question is how those fees should be structured. Specifically, should there be a fixed charge that applies to all degrees at all universities, or should each university have some choice over the fees it charges for different degrees?

Are price signals useful?

The usefulness of price signals can be shown by considering what can happen in their absence: much of the reason for the collapse of the Communist system was pervasive adverse incentives, of which the absence of price signals was a major component. Price signals work well for many commodities, including food and clothing, cars and computers. But they are not universally useful. Markets can fail – information failures being key – giving a robust case for state intervention in areas like healthcare and school education (Barr, 2004a).

Students in higher education are generally well informed and can be made better informed, suggesting that the model of well-informed individual choice applies to higher education in a way that it does not to school education (Barr, 2004b). If so, price signals are useful, and competition will improve welfare by making universities more responsive to the preferences of students and, indirectly, of employers. This theoretical argument underpins the case for variable fees.

Although that argument is powerful, there are two caveats. It might fail for some students from poorer backgrounds, who may not be well informed. Second, the argument for consumer choice, competition and market forces does not mechanistically point to unrestricted markets. Rather, the analysis points to regulated markets, with an important continuing role for government.

Variable fees: more efficient

Given mostly well-informed consumers and a large, diverse system of higher education, resources will be misallocated if students do not face price signals. Employers want people with quantitative skills and computer literacy. Both mathematics and engineering graduates have those skills, but one degree is much more expensive than the other.

In the absence of price signals students are indifferent; the taxpayer is not. The same is true in choosing a university: a well-taught, cheaper course at a local university might suit a student better than a more expensive course. There are gains for the student, the taxpayer and (through competition) the university system from student choice in response to the price mechanism.

A fixed price also has adverse incentives on the supply side. Price ceilings erode incentives to raise quality (since extra quality brings no extra income); price floors erode incentives to efficiency (since increased efficiency cannot be translated into lower prices). A fixed fee is both a floor and a ceiling and hence deeply inefficient.

Alongside such microeconomic arguments, variable fees also make higher education funding open-ended, strengthening the autonomy of universities and promoting quality and efficiency. If there is a fixed fee, government controls the volume of resources going into higher education. Thus universities compete in a zero sum game. This arrangement puts a strain on scarce fiscal capacity, leads to an inefficiently low level of funding for universities, and weakens incentives to efficiency, since government continues to decide on the division of resources between institutions.

Variable fees: fairer

Variable fees are not only more efficient than fixed fees but – counterintuitively – also fairer.

Variable fees facilitate redistribution from better off to worse-off. The strategy has two elements:

- Fees introduce higher charges for those who can afford them (note that with income-contingent loan repayments, 'can afford' refers to a person's earnings as a graduate, not to family circumstances while a student).
- Redistributive policies such as grants help poor people to pay those charges.

To an economist, these elements are staggeringly familiar: the first, a price increase, represents a movement *along* the demand curve. Taken alone, this element would harm access. However, when combined with targeted transfers to groups for whom access is fragile, this policy moves their demand curve *outward*. This line of argument lies at the heart of the strategy that underpins the 2006 reforms.

Variable fees are also fairer at an institutional level. If funding is closed-ended, prestigious universities and local institutions compete for allocations from the same pot of money. Variable fees start to address this gridlock, making it easier to redistribute taxpayer resources to institutions whose student body requires more intensive teaching.

Third, variable fees are directly fairer. It is inequitable if the student at a little-known local institution pays the same fee as the student at Oxford.

Why loans?

Two lines of argument support widespread student loans. The first, already noted, is that it is not feasible to rely on taxation to finance high-quality mass higher education. But tax finance is not only infeasible but also undesirable, for at least three reasons.

First, tax finance has failed to widen access. In 2002, 81% of children with parents from professional backgrounds went to university; the comparable figure for children from poorer backgrounds was 15% (UK Education and Skills Select Committee, 2002, p 19). The issue is taken up more broadly in Glennerster and Sparkes, (2002). In contrast, contributory finance is unambiguously progressive (Falkingham et al, 1995).

Second, tax finance has been unable to protect quality. Real funding per student almost halved in the 20 years to 2000 (Greenaway and Haynes, 2002, Figure 1), creating worries about quality. The days are gone when the higher education sector is small and competing claims on public funds less powerful.

Third, tax finance is regressive. Participating in higher education is a matter of choice, and that choice is highly skewed to the better off. Some people argue that the answer is to make Income Tax more progressive, for example the Liberal Democrats have proposed a higher rate of Income Tax on earnings above £100,000 per year. But proponents of that view have to justify why the proceeds should be spent on students (on average the best and the brightest, disproportionately destined to be among the richest), rather than on nurses' pay, schools, Child Benefit and targeted measures to promote access.

Thus the case for loans is twofold: well-designed loans bring in private sector sources (graduates' repayments) to supplement tax revenues; and they address the regressivity of tax finance. Loans are an essential element in the strategy to widen access set out in the opening part of the chapter.

Why income-contingent repayments?

The structure of repayments

The efficiency case for income-contingent repayments is that they address the capital market imperfections discussed earlier: borrowers from disadvantaged backgrounds may be badly informed about the value of a degree; and all borrowers face substantial risk and uncertainty. Thus there are technical problems on the demand side of the market for loans and, as a result, borrowing to finance investment in human capital will be inefficiently low.

On the supply side, lenders are uncertain about the riskiness of an applicant for a loan and will therefore charge a risk premium. A risk premium assessed by a well-informed lender is efficient (analogous to higher car insurance premiums for bad drivers). But lenders are not well informed about the riskiness of an applicant, not least because of adverse selection.[7] Thus risk premiums will be inefficiently high, again leading to an inefficiently small amount of borrowing. A consequential supply-side problem is that lenders face incentives to lend only to the best risks, analogous to incentives to cream-skimming facing private medical insurers. An obvious way to do so is to lend only to students who can provide security, for example from a home-owning parent.

For all these reasons, in a conventional loan system, capital market imperfections lead to a level of borrowing that is inefficiently low: the interest of lenders is in secure loans; the national interest is in the optimal quantity and mix of investment in human capital. In a world of perfect information the two interests coincide; with imperfect information they do not.

What interest rate?

To complete the story it is necessary briefly to discuss the appropriate interest rate. Some countries with income-contingent loans, notably Australia and the UK, charge an interest rate equal to the rate of inflation, that is, a zero real rate. Since this is less than the rate at which government can borrow, the arrangement represents an interest subsidy. It seems intuitively plausible that interest subsidies help access. But intuition in this case is profoundly wrong.

Blanket interest subsidies cause inefficiency and inequity: they are costly; they impede quality because student support, being politically salient, crowds out resources going to universities; and they impede access – loans are expensive, therefore rationed and therefore too small. Finally, interest subsidies are deeply regressive. They do not help students (graduates make repayments, not students). They help low-earning graduates only slightly, since unpaid debt is eventually forgiven. They do not help high-earning graduates early in their careers: with income-contingent loans, monthly repayments depend only on earnings; interest rates only affect the duration of the loan. Thus the major beneficiaries are successful professionals in mid-career, whose loan repayments are switched off earlier because of the subsidy (for fuller discussion see Barr, 2004b).

Instead, loans should attract an interest rate broadly equal to the government's cost of borrowing, with targeted interest subsidies for low earners.

Income-contingent repayments have a profound effect in ways that are not widely understood. Low earners make low or no repayments. People with low lifetime earnings do not fully repay. A larger loan or a higher interest rate has no effect on monthly repayments, which depend only on the person's income; instead, a person with a larger loan will repay for longer. In efficiency terms, income-contingent repayments are designed to protect borrowers from excessive risk arising from imperfect information and the lack of collateral; in equity terms, they assist access because they have built-in insurance against inability to repay.

Implementing policy[8]

Fiscal pressures make loans attractive to Ministries of Finance. However, loans are not easy to implement, so many countries have a lamentable record of collecting repayments. It is one thing to design a good loan system, quite another to make it work in practice.

Implementing an effective loan system has major administrative implications of which the following is a very incomplete listing.

Establishing a scheme includes ensuring enough people with the necessary skills, legislative preparation, information technology development, proper project management and strong political support. A number of problems are common:

- Policy makers may introduce changes to the scheme once work is under way; such changes are often incompatible with the planned administrative structure.
- The political timetable for the introduction of a scheme is often incompatible with the timetable necessary for administrative purposes.
- Ownership of the scheme may be unclear or diffuse.

Running the scheme once it has been established involves identification of the student, record keeping (amounts borrowed, repayments, accumulation of interest), and collection of repayments within the country and from graduates working abroad.

Merely to list these elements indicates the size of the task. The following tales from the front are intended to convert the sceptical and amuse the converted:

- Some institutions have a large peak in communications from the customer, for example tax returns around the filing deadline, or student loan applications in the period between A-level results and the start of the academic year. If such a system is paper-based, as until recently, how does one deal with tasks like opening envelopes when there can be millions of them to open?
- Where the system is electronic, the analogous problem is whether the system can cope with a huge peak without crashing.
- If a loan scheme processes loan applications by optically scanning handwritten paper applications, can the scanner cope with an application that has spent two weeks folded in a student's pocket or has a large coffee stain on it?
- Does the system have a way of coping where an applicant for a loan misspells (paper-based) or mistypes (electronic) his or her own name (this is not fanciful)?
- Can the system cope with a massive peak of phone enquiries, for example by automatically moving people from other tasks to staffing the phones at such times. Again this is not fanciful. If any element in the system breaks down (for example the system of loans disbursement), there will be a large surge of telephone enquiries; if nothing is done, a breakdown in disbursement is rapidly followed by a breakdown in the system of telephone enquiries.

These matters are a long way from the economics of information or debates about equity finance versus loan finance – but they are equally important; as examples, see Glennerster (1983, 1994) and Glennerster and Lewis (1996).

Income-contingent loan or graduate tax?

Discussion thus far has followed Friedman and Glennerster in arguing for income-contingent repayments, largely setting to one side the question of which of two forms they should take:

- A graduate tax is a form of equity finance, with repayments continuing permanently or until some date such as turning 65.
- An income-contingent loan is a form of loan finance; repayments stop once the borrower has repaid what he or she has borrowed, plus interest.

The original Glennerster et al (1968) paper argued for a graduate tax. My own work (Barr, 1989, 2004b; Barr and Crawford, 2005) is based round the loans approach. What are the arguments?

Arguments for the graduate tax approach

Two lines of support have been offered – by very different groups of people:

1. A graduate tax is a type of equity finance that can address capital market imperfections. Friedman (1955, p 140) is explicit: 'The desideratum is not to redistribute income but to make capital available for investment in human beings on terms comparable to those on which it is available for physical investments'. Reflecting on the government-run scheme that he had proposed, he is clear that '[a]n alternative, and a highly desirable one if it is feasible, is to stimulate private arrangements directed towards that end' (p 144).[9]
2. With a graduate tax, high earners repay more than they have borrowed and low earners less; thus a graduate tax is more strongly redistributive than an income-contingent loan, which redistributes only to those with low lifetime earnings.

Another argument is one of practicality:

3. A graduate tax is easier to implement than a loan. It is necessary to identify individuals and to establish that they have gone to university, but it is not necessary to track repayments, nor to cumulate across years, nor to do complex interest calculations. Thus a graduate tax might be feasible in a developing country earlier than it is possible to implement a loan scheme effectively.

Arguments for the income-contingent loan approach[10]

1. *An analytical error:* a standard principle of public finance is that what matters is the redistributive impact of a system as a whole. To argue

(as I do) that the system as a whole should be redistributive does not mean that *every* element of it must be. Income-contingent loans redistribute to people who are lifetime poor and hence do not repay in full – a purpose that the loan was explicitly designed to achieve – but the main redistributive thrust of higher education finance is in the third element described in the opening section, whose explicit purpose is to promote access through measures much broader than cash redistribution.

2. *Loans bring in private finance more quickly* than a graduate tax. With care, it is possible to design an income-contingent loan scheme that is privately financed. A graduate tax, being by definition a tax, rules out that option. The costs of expansion come immediately, while the revenue gains accrue to future governments.

3. *Open-ended finance, hence less government control.* The combination of loans and variable fees makes finance open-ended. With a graduate tax, funding remains closed-ended since government continues to control the volume of resources going into higher education, thus perpetuating central planning.

4. *Stronger incentives to efficiency* arise in two ways. First, it is possible for students to take out a larger loan if they go to a university with higher fees, which is essential if the system is to be free at the point of use. Thus loans, by supporting variable fees, create incentives to efficiency at the institutional level through stronger competition. A graduate tax creates no such incentives.

Loans also have better incentives at the individual level. With a graduate tax the duration of repayments is independent of the amount repaid; thus repayments will be perceived as a tax, with potential adverse effects on work effort. Loan repayments are not a tax: larger repayments hasten the day when the repayment will be switched off; thus repayments are less likely to be perceived as a tax, and will thus tend to have weaker adverse incentives.

5. *Loans facilitate repayments from students from other European Union (EU) countries.* Under present EU law, countries are allowed to restrict social security to their own nationals but, as a single market, have to charge the same price throughout the EU. Thus the UK can (at least for the moment) restrict maintenance loans to UK nationals, but has to offer fees loans to all EU students. This is not a problem for a loan system, where each borrower has an individual contract with the Student Loans Company, which can be (and is) enforced

where a borrower lives abroad after graduation. With a graduate tax, in contrast, a person with no UK tax liability does not repay.

6. *Loans are fairer.* A graduate tax is unfair and hence politically difficult. People are compelled to make continuing contributions, with no option to pay upfront if they wish. Those contributions are unrelated to the cost of their higher education; and the contributions will be considerable for a successful professional, without having to refer to extreme cases like Mick Jagger or Stelios Haji-Ioannou. This argument – a value judgement – is the direct mirror-image of the argument that a graduate tax is beneficial because it is strongly redistributive.

Thus income-contingent loans have major advantages over a graduate tax. Perhaps the great advance of the graduate tax proposals was to highlight the centrality of income-contingent repayments, leaving open the question of specific design. A graduate tax made sense for a small and simple system, and hence might be relevant in a developing country, but income-contingent loans are a more suitable instrument for large and complex systems.

The general case

With a simple income-contingent loan, repayments stop when a person has repaid the loan. Nobody repays more than he or she borrowed. Losses associated with graduates with low lifetime earnings are picked up by the taxpayer. This is the pure case of loan finance. With a simple graduate tax, repayments continue until, say, age 65. Thus high earners repay many multiples of their initial investment – the pure case of equity finance.

While there are problems with an arrangement in which there is no relation between the cost of a person's higher education and the amount the person repays, it does not follow that the optimal repayment is 100%. It is possible to design a graduate tax that incorporates a ceiling on a person's total repayment; thus high earners repay more than low earners but the disparity is bounded; the upper bound could be chosen so that, ex ante, the cohort as a whole repays its total borrowing. Similarly, it is possible to design a loan scheme with a risk premium added to the interest rate of all borrowers, the premium chosen so that, ex ante, the cohort repays 100% of its borrowing. Thus the two approaches – a graduate tax with a ceiling on an individual's repayment or an income-contingent loan with a cohort risk premium – converge. To what?

The converged arrangement has all the major characteristics of social insurance: nobody is excluded; everyone is in the same risk pool; and the losses from low earners in the cohort are made up by the high earners so that the scheme is self-financing.[11] The 'insurance' part, as with actuarial insurance, is that those who are lucky (stay in work, live to old age) subsidise those who are unlucky (become unemployed, die young). The 'social' part, in contrast with actuarial insurance, means that the system can cover everyone, including bad risks, and can redistribute from higher to lower earners. A major example of social insurance is old-age pensions, which redistribute from a person's younger to their old self. The arrangements suggested by Friedman (1955) and Glennerster et al (1968) allow young people to redistribute from their middle years to their earlier years to finance their investment in education. Thus the benefit principle and ability-to-pay principle are compatible not only with each other but also with the idea of social insurance. Social insurance is the general case where the two pure cases meet. That, perhaps, explains the power of the idea.

Conclusion: a view ahead

Returning to the discussion at the start of the chapter, the 2006 reforms are a major advance, but reform is never finished. Each of the three elements in the first section — deferred variable fees, a good loan scheme, and active measure to promote access – requires attention.

Action on fees: there are good reasons for imposing a maximum on fees. But some argue that £3,000 is too low and/or that it will be kept in place for too long. This is an area where economics and politics must flow together: if the cap is too low for too long, fees will bring in only limited resources, compromising quality, and will fail to create competition, forgoing efficiency gains; but if the cap rises too far too fast, the risk is that the political settlement underpinning the reform will fracture.[12] Policy makers need to find a meeting point between these pressures.

Action on loans: the blanket interest subsidy is expensive and regressive. There are major gains to replacing the blanket subsidy with targeted interest subsidies for people with low earnings or who are unemployed. The resulting savings make it possible to offer larger loans, and to offer all students a full loan; they would also free considerable resources for policies to promote access.

Action on access: more could be done to protect low-earning graduates by progressively writing off loans for some public sector workers, for example in teaching or the health service, and offering loan remission for people caring for young children or elderly dependants. That said, the saddest barrier to access is someone who has never even thought of going to university. Thus major and continuing work is necessary to raise aspirations and improve information.

Notes

[1] I am grateful to Howard Glennerster for conversations over many years – when rain stopped play and at other times – about higher education finance and much else. Thanks are due also to Hugh Macadie on whose work part of the fourth section of the chapter 'Implementing policy' draws and to John Hills for helpful comments.

[2] For a recent study in a Canadian context, see Usher (2006).

[3] For fuller discussion, see Barr (2001a, Ch 11).

[4] Coincidentally, a chapter in a Festschrift.

[5] For fuller discussion, see Barr (2001a, Chs 10-13, 2004b).

[6] On the analytics, see Barr and Diamond (2006).

[7] Adverse selection arises where a borrower knows that he or she is a bad risk but can hide the fact from the lender. In a market system, the lender would not be certain that I would become an accountant rather than an actor, nor that I would work hard.

[8] For fuller discussion, see Barr (forthcoming).

[9] For a recent proposal for privately arranged income-contingent loans, see Palacios Lleras (2004).

[10] For discussion of income-contingent repayments more broadly, see Chapman (2006).

[11] For such reasons, my original proposal (Barr, 1989) was for student loan repayments added to National Insurance contributions rather than to income tax; for fuller discussion, Barr (2001a, Ch 14).

[12] In the crucial parliamentary vote in January 2004, a government with a parliamentary majority of 160 got the Higher Education Bill through with a majority of five.

References

Barr, N. (1989) *Student Loans: The Next Steps*, Aberdeen: Aberdeen University Press for the David Hume Institute, Edinburgh, and the Suntory-Toyota International Centre for Economics and Related Disciplines, London School of Economics and Political Science.

Barr, N. (2001a) *The Welfare State as Piggy Bank: Information, Risk, Uncertainty and the Role of the State*, Oxford and New York, NY: Oxford University Press.

Barr, N. (ed) (2001b) *Economic Theory and the Welfare State, Vol. I: Theory, Vol. II: Income Transfers, and Vol. III: Benefits in Kind*, Edward Elgar Library in Critical Writings in Economics, Cheltenham and Northampton, MA: Edward Elgar.

Barr, N. (2004a) *The Economics of the Welfare State* (4th edition), Oxford and Stanford, CA: Oxford University Press and Stanford University Press.

Barr, N. (2004b) 'Higher education funding', *Oxford Review of Economic Policy*, vol 20, no 2, summer, ISSN 0266-903-X, pp 264-83, downloadable from http://oxrep.oupjournals.org/cgi/content/abstract/20/2/264?ijkey=20GIFCugfcjFz&keytype=ref

Barr, N. (forthcoming) *Financing Higher Education: Lessons from Developed Economies, Options for Developing Economies*, Washington, DC: World Bank.

Barr, N. and Crawford, I. (2005) *Financing Higher Education: Answers from the UK*, London and New York, NY: Routledge.

Barr, N. and Diamond, P. (2006) 'The economics of pensions', *Oxford Review of Economic Policy*, vol 22, no 1, spring, ISSN 0266-903X, pp 15-39, http://oxrep.oxfordjournals.org/cgi/reprint/22/1/15?ijkey=9DjQZbG8zPR17qI&keytype=ref

Barr, N., Glennerster, H. and Le Grand, J. (1988) 'Improving the National Health Service', in *Resourcing the National Health Service*, House of Commons Social Services Committee, Memoranda laid before the Committee, Session 1987-88, HC 264-IV, London: HMSO, pp 11-21; also published as 'Working for patients? The right approach?', *Social Policy and Administration*, vol 23, no 2, August 1989, pp 117-27.

Blundell, R., Dearden, L., Goodman, A. and Reed, H. (2000) 'The returns to higher education in Britain: evidence from a British Cohort', *Economic Journal*, vol 110, no 461, February, pp F82-F99.

Chapman, B. (2006) *Government Managing Risk: Income contingent Loans for Social and Economic Progress*, London and New York, NY: Routledge.

Falkingham, J., Glennerster, H. and Barr, N. (1995) 'Education funding, equity and the life cycle', in J. Falkingham and J. Hills (eds) *The Dynamic of Welfare: The Welfare State and the Life Cycle*, Hemel Hempstead: Prentice Hall/Harvester Wheatsheaf, pp 150-66.

Feinstein, L. (2003) 'Inequality in the early cognitive development of British children in the 1970 cohort', *Economica*, vol 70, no 277, pp 73-98.

Friedman, M. (1955) 'The role of government in education', in R.A. Solo (ed) *Economics and the public interest*, New Brunswick, NJ: Rutgers University Press, pp 123-44.

Friedman, M. and Kuznets, S. (1954) *Income from Independent Professional Practice*, New York, NY: National Bureau of Economic Research.

Glennerster, H. (1983) *Planning for Priority Groups*, London: Martin Robertson.

Glennerster, H. (1994) *Implementing GP Fundholding*, Buckingham: Open University Press.

Glennerster, H. and Lewis, J. (1996) *Implementing the New Community Care*, Buckingham: Open University Press.

Glennerster, H. and Matsaganis, M. (1993) 'The UK health reforms: the fundholding experiment', *Health Policy*, vol 23, pp 179-91.

Glennerster, H. and Sparkes, J. (2002) 'preventing social exclusion: education's contribution', in J. Hills, J. Le Grand and D. Piachaud (eds) *Understanding Social Exclusion*, Oxford: Oxford University Press.

Glennerster, H., Merrett, S. and Wilson, G. (1968) 'A graduate tax', *Higher Education Review*, vol 1, no 1, pp 26-38; reprinted in Barr (2001b) vol 3, pp 570-82; and in *Higher Education Review*, vol 35, no 2, spring, pp 25-40.

Greenaway, D. and Haynes, M. (2002) 'Funding higher education in the UK: the role of fees and loans', *Economic Journal*, vol 113, pp F150-F166.

Palacios Lleras, M. (2004) *Investing in Human Capital: A Capital Markets Approach to Student Funding*, Cambridge: Cambridge University Press.

UK Committee on Higher Education (1963) *Higher Education* (The Robbins Report), Cmnd 2154, London: HMSO.

UK Education and Skills Select Committee (2002) *Post-16 Student Support*, Sixth Report of Session 2001-2002, HC445, London: The Stationery Office, downloadable from www.parliament.uk

Usher, A. (2006) *Grants for Students: What They Do, Why They Work*, Toronto, Ontario: Educational Policy Institute, downloadable from www.educationalpolicy.org

SEVEN

Quasi-markets in healthcare

Julian Le Grand

One of Howard Glennerster's most significant areas of work has concerned the use of quasi-markets in the public provision of healthcare and education. His many contributions include his analyses of the British Conservative government's quasi-market in education (Glennerster, 1991) and of the same government's internal market in healthcare (Glennerster and Matsaganis, 1994a; Glennerster, 1995), work on the development of quasi-markets in public services (Glennerster and Le Grand, 1995) and, perhaps most important, his influential study of general practitioner (GP) fundholding (Glennerster et al, 1994; Glennerster, 1996).

The Labour government that took power after 1997 initially rejected many of the quasi-market principles that underlay the Conservative reforms, especially in healthcare. This was partly for ideological reasons, but partly also because in some areas they were perceived as not to have worked – or at least not to have delivered the dramatic changes in behaviour and performance that their advocates had expected (or indeed that their critics had feared). However, that government's experiments with alternative ways of running the National Health Service (NHS), including an attempt to assert command and control over the system, convinced many key actors that some elements of quasi-markets should be retried – at least within the English NHS (Stevens, 2004)[1].

More specifically, the government has introduced reforms that (a) extend patient choice of hospital for elective surgery, (b) enable the money to follow the choice (through so-called payment-by-results[2]) thus encouraging competition between providers and (c) give hospitals and other NHS organisations greater independence, through the institution of foundation trusts. The government has also effectively reintroduced GP fundholding, under the name of practice-based commissioning. Indeed, in some respects it has gone further than its predecessor, contracting with private sector firms to provide specialised treatment centres for elective surgery and diagnostics, and by trying to expand the range of possible providers of primary care beyond the traditional GP practice.

It therefore seems appropriate, and in the spirit of Howard Glennerster's commitment to making social policy work, to ask how these reforms will operate in practice and whether they can be designed in such a way as to avoid the mistakes made in the previous quasi-market experiment. And that is the principal aim of this chapter. It begins with a brief review of the theory behind the use of quasi-markets as a mechanism for delivering healthcare. It then considers some of the empirical evidence concerning quasi-markets in practice, concentrating on the impact of patient choice and competition – the principal elements of the new quasi-market – in healthcare systems that have already tried them, including the UK Conservative government's internal market. Finally, it draws on that experience to discuss some of the conditions necessary for the quasi-market to deliver high-quality, efficient and equitable healthcare – that is, for the healthcare system to work.

Quasi-markets in theory

The theory of quasi-markets (or, more accurately, the theoretical predictions that emerge concerning their likely benefits) derives in large part from the failure of other models of service delivery. Essentially, there are three other such models, all of which have been tried in one form or another within the Health Service.[3] First there is the *trust model*, where professionals and managers are simply trusted to know what is best for their users, and to deliver high-quality services without interference from government or any other source. Second is what we might consider the opposite of trust: a version of command and control that we might term the *targets and performance management model*, where central management sets targets for providers, rewards them if they succeed in meeting those targets, and penalises them if they fail. Third is the *voice model*, where users express their dissatisfaction (or satisfaction) directly to providers through face-to-face conversations, or through complaints to higher managers or elected representatives.

There are well-known problems with all of these. The trust model assumes that providers are solely motivated by the desire to provide exactly the services patients want and need, and that they have no more self-interested concerns. That is, in terms of a metaphor I have used extensively elsewhere, they are 'knights', not 'knaves' (Le Grand, 2006). In fact, of course, like everyone else, professionals and managers who work in health systems are a mixture of knight and knave; and inevitably therefore at times the service concerned is likely to be organised more in the interests of the provider than of the user. Moreover, even when providers do behave in a knightly fashion, they are more likely to provide what they think users want or need, rather than what users may actually want. As Rudolf Klein (2005, p 92) has put it:

> From the perspective of users, knights may be authoritarian paternalists acting in the sure faith that they are altruists who know best. If the pursuit of self-interest at the expense of the public interest is the pathology of knavery, self-righteous rectitude is the pathology of knighthood.

Targets and performance management is a model that is a form of command and control. Its chief merit is that it can work – at least in the short term. In the early years of this century, the English NHS adopted a wide variety of targets coupled with heavy performance management and in consequence some key aspects of service delivery (notably patient waiting times) sharply improved. For instance, in 2002 the target was set that 98% of accident and emergency attendees should be treated, discharged or admitted to hospital within four hours of their arrival (at that time it was less than 20%). By 2005, this target had been achieved – and this despite an increase of over a quarter in the number of people attending accident and emergency admissions in that period (DH, 2005, Statistical Supplement). Another example concerns elective surgery. In 1999, more than a quarter of the relevant patients in England were waiting longer than six months for surgery, and over 4% for more than a year. Key targets were set and by 2005 there was nobody waiting longer than a year and only 5% waiting longer than six months (Bevan and Hood, 2006, p 420, Table 1).

But, however well they work in the short run, in the long run targets and performance management suffer from all the standard problems associated with command and control. Of these perhaps the most significant is the demoralisation and demotivation of those on the front line of service delivery – especially if they are professionals who are not used to receiving orders and have been trained to believe that they will have substantial autonomy and independence in their work. Other problems include the distortion of priorities (hitting the target and missing the point), and the incentive for 'gaming' behaviour of various kinds, ranging from straightforward fiddling of the figures to more subtle ways of meeting the target by changing other untargeted behaviour in undesirable ways.

Voice, as defined by the man who originated the term in this context, Albert Hirschman, is

> any attempt at all to change, rather than to escape from, an objectionable state of affairs, whether through individual or collective petition to the management directly in charge, through appeal to a higher authority with the intention of forcing a change in management, or through the various types of actions and protests, including those that are meant to mobilize public opinion. (Hirschman, 1970, p 30)

In fact, voice is shorthand for all the ways in which users can express their dissatisfaction (or indeed their satisfaction) by some form of direct communication with providers. This could be through informally talking to them face to face – patients chatting to their GP. It could be more indirect: speaking at a patient or public consultative forum, joining the board of a hospital. It could be more formal: invoking a complaints procedure, complaining to elected representatives and so on. And it could be collective, through the process of voting for those representatives.

Now the voice model has its advantages as a means of public service delivery. Obviously it takes direct account of users' needs and wants, at least as they themselves perceive them. Moreover, individual voice mechanisms, especially, can be rich in useful information. Telling providers what is wrong with the service they provide (and indeed what is right with it) can be very helpful to providers who desire to improve – indeed much more so than simply not turning up for appointments or, as with the choice model, just switching to another provider.

However, it also has its difficulties. In a no-choice world of publicly funded healthcare, patients who are dissatisfied with the quality of the treatment they are getting, or the responsiveness of the medical professionals or managers with whom they are dealing, have only a limited range of options open to them. If there is a private healthcare sector running in parallel to the public one, they can use that – or, at least, the wealthier among them can do so. Those who cannot afford this option can only complain, either directly to the professional or manager concerned or to their superiors. In each case, the individual has to depend for a response on the goodwill, or indeed on the knightliness, of the person to whom they are complaining. As well as being demanding to undertake, this is a fragile mechanism for improving quality. It offers little or no direct incentives for improvement to the knavish or self-interested professional or manager; and even knightly, more altruistic, ones do not respond well to being challenged by pushy patients.

Moreover, insofar as complaining works at all, it favours the self-confident and articulate middle classes, thus tending to steer services in their direction at the expense of those for the less well off. The middle class thus have a double advantage over the less well off. They are better placed to persuade the key decision makers in the public service to meet their needs. And, if that fails, they can use the private sector. In neither case are equity and efficiency being served.

All of these models of service delivery thus have significant problems associated with them. So what about the model that is our principal concern here: the quasi-market model? It has some clear advantages over the others. Unlike the trust model, it channels both self-interest and altruism to serve the public good. If the money follows patient choices, then the hospital or practice that provides the better service will gain resources; that which provides the inferior service will lose. Whether the unsatisfactory providers are knights or knaves, they will wish to continue in business; the knaves because it is in their self-interest to do so, the knights because they want to continue to provide a good service to needy patients. But, to continue in business, they will have to improve the quality and responsiveness of the service they provide in order to attract patients, as well as the efficiency with which the service is delivered. Unlike the command and control model, it gives freedom and autonomy to professionals and managers, encouraging them to engage in innovation and creativity, and with no outside authority continuously telling them what to do. Unlike voice, in a quasi-market world where patient choice and provider competition is the norm, patients dissatisfied with the general quality of the service they can get from one provider – a hospital or a GP practice – have the opportunity to go to another who can provide them with a better service. This gives considerable leverage to anyone who does want to voice their dissatisfaction. If the listeners to a complaint know that in the last resort the complainant can go elsewhere, they are much more likely to respond positively to the issues being raised. Choice gives power to voice. Moreover, the facts that now both poor and rich can exit if necessary, and that the less well off are no longer dependent on their ability to persuade professionals to get the service they want, can improve the equity of service delivery.

Of course, there are limitations to the applicability of these kinds of arguments to all forms of healthcare. Patients who have suffered an accident or are seriously ill are unlikely to be able to make any kind of choice of provider, and may have to rely on others (attending doctors or ambulance crews) to make the choice for them. Some forms of medical treatment are one-off (your appendix can only be taken out once); in such cases information gained about the quality of treatment may be of little use in deciding where to go for other forms of treatment. Some people – perhaps an older person or one suffering from a debilitating long-term condition – may prefer not to have to make the necessary decisions.

However, the number of conditions where choice is impossible or unwanted should not be exaggerated. Experience of one form of treatment at a hospital can give insights into the quality of care provided for other treatments at the same facility. And the recent British Social Attitudes Survey showed that most people do want choice of medical facility – with, interestingly, larger majorities in favour of choice among the less well off than the middle classes (Appleby and Alvarez, 2005).

So, in theory at least, elements of quasi-markets, especially patient choice and provider competition, can be used to promote responsiveness, quality, efficiency and equity across wide areas of healthcare. But do things really work out that way in practice?

Quasi-markets in practice

Carol Propper and colleagues have recently produced a comprehensive survey of the US and other international evidence concerning the effects of competition between providers, especially hospitals (Propper et al, 2006). They found evidence that, as the model would predict, competition in the US both reduced costs and increased quality, so long as prices were fixed. But the US also provides examples of where problems can arise. Information provided to patients on quality was often too complex to be used effectively by them or indeed by institutional buyers of healthcare. In fact it was most widely used by the providers of that care itself, sometimes in ways that may have harmed patients. Providers concentrated on improving what was measured, which was not necessarily that which contributed to health. The fixed price system may have induced 'cream-skimming', whereby hospitals try to attract patients whose treatment costs they expect to be below the fixed price they are being offered, and to 'dump' patients whose costs they expect to be above that price.

There are also useful lessons to be derived from the British experience with the Conservative government's NHS internal market mentioned above. The principal feature of that market (and one that remains under the current system, at least in England) was a splitting up of the old state monolithic bureaucracy into purchasers and providers. The providers, mostly hospitals, became semi-independent 'trusts', with freedom to price their services and to compete for custom from the purchasers. The purchasers were of two kinds. There were 'GP fundholders': family practices that not only provided primary care for the patients registered with the practice, but also held a budget to purchase some forms of secondary care (mostly elective surgery) for them. And there were health authorities, geographically defined organisations that purchased secondary care services for all those who lived in their area, except for those purchased by fundholders.

Under the auspices of the King's Fund, I with colleagues undertook a comprehensive review of the evidence concerning the effectiveness of the internal market with respect to quality, efficiency, responsiveness, accountability and equity (Le Grand et al, 1998) – including the evidence on GP fundholding produced by Howard Glennerster (Glennerster et al, 1994). During the period from 1991 to 1997, NHS activity rose faster than resources (and rose at a relatively faster rate than before the reforms). This suggests that overall, despite some well-publicised increases in transaction costs, there was an increase in efficiency in the NHS that was attributable to those reforms. Moreover, following the partial roll-back of the internal market that was carried out by the new government in 1997, efficiency fell (Le Grand, 2002).

Although many analysts predicted that cream-skimming would cause equity problems, no cream-skimming was observed in practice. The principal equity concern arose from the differences between the two types of purchasers, one of which, GP fundholders, was more successful in getting a better deal for their patients. In particular, GP fundholders were effective in bringing down waiting times, reducing hospital referrals and holding down prescription costs. They were also better able to generate surpluses on their budgets than health authorities, and were able to generate improvements in the responsiveness of providers.

There was no evidence of any increase in choice for patients, and although there were changes over the period in indicators of quality such as waiting lists and patient satisfaction surveys, it was difficult to attribute these to the reforms. One study, however, found an increase in mortality from heart attacks in hospitals that were under greater competitive pressure (Propper et al, 2004).

Overall, despite some changes in culture, measurable changes were relatively small, and perhaps not as great as was predicted by the reforms' advocates, or as was feared by their critics. This appears to have been because competition within the market was limited, and this in turn may have been because some of the essential conditions for the market to operate were not fulfilled. More specifically, the incentives for the market players were too weak and the constraints imposed by central government were too strong. This interpretation is reinforced by the fact that the area where there were the greatest changes, GP fundholding, was the one where the incentives were greatest and the constraints the weakest.

Finally, there is evidence from the choice experiments that were tried out in England under the Labour government in the early years of this century (Dawson et al, 2004; Coulter et al, 2005). These offered a choice of hospital to patients who had been waiting more than six months for certain kinds of surgery (chiefly cataract and heart operations). Help was provided with transport costs, and patients were given a 'patient care adviser' to help them with the relevant choices: points to which I return below.

Take-up of choice was high – perhaps not surprisingly given that the patients concerned had already been waiting six months. Significantly, there was no difference in take-up between socioeconomic groups defined in terms of income, class or education, although the unemployed took up the offer of choice less frequently than the employed. The pilots also had a significant impact on waiting times in the areas in which they operated. For instance, in all of England except London, in the six months ending in March 2003 compared with the same period in the previous year, there was a fall of 2% in ophthalmology referrals received and seen, and a decline in the mean waiting time of 6%. However, in London where the choice project was in operation there was an *increase* in referrals of 5-6%; but this was accompanied by a *decrease* in waiting times of 17%.

So what are the lessons that can be learned from all this about policy design? The principal ones may be summarised under the headings of competition, information and cream-skimming.

Competition

For the quasi-market model to work – that is, for it to provide the necessary incentives for greater quality, efficiency and responsiveness – there have to be competitors, actual and/or potential. That is, there have to be alternative providers from which to choose; there have to be easy ways for new providers to enter the market, and, correspondingly, for failing providers to leave or exit from it; and there have to be ways of preventing existing providers engaging in anti-competitive behaviour, such as colluding with one another against the interests of users, or trying to create local (or even) national monopolies. In short, the competition must be real.

It is often argued that the condition for choice to exist – that there be alternative providers – is generally not fulfilled, and hence that offering choice is illusory, especially in healthcare. In Britain, London is usually cited as an exception; most of the population outside of London cannot realistically be offered a choice of hospitals simply because there are not enough of them within easy travelling distance – or so the argument goes.

However, the facts do not bear out this claim, at least for English hospitals. A study by the King's Fund and the University of Bristol found that 92% of the population had two or more acute NHS trusts within 60 minutes travel time by car (Damiani et al, 2005). Further, 98% of the population had access to 100 available and *unoccupied* NHS beds and 76% to 500. The only areas that came close to monopolistic provision were the relatively lightly populated parts of Cornwall, North Devon, Lincolnshire and Cumbria.

That said, there is evidence that some patients, notably those from poorer backgrounds, do have problems with transport to medical facilities. A survey of the evidence undertaken by myself and colleagues at the Department of Health and the London School of Economics and Political Science (LSE) suggested, perhaps rather surprisingly, that the poor did not necessarily have to travel further in terms of distance than the better off to access good medical facilities in the UK at present. However, even if the actual distances were not a factor in deterring the poor from using the NHS, the *cost* of travelling those distances, or more generally access to transport, was important. More specifically, lower car ownership and the consequent dependence on public transport among lower-income groups was a significant factor in lower utilisation rates and higher rates of did-not-attend-appointments (Dixon et al, 2003).

So, to promote both equity and to help make competition real, an essential element of any policy aimed at encouraging choice is the provision of help with transport and travel costs. This might involve the better planning of public transport infrastructures and timetables to enable easier access to a range of health facilities at all times, or transportation arrangements made on behalf of patients by the NHS. Ideally, financial help would cover the full range of costs, including the costs of time off work and costs associated with an accompanying partner or carer.

A second condition concerns the ability to enter and exit the market. New providers face barriers to entry into any market. An obvious one in healthcare is the capital cost of setting up a new facility; this could be quite considerable, especially if high technology equipment is required. A less obvious one concerns the habits of users; if people are used to being referred to their local hospital (and if GPs are used to referring them there) then it can be difficult to persuade them to use a new or a different provider. In such cases it may be necessary to offer some kind of assistance to new providers, for instance, through guaranteeing them a higher price for their services, or guaranteeing a specific volume of business. However, such assistance should be strictly time-limited.

Then there is the crucial question of 'exit' – or, more generally, how to deal with failing hospitals or other medical facilities. It is critical for the choice and competition model that there is some mechanism for dealing with failure that imposes costs on failing institutions. For, if there is no cost to failure, then much of the incentives that are so important for generating the desired outcomes disappear.

This absence of penalties for failure was, arguably, one of the reasons why the internal market of the 1990s' NHS failed to generate large changes in behaviour. Relatively early in the market's lifetime, a major teaching hospital in London got into trouble because it was losing business to outer London hospitals. There was considerable political protest, a consequence of which was that it was bailed out, and the internal market in London suspended. As a result, not only was the incentive for that hospital to improve removed, but, even more seriously, it had the effect of serving notice on hospitals, managers and consultants round the country that financial failure would not only not be penalised, but may even be rewarded – with a consequent dramatic weakening of incentives throughout the system.

Now dealing with inefficient or ineffective providers presents perennial difficulties for all systems for delivering public services. One advantage of quasi-markets in this respect is that failure under choice and competition is obvious. If a hospital or other medical facility is failing in terms of quality, and if it is recognised as such by potential users, then it will not be chosen. In consequence its revenues will fall, and its quality failure will be reflected in a financial failure. The failure will be clear; moreover, since few people will be choosing the facility, it will affect a relatively small number of people directly. Hence it will not be necessary to have some additional mechanism for checking quality; and, if it becomes necessary to close the facility, there will be relatively few patients affected.

It is necessary to have procedures for dealing with failure that are rule-driven, and that allow for little opportunity for discretion, and hence for political intervention that might otherwise blunt the relevant incentives. One such rule could be that intervention would be triggered automatically if a provider has deficits exceeding 3% of total income for two consecutive years (Palmer, 2005, p 21). But possibly even more important than the existence of rules governing the process of intervention is that both the decision to intervene and the intervention itself are undertaken by an agency independent of government. This could be an industry regulator, as in the privatised utilities in the UK where regulators have statutory powers to act to protect consumers in the event that the utility should face financial distress or fail. In those cases the regulator does not have to wait until a firm becomes insolvent to act and its powers enable it to approve or reject a financial restructuring.

Also, there is a danger in any market that the actors in the market will behave in ways that damage competition. Examples include agreements to drive up prices, arrangements to divide up the market and not to poach on each other's territory, and attempts to try to take over competitors so as to create a monopoly. Again to prevent unwarranted or unhelpful political interference, the answer here would seem to be to have a rule-driven system implemented by an independent regulator. It would in fact be sensible for this regulator to be the same as that for deciding on the entry and exit of providers; for all the relevant decisions are aspects of competition and indeed all are part of the business of making competition real.

Information

Information is crucial to the quasi-market model. More specifically, if patient choice is to act as an effective driver of quality, it is necessary to rely on the user's judgement about the quality and responsiveness of the service and necessary for providers to react to choices made on the basis of those judgements.

In healthcare this is clearly a key issue, since much of the relevant information is of a technical nature that most patients will have difficulty dealing with. And in fact there is little evidence that, when, for instance, presented with information about the quality of outcomes by individual surgeons, patients actually use that information to make the appropriate judgements (Marshall et al, 2000; Burgess et al, 2005).

However, all is not lost. Even if not driven by patient choice, there is evidence that providers do use published information to improve their performance – even if, as noted earlier, they may on occasion game the system. This may be because of professional pride or because they believe that, although patients do not directly use the information, it will eventually affect patient choice through the impact on their reputation and other less direct factors.

Moreover, there are ways of making information more accessible to patients. One method that proved very successful in helping overcome the patient information problem and encouraging user choice in the UK was the Patient Care Adviser (PCA) used in the choice pilot experiments mentioned above. Patient Care Advisers were trained staff, sometimes with a clinical background, who advised on choice of provider; they also gave advice on other matters, including (from those who were clinically trained) clinical ones, and offered support and reassurance.

Depending on what model of support was implemented, one potential criticism of extending the PCA idea is that it could be resource-intensive. This would be especially likely if a new professional role was created, generating an 'army of bureaucrats'. On the other hand, this would be less likely if it drew upon existing skills. And there could be resource savings. It could lead to better use of hospital capacity, more informed and active patients taking responsibility for their health and care, lower rates of non-attendance, and better coordination and planning of care. It could release GPs' and consultants' time. Further, the cost could be reduced if the scheme were targeted at patients in poor areas— areas where the biggest equity problems are likely to arise.

Cream-skimming

Any quasi-market system carries within it the danger of cream-skimming, whereby, instead of users choosing providers, providers choose users and do so on the grounds of cost. So in healthcare there is the possibility that popular GPs or hospitals, perhaps with waiting lists or queues for treatment, will only choose to treat those patients who are easiest or the cheapest to treat.

One possibility for dealing with this is to introduce some kind of stop-loss insurance scheme whereby hospitals faced with a patient whose treatment costs lie well outside the normal range get allocated extra resources once the cost has passed a certain threshold. These would have to be justified as catastrophic costs (not as the result of poor-quality care). This has the advantage of removing the incentive to discriminate against high-cost patients; but carries with it the problem that the hospitals concerned have no incentive to economise on treatment once the threshold has been passed. A similar scheme was used to stop cream-skimming by GP fundholders (which had been signaled as a potentially significant problem for the scheme on its introduction; Scheffler, 1989).

As Howard Glennerster has observed, in fact, the scheme seemed to have worked with little or no cream-skimming being seen (Glennerster and Matsaganis, 1994b; Goodwin, 1998).

A second possibility is to take the admission decisions completely away from hospitals. The Primary Care Trusts (PCTs) or GP practices would 'own' the waiting or referrals list, and hospitals and other treatment centres would be required to accept whoever was referred to them by PCTs or GPs. In fact, this is already envisaged with the introduction of e-booking and choice at the point of referral.

A third alternative is to risk-adjust the tariff system such that higher-risk patients have a higher tariff associated with them. A certain amount of this is already going to happen under the payment-by-results national tariff system. If fully risk-adjusted, this could eliminate the incentive to cream-skim completely. However, as has often been demonstrated, not least by Howard Glennerster (1996), risk-adjustment is a complex and difficult business; perfectly accurate risk-adjustment is arguably an impossible one. But so long as risk-adjustment is not perfect, there will remain an incentive to cream-skim. Risk-adjusted payments also provide the incentive to up-code patients to more lucrative high-price categories.

Overall, we do not know whether risk selection or cream-skimming will turn out to be a problem associated with the new quasi-market. As the policy is implemented, an equity audit needs to be undertaken, partly to check on the progress of the supported choice package, but also to assess whether there are adverse equity consequences arising from risk selection. If this does emerge as a concern, policy options for dealing with it such as these need to be explored.

Conclusion

Publicly funded healthcare systems that incorporate quasi-market elements such as user choice and provider competition can achieve the ends of healthcare policy. But they must be properly designed so as to meet the conditions for effectiveness. There must be mechanisms for ensuring that the entrance for new providers is easy; that exit can take place and that the relevant decisions are immune from political interference; that patients are given the relevant information and help in making choices, especially the less well off; that there is help with transport costs, preferably again targeted at the less well off. And the opportunities and incentives for cream-skimming should be eliminated, either through not allowing providers to determine their own admissions or through properly risk-adjusting the fixed price system.

Notes

[1] Scotland and Wales continued, temporarily at least, to reject quasi-market principles.

[2] Since it actually involves payment for procedures undertaken and not for the results of those procedures in health terms, a more accurate label would be payment-by-activity.

[3] For a longer version of much of the material in this chapter and a fuller discussion of both these models and the quasi-market model, see Le Grand (2007).

References

Appleby, J. and Alvarez, A. (2005) 'Public response to NHS reform', *British Social Attitudes Survey, 22nd Report*, London: Sage Publications.

Bevan, G. and Hood, C. (2006) 'Have targets improved performance in the English NHS?', *British Medical Journal*, vol 332, pp 419-22.

Burgess, S., Propper, C. and Wilson, D. (2005) *Will More Choice Improve Outcomes in Education and Healthcare? The Evidence from Economic Research*, Bristol: The Centre for Market and Public Organisation, University of Bristol.

Coulter, A., le Maistre, N. and Henderson, L. (2005) *Patients' Experience of Choosing Where to Undergo Surgical Treatment – Evaluation of the London Patient Choice Scheme*, Oxford: Picker Institute.

Damiani, M., Dixon, J. and Propper, C. (2005) 'Mapping choice in the NHS: cross-sectional study of analysis of routinely collected data', *British Medical Journal*, vol 330, p 284.

Dawson, D., Jacobs, R., Martin, S. and Smith, P. (2004) *Evaluation of the London Patient Choice Project: System-Wide Impacts, Final Report*, York: Centre for Health Economics, University of York.

DH (Department of Health) (2005) *Chief Executive's Report to the NHS: December 2005*, London: DH.

Dixon, A., Le Grand, J., Henderson, J., Murray, R. and Poliakoff, E. (2003) *Is the NHS Equitable?*, LSE Health and Social Care Discussion Paper no 11, London: London School of Economics and Political Science.

Glennerster, H. (1991) 'Quasi-markets for education?', *Economic Journal*, vol 101, pp 1268-76.

Glennerster, H. (1995) 'Internal markets: context and structure', in M. Jerome-Forget, J. White and J.M. Wiener (eds) *Healthcare Reform through Internal Markets*, Washington, DC: Brookings Institution.

Glennerster, H. (1996) 'Fixed budgets for fundholding: general practitioners in the UK', in F.W. Schwartz, H. Glennerster and R.B. Saltman (eds) *Fixing Health Budgets: Experience from Europe and North America*, Chichester: Wiley.

Glennerster, H. and Le Grand, J. (1995) 'The development of quasi-markets in welfare provision in the United Kingdom', *International Journal of Health Services*, vol 25, pp 203-18.

Glennerster, H. and Matsaganis, M. (1994a) 'The English and Swedish healthcare reforms', *International Journal of Health Services*, vol 24, pp 231-51.

Glennerster, H. and Matsaganis, M. (1994b) 'The threat of "cream skimming" in the post-reform NHS', *Journal of Health Economics*, vol 13, pp 31-60.

Glennerster, H., Matsaganis, M. and Owens, P. (1994) *Implementing GP Fundholding*, Buckingham: Open University Press.

Goodwin, N. (1998) 'GP fund-holding', in J. Le Grand, N. Mays and J. Mulligan (eds) *Learning from the NHS Internal Market*, London: King's Fund.

Hirschman, A. (1970) *Exit, Voice and Loyalty*, Cambridge, MA: Harvard University Press.

Klein, R. (2005) 'The great transformation', *Health Policy, Economics and Law*, vol 1, pp 91-8; reprinted in J. Le Grand (2006) *Motivation, Agency and Public Policy: Of Knights and Knaves, Pawns and Queens* (revised edition), Oxford: Oxford University Press.

Le Grand, J. (2002) 'The Labour government and the National Health Service', *Oxford Review of Economic Policy*, vol 18, pp 137-53.

Le Grand, J. (2006) *Motivation, Agency and Public Policy; Of Knights and Knaves, Pawns and Queens* (revised edition), Oxford: Oxford University Press.

Le Grand, J. (2007) *The Other Invisible Hand*, Oxford: Princeton University Press.

Le Grand, J., Mays, N. and Mulligan, J.A. (1998) *Learning from the Internal Market: A Review of the Evidence*, London: King's Fund.

Marshall, M., Shekelle, P., Leatherman, S. and Brook, R. (2000) *Dying to Know: Public Release of Information about the Quality of Healthcare*, Nuffield Trust Series 12, London: Nuffield Trust.

Palmer, K. (2005) *How Should we Deal with Hospital Failure: Facing the Challenges of the New NHS Market*, London: King's Fund.

Propper, C., Burgess, S. and Green, K. (2004) 'Does competition between hospitals improve the quality of care? Hospital death rates and the NHS internal market', *Journal of Public Economics*, vol 88, pp 1247-72.

Propper, C., Wilson, D. and Burgess, S. (2006) 'Extending choice in English healthcare: the implications of the economic evidence', *Journal of Social Policy*, vol 35, pp 537-57.

Scheffler, R. (1989) 'Adverse selection: the Achilles heel of the NHS reforms', *The Lancet*, vol 29, pp 950-2.

Stevens, S. (2004) 'Reform strategies for the English NHS', *Health Affairs*, vol 23, pp 37-44.

EIGHT

Social care: choice and control

Martin Knapp

The 'mixing' of the social care economy in the UK has been one of the most notable features of the past two decades, with attention initially focusing on changes to the balance of provision and more recently turning to the sources, balance and routes of funding. Throughout the past two or three decades there has been emphasis on shifting the administrative centre of gravity – initially towards and later somewhat away from local authorities. These broad changes are discussed in this chapter as a platform for considering current quite radical efforts to shift responsibility and power to service users – for example through direct payments and individual budgets – linked to the broader choice agenda and obviously with deep roots in social work practice and personal empowerment.

Introduction

As the other chapters of this book describe, almost every area of social policy in the UK has seen shifts in the balance of provision and responsibility over recent decades. Many areas have also seen changes in financing and expenditure routes. In some cases, those organisational and economic changes promise to alter the fundamental architecture of the policy area. Social care is no exception. Of all the various changes across the social policy spectrum, in fact, some in the social care area have been particularly adventurous in both intent and implementation. Most obviously, while the UK health system has been introducing a series of quasi-market structures since the early 1990s, the social care system has been forging ahead with *real* markets. And while the National Health Service (NHS) has been experimenting with money that follows the patients, the social care system is now handing the money over *to* service users so that they can decide how best to meet their own needs. New arrangements in the NHS will very gradually broaden patient choice, but the social care sector is experimenting with ways to promote user *control*. It is this latter policy area that is the main focus of this chapter.

Underlying these shifts in social care are a number of fundamental principles. One has been the long-term social work commitment to empowering marginalised individuals and groups. Another has been to emphasise the roles of families, although sometimes this admirable principle has been misused to dress up a policy of benign neglect. Then there is the wider community development agenda, encouraging communities to assume greater responsibility for identifying and meeting the needs of vulnerable members, with or without support that is structured and/or financed by the state.

The 'administrative anthropological' approach to understanding policy and practice development, to focus on an enduring theme of Howard Glennerster's work across a number of social policy fields, would therefore be called upon to record and interpret some fairly fundamental changes. Perhaps none is more fundamental than the efforts now in train to shift some of the funding from what some would see as the clutches of state-employed case managers (more often in fact their line managers) to those individual people assessed as qualifying for state-supported care. Consequently, the focus of any 'administrative anthropological' work today would need to move partly away from structures dominated by public sector rules and roles about how to channel funds and commission services, and also partly away from the motivations and modus operandi of the independent provider organisations that deliver them, to the personalised, idiosyncratic arrangements that individual people put in place to identify, access and pay for their own care. The emphasis, as just noted, is not just on choice but on *control*: for many advocates in the social care field, choice is too passive, too vulnerable to bureaucratic manipulation – in sum, too 'controlled'.

However, it all started with expanding choice. At a macro level, we might expect choice to be broadened by, for example, stimulating new providers to enter care markets – a strategy at the heart of the Conservative government's push to expand choice in the early 1990s, intimately tied up with its push to substitute independent sector for state services. There were also efforts, at a micro level, to promote choice by helping older people and other social care users to make informed decisions about the services they receive and who provides them. Again one can see this as a feature of the early 1990s: the 1989 social services White Paper (DH, 1989) and the 1990 NHS and Community Care Act were the main prompts for many of the most significant changes witnessed in social care for half a century. One of the most widely quoted passages from that White Paper was the objective 'to give people a greater individual say in how they live their lives and the services they need to help them to do so' (Secretaries of State, 1989, p 4). A few years later, the so-called *Direction on Choice* (DH, 1992) specified the operational meaning of choice for people considering or facing admission to a care home.

But the expansion of choice and control requires more than this. The two elements promoted in the early 1990s were clearly fundamental ingredients:

* developing a range of services that vary sufficiently to offer meaningful *diversity*;
* providing *information* so as to make the pertinent details of those services known to current and potential users and their carers in ways that are accessible and understandable.

But two more elements also need to be in place:

* *empowering* users and carers so that they can select in an informed way from the options available;
* allowing users to have *control* – albeit probably with a degree of support and/or monitoring – over those selections.

Although the 1990 legislation encouraged individual flexibility and devolved budgets (to case/care managers) and although the Independent Living Fund had been established in the 1980s to channel state funding to disabled people in part to compensate for difficulties encountered and anticipated as social security support was reformed, real progress has been made only comparatively recently. Direct payments (transfers of funding to individuals to spend on care services) for physically disabled people have really only been given concerted encouragement since the mid-1990s – by the 1996 Community Care (Direct Payments) Act – followed by extension to older people (since 2000) and other user groups. It is now mandatory for local authorities to offer direct payments to all 'suitable' users, and national performance monitoring systems now look at the numbers of people who receive them. More recently, more adventurously, and certainly with more attendant risks, *individual budgets* have been launched. They were heralded in Labour's general election manifesto as the centrepiece of ambitions to 'modernise' social care in England (Glendinning et al, 2006), first being proposed by the Cabinet Office (2005) and propounded with growing enthusiasm in subsequent Green and White Papers (DH, 2005, 2006).

In considering how choice and control have been addressed in the social care field, it is therefore instructive to organise discussion of recent developments under the four headings defined by the elements distinguished above (*diversity, information, empowerment, control*), and then to set out what is being done in relation to direct payments and individual budgets. In what follows I shall tend to concentrate on older people, as these people as a group account for the single largest element of public expenditure on social care. But it is also helpful to look at other user groups, and so I subsequently also offer some reflections on choice for mental health service users and people with intellectual (learning) disabilities.

Diversity

Diversity of provision was an explicit aim of the 1989 White Paper (Secretaries of State, 1989) and was one reason for the Conservative government's encouragement of private and voluntary sector provision of social care, although whether this was really or primarily linked to an underlying desire to empower service users is a moot point. Indeed the changes to the availability of social security funding for care home placements actually represented a considerable reining in of choice for people who were eligible for state support, as Howard Glennerster has himself described:

> The paradox was that this [the pre–1990 Act social security eligibility] was an almost perfect voucher scheme that had grown up by accident. Families could choose a home for their elderly relative and the state would pay. This maximised choice and consumer power. Unfortunately, it also maximised the growth of public expenditure on this group. (Glennerster, 1995, p 208)

Nevertheless, the emphasis on changing the balance of provision undoubtedly proved successful. Service variety has increased over the past 15 years or so, although not yet sufficiently, as is made plain by a review of inspection and audit evidence on unmet needs and service development:

> Indisputably, between 1996 and 2003, a wider range of services has been developed to support vulnerable people in the community. This has been driven, in part, by action from the Government in the form of national priorities, hypothecated investment and performance assessment. However, the impact locally varies markedly depending

on the coherence of council planning, the quality of local partnerships and the extent to which that planning has sought to involve people using services. (Social Services Inspectorate and Audit Commission, 2004, p 12)

Expanding choice requires the commissioning framework to allow (or, more likely, actively to encourage) the development of a range of services at an affordable cost to the state and to self-funding users. Diversity is also needed in other dimensions. For example, for an older person about to enter a care home, there should be more than one option not just in relation to the features of that particular home and its location, but also in relation to when to enter a home and whether to stay there once the choice and initial move have been made (Challis and Bartlett, 1998). For the majority of older people, such a move is likely to be a choice about where they will spend the rest of their lives. For older people receiving services in their own homes, there might need to be the option of choosing the provider (although a few years ago most older people appeared not so bothered about this particular choice; see Hardy et al, 1999; Ware et al, 2003), the regularity and timing of the visits, and perhaps the tasks to be performed. They would certainly like to have fewer changes in the people who come into their homes to perform what are often quite personal care tasks.

What factors limit diversity and hence the 'choice range' (in this narrow sense)? Budgetary restrictions that constrain the development of new services obviously limit choice. So, too, does a contractual regime that rules out diversity through the imposition of uniform standards or the block purchasing of large numbers of places from a single provider. 'In-house first' practices (local authorities purchasing services from local authority providers first, and only then turning to independent providers) are clearly also likely to be damaging in this respect (Audit Commission, 1997; Ware et al, 2003). Clearly, therefore, the basic 'institutions' of a mixed economy can be highly influential. Underdevelopment of home care services could leave little option but for someone to go into a home (Ryan and Scullion, 2000). Admissions policies operated by care homes might deny a full free choice.

Fears have also been expressed that the introduction and growing influence of national care standards could narrow the difference between providers (Holden, 2002). There might be a tension between the tendency for the standardisation of provision and the individualisation of services in response to individual users' preferences, particularly the 'routinisation' and increasing regulation of home care services (Patmore, 2001). This is the longstanding (and elegantly named) 'coercive isomorphism' thesis of DiMaggio and Powell (1983). Concentration of provision in a small number of organisations as a result of mergers and acquisitions – which is beginning to happen in care home markets in England, for example, although the pace of change remains modest – could reduce the diversity of provision (Holden, 2002), although it should not be seen as inevitable. Another problem is the 'ratcheting up of eligibility criteria' (Ware et al, 2003, p 422), denying older people with 'lower-level' needs the access to publicly supported services. For these people, the range of options is limited to what they personally can afford or what their relatives can provide informally.

Diversity, interpreted in the multidimensional sense set out here, is a clearly rate-limiting factor in the promotion of choice. If there is insufficient diversity in provision or approaches to meeting needs, then there is an obvious constraint on choice. But diversity is only a necessary and not sufficient ingredient for choice.

Information

The second ingredient is development of better information systems, particularly ensuring that accessible, meaningful information reaches people who, through dint of language, culture, cognitive impairment, frailty or other reasons, may have difficulty with comprehension or some forms of communication. Accounts of the failings of available information arrangements, including for older people from black and minority ethnic groups and for older people with mental health problems, are legion (Audit Commission, 2000; Reed et al, 2003).

Three particular barriers to accessing information, advice and advocacy can be distinguished: lack of awareness that helpful information is available, difficulties in gaining access to that information, and difficulties in gaining practical assistance to act on the information obtained (Quinn et al, 2003). Over-bureaucratisation and fragmentation of the care management and assessment processes have made it harder for information to flow efficiently through the system (Ware et al, 2003). Certainly, care management has not been operating in the manner evaluated in the path-breaking Personal Social Services Research Unit projects of the 1980s or as envisaged in the 1989 White Paper (Davies and Challis, 1986). There has also been a tendency to underestimate the abilities of older people (Godlove-Mozley et al, 1999).

There has nevertheless been progress. Local authorities today collate and distribute information on care homes to prospective new residents and their families, although usually relatively little is given on the quality of providers – understandable in part because of the inherent difficulties in doing so, and anyway authorities express hesitation about being seen to be favouring or recommending particular homes or providers (Audit Commission, 1997). Annual or more frequent sample satisfaction surveys allow information to flow in the other direction. Improving inter-agency coordination should also reduce the confusion among users and carers, although it might actually make things worse in the short run. On the other hand, many older people are still admitted to care homes with little preparation (because of sudden changes in either their needs or in the abilities of their caregivers), and when there is a degree of planning, the information provided to them can be quite limited. Wigley et al (1998), for the Office of Fair Trading (1998), found that a majority of care home residents were able to express views on the care they received, but many had been poorly informed about what admission to the home would entail or the options available to them: 'Nearly six out of ten said they had no choice about moving into a home' (Wigley et al, 1998, p 53). People going into local authority homes received less prior information than those entering independent homes. Very few made complaints about their care, and when they did, it was usually via a third party (a relative). Wright (2003) found that people who were paying the full cost of their long-term care home were given little professional advice about placements or alternatives to care in a home. The situation was little different for older people moving into extra-care housing (Oldman, 2000) or facing healthcare interventions (CHI, 2004).

Empowerment

Diversity and information are clearly necessary, but options need to be turned into genuine choices (Myers and MacDonald, 1996). Evidence from a study I conducted a few years ago with colleagues illustrates some of the issues (Ware et al, 2003).

We looked at the choices available to 55 older people, their carers and care managers (drawn from 11 areas of England). Users and care managers were asked what choices they had over providing agency, service and timing. The overriding impression was of users being offered little choice in any of these dimensions. Care managers confirmed that users were rarely offered a choice in selecting a home care agency, but argued that it made little sense to users without them having prior knowledge of what services were available. It is difficult to gain experience by 'shopping around' for a product such as personal care. Moreover, these care managers argued, users' choices would clearly be restricted by the availability of services and the nature of contractual relationships between purchasers and providers. Block contract or cost-minimisation purchasing arrangements were restricting choices. So, too, were the 'in-house first' policies then operating in three of the 11 localities included in the study. In a fourth area, care managers said they had a personal preference for in-house services. Most users said they did not mind which sector provided their care. Another restriction on choice came from tightened eligibility criteria, in that domestic tasks were increasingly being taken out of the range of services supported by local authorities, even though this limited older people's abilities to maintain their independence. Clearly, empowering users was a long way off.

The choice of care home was subject to the 1992 *Direction on Choice* (DH, 1992), and it was not surprising that older people in this study who had moved into care homes reported that they had been offered some options. They were given more written information and could visit the homes prior to making a decision. However, some users were presented with just two bald choices – stay at home or go into care – and a number said they had accepted the latter reluctantly. There was no involvement of users or carers in decision making in two out of 12 cases. Again, choices were constrained, in this case by service costs (in relation to authorities' contractual arrangements), the availability of vacant places, and the speed with which funding could be allocated.

Information provided to users of domiciliary (home-based) care was limited, but generally appeared to be better than in the past. Care managers said that they had too little information about providers in the independent sectors, and some said that they did not have confidence in their purchasing colleagues' assurances on the quality of such services. Information on user charges was also sometimes less than complete. Service users' satisfaction levels, as other studies have found, were generally high, but a number of difficulties with home care packages were mentioned, mainly related to having too many changes of worker, or workers arriving late or not at all. Some users complained that their care workers came too early to put them to bed, a lament familiar from Lewis and Glennerster's (1996) earlier work.

Other research in a variety of settings has shown how active participation of service users in decisions about their care has remained elusive in many settings. Based on evidence collected a decade ago, Hardy et al (1999) reported that no one in a sample of 24 users of local authority and independent sector home care services (sampled from four localities) had been offered a choice between sectors or providers, and few had been consulted about the composition or timing of services. The District Audit (2002) summary of their auditing of rehabilitation services found that few services had a user-centred approach or offered them much choice. Shortages of professionally qualified staff – particularly of speech and language therapists and physiotherapists – were contributing to these difficulties.

There are concerns that the development of performance measurement regimes might be encouraging standardised methods of information gathering, rather than efforts to engage with residents in order to elicit a better understanding of their needs and preferences (for example, see Foord et al, 2004, on sheltered housing). These authors could find little evidence that the emphasis in *Quality and Choice for Older People* (DETR, 2001) on gauging user quality of life was reflected in the performance measures being introduced.

Bland (1999) focused 'on the translation of the core values of independence, privacy, dignity, choice and rights into a daily reality for residents' of care homes (p 539). She traced the historical development of what she called a 'social care' approach to residential care for older people that:

> assumes responsibility for their [residents'] welfare because they are seen as no longer able to manage it for themselves. By applying for residential care or, more typically, being referred by professionals or relatives, older people become by definition, 'socially incompetent' or incapable of remaining independent. (p 545)

This is consistent with Walker's (1982) thesis on the social construction of 'dependency'. Bland argued that care home staff interpret the objective of promoting independence as enabling physical activities, rather than allowing residents to exercise autonomy and self-determination. She compares this approach with what she calls the 'service approach', which emphasises autonomy and independence, gives residents greater control over their lives, ensures that they are treated as socially competent rather than as frail and vulnerable, and sees them as experts in relation to their own needs and wishes. As she notes, by returning to the original Bevanite conception of care homes as hotels, we would be paying greater attention to service user choice and control.

Control

To what extent should service users be given the freedom to decide what care they receive, and that includes the freedom to choose risky behaviours (Clark et al, 1996)? Paying for their own care, an option now (slowly) being offered to older people through direct payments and individual budgets, obviously gives a much greater degree of control, although – as discussed in more detail below – older people will still need information and support in order to exercise their powers (Roberts, 2001).

The Office of Public Management (1995) reported significant changes in user and carer involvement across the range of community care activities in four sites following initiatives to improve user- and carer-centred services. Resources were allocated to individual service users to allow them to purchase some services for themselves (communication aids, respite care, travel and so on). These early explorations of direct payments for older people pointed to some potential benefits.

At the heart of an Audit Commission (2004a) report on services for older people sat choice as control:

> Older people have strong and consistent views about what helps them to stay independent.... At the heart of older people's sense of independence and well being lies their capacity to make choices and to exercise control over their lives. (p 7)

Both independence and interdependence were emphasised. The work underpinning this report found that many older people had very few opportunities to express their preferences, those most disadvantaged in this respect being 'very frail or housebound older people, black and minority ethic elders or older people with mental health problems' (p 11). In follow-up work, the Audit Commission (2004b) argued that older people's expectations are changing, but that systems of support and care have failed to adapt. The message was not new (Harding, 1997).

Before describing the development of the two mechanisms that have sought genuinely to impact on choice by giving social care users *control* (direct payments and individual budgets), it is instructive to consider the experiences of people with intellectual disabilities and, first, people who use mental health services.

Experiences for mental health service users

One user group for whom choice has for long been especially limited is people who use mental health services, many of whom are today supported quite extensively by social care services. Some years ago Barnes (1997) set out steps to improve choice that are congruent with the elements above: there needs to be service alternatives, information on them needs to be accessible to service users, moving from one option to another must be possible, and moving from one option to another should not in itself be harmfully disruptive. The last of these raises interesting questions about the domains over which individuals should be allowed freedom of choice and action. What is clear from a review of the evidence in this area, with its close links with the health system, is that action has until recently not moved much beyond user involvement – essentially the second of our four elements. There almost seems to have been an implicit but myopic assumption that promoting service diversity and encouraging care managers to consult mental health service users is sufficient to establish 'choice'.

Recent policy announcements and practice guidance documents have set out plans and recommendations for a more inclusive, 'involving' strategy. The Department of Health (DH, 2001b), for example, has argued that: 'Improved information will support service user empowerment and improved safer care' (p 22). A booklet by the National Institute for Mental Health in England (NIMHE, 2003b) booklet identified five reasons for involving service users and the general public in decision making: accountability, developing local understanding, strengthening public confidence, encouraging services to become more responsive, and challenging any paternalistic models of provision. User involvement brings a particular expertise and a different perspective to the decision-making forum, it can be therapeutic, and it can help new approaches to meeting needs to emerge.

A useful review by NIMHE (2003b) traces service user involvement since the 1980s, identifying barriers, influences and successes. Service user involvement in planning and monitoring of services was 'fairly promising' according to the former Social Services Inspectorate (Robbins, 2004, p 15), with 60% of local implementation teams (LITs) 'meaningfully involving some service users in the planning and monitoring of services', and the remaining 40% having 'effective structures and systems for ensuring that a wide network of service users is involved in the planning and monitoring of services'. In relation to user-led services, 76% of teams were rated as 'working to establish or increase the provision of user-run or led services within the LIT area', and 17% had 'user-run or led services ... provided at a level that the LIT deems to reflect an adequate mix within the overall provider arrangements'.

Progress in this respect is indeed therefore encouraging, but there is still some distance to travel in ensuring that all service users have the opportunity to be involved in service planning and decision making if they wish (CHI, 2003; Langan and Lindow, 2004). The authors of a NIMHE (2003b, p 4) publication expressed concern that 'the often very good intentions of service providers can sometimes fail to move beyond the rhetoric into reality'. Barriers include lack of information for service users, the time and money costs of user involvement, concerns about 'representativeness', and the experience of some users that involvement can actually be disempowering. The Healthcare Commission survey of NHS patients in 2004 (Healthcare Commission, 2005) found that 15% of 27,000 mental health service users did not have enough say in care decisions, and another 44% only had a say to a limited extent. This matched the SSI conclusion that:

> The active involvement of service users in their own care planning was too often very limited, with insufficient focus given to the need – and potential – for people to participate in socially inclusive activities. Greater transparency around care planning, with better sharing of information at all stages would help here. (Robbins, 2004, p 16)

Diversity also remains limited. One emphasis in recent policy literature, and identified as a failing by many reports and studies, is the provision of culturally sensitive services. The poor targeting of services and support on the needs of black and minority ethnic service users is unfortunately prevalent in today's health service. Robbins (2004) reports that two-thirds of local authorities were, at that time, not yet sure whether their Race Equality Schemes would directly result in service improvements. There was a particular problem with slippage in the development of 'plans for improving the provision of services which would be accessible to black and ethnic minority service users' (p 19).

There is certainly scope for empowerment and control for mental health service users, but perhaps only in the face of some professional opposition. As discussed below, take-up of direct payments by mental health service users has been very slow (Davey et al, 2006; Fernandez et al, 2007), and few of the pilot schemes for individual budgets are involving this user group.

Experiences for people with intellectual disabilities

Valuing People, the 2001 White Paper on people with intellectual (learning) disabilities (DH, 2001a), offered an array of proposals that were intended to:

- 'tackle social exclusion and achieve better life chances;
- ensure value for money from the large public investment in learning disability services;
- reduce variation and promote consistency and equity of services across the country;
- promote effective partnership working at all levels to ensure a really person-centred approach to delivering quality services;
- drive up standards by encouraging an evidence-based approach to service provision and practice.' (p 22)

Underpinning these proposals was the core objective of promoting independence, choice and control.

> Like other people, people with learning disabilities want a real say in where they live, what work they should do and who looks after them. But for too many people with learning disabilities these are currently unattainable goals. We believe that everyone should be able to make choices. This includes people with severe and profound disabilities who, with the right help and support, can make important choices and express preferences about their day-to-day lives.' (DH, 2001a, p 24)

Choices have been and remain constrained in a number of ways, including: failure to recognise the rights of individuals with intellectual disabilities as ordinary citizens; patchy provision of advocacy services; very limited involvement in decision making, such as in planning or review meetings; not acting on the expressed preferences of those people who *do* participate; and low take-up of direct payments because of poor support arrangements (Baines et al, 2001; Cambridge and McCarthy, 2001; Carr, 2004).

Proposals were set out in *Valuing People* to address these deficiencies, including establishment of a group to advise the Disability Rights Commission. Another initiative was to fund (albeit modestly) further services to develop both self-advocacy and citizen advocacy, aiming to offer a choice of independent advocacy services in each area. The Department of Health's first annual report on intellectual disability (DH, 2003) noted some progress in this last respect, with the establishment of more local advocacy groups, although not enough to satisfy the Learning Disability Task Force (LDTF, 2004). In 2002-03 local authorities were reported to have spent about a third more on advocacy than in the previous year, although there was wide variation across the country.

Guidance was issued on housing, care and support options, although not as quickly as hoped because of the need for local consultation with Partnership Boards. A great deal of reliance was clearly placed on Supporting People funding – from outside the social care budget, of course – for independent living arrangements. One concern expressed by the LDTF (2004) was that 'the new draft Mental Incapacity [later Capacity] Bill could be used to stop people with learning disabilities from making their own decisions' (p 39). Other initiatives pertinent to choice and control included rewording of the 2003 Sexual Offences Act 'to reflect the right of people with learning disabilities to a full sexual life' (DH, 2004, p 23) and facilitation of the use of Consumer Direct, a helpline set up by the Department of Trade and Industry.

Using our 'diversity, information, empowerment, control' framework we can see some progress for people with intellectual disabilities. For example, the range of day activity services is gradually being widened away from the traditional and sometimes rather institutional adult training and social education centres (although they are not necessarily unpopular with users). Today there is more emphasis on supported employment arrangements. Accommodation options are also growing, but very unevenly, as a summary of inspection reports concluded a few years ago:

> Choice of services varied greatly. Most councils were well on the way to modernisation, and offered a wide range of community-based flexible options, but some provided relatively inflexible accommodation, day care and short-term break options. Surprisingly, there were some councils which did not have any form of adult placement scheme – either for respite or long-term care. This was a serious omission as such schemes were well liked by carers and offered a cost-effective solution to the challenge of re-providing services. (Cope, 2003, p 23)

Information on that diversity was similarly mixed in availability and appropriateness:

> Some councils provided information in a range of formats, including the internet, and supported this by advocates and specialist disability information services.... However, most people still use the telephone or visit an office to gain information. Best practice would suggest that information should be available in the format preferred by service users

and carers. Unfortunately this was still not the norm. In some councils information was available in day centres but not area or district offices. (Cope, 2003, pp 3, 18)

Hatton (2004) discussed the definition of choice and the tendency (wrongly, he argued) to see it as synonymous with, rather than one (key) element of, control and self-determination. He discussed the capacity of people with intellectual disabilities to make choices, which constitutes a 'substantial strand of research'. Williams and Robinson (2001, p 30) opined that 'a greater degree of informed choice for individuals with intellectual disabilities will in itself resolve many potential conflicts of interest'.

Hatton (2004) reviewed studies that assessed the extent to which people have opportunities to make choices (see also earlier work by Stalker and Harris, 1998, and Harris, 2000). A systematic review by Algozzine et al (2001) looked at evaluated efforts to improve choice-making behaviour, and Kern et al (1998) looked at choice making as an intervention to improve behaviour. Community-based settings are superior to hospital in offering choice and facilitating empowerment, although there is great variation across settings. Smaller, newer facilities generally perform better than larger facilities. The domains over which choice can be exercised also show some variation between settings, and people with mild or moderate intellectual disabilities have more opportunities to exercise choice than people with more severe disabilities or with challenging behaviour (Stalker and Harris, 1998).

In 2001, *Valuing People* noted that:

> Many people with learning disabilities have little choice or control in their lives. Recent research shows only 6% of people with learning disabilities having control over who they lived with, and 1% over choice of carer. Advocacy services are patchy and inconsistent. Direct payments have been slow to take off for people with learning disabilities. (DH, 2001a, p 19)

Since then, efforts by non-statutory bodies such as In Control and the introduction of individual budgets in 13 pilot areas have moved things forward for those people directly affected.

Direct payments

Direct payments transfer social care funding to service users, who then have the opportunity to spend their budgets on a range of services to meet their personal (care) needs. Direct payments were introduced in England and Wales under the 1996 Community Care (Direct Payments) Act, coming into effect in 1997, and extended to older people in 2000. Direct payments must now be offered to everyone assessed as needing social care. Although formally introduced in the 1990s, in fact there were variants earlier, particularly through the Independent Living Fund, which was established in the 1980s. Also during that earlier period, some local authorities had experimented with 'third party payment' schemes, which allowed funding to reach users via voluntary sector bodies.

Direct payments cannot be spent on local authority in-house services or on informal care support. Nevertheless, direct payments clearly give greater control to people eligible for state-funded social care support and for that reason have been widely welcomed. Surprisingly, therefore, the roll out of direct payments to social care users has been slow – and certainly disappointingly slow to central government. As can be seen from Table 8.1, the numbers of people in England with direct payments grew between September 2005 and March 2006 but are still very modest. For example, less than 1% of older people supported by English authorities are in receipt of direct payments, and even for disabled people the proportion is only around 7%.

Table 8.1: Numbers of people with direct payments, England

Service user group	Numbers of people with direct payments	
	September 2005	March 2006
Older people	7,566	9,733
People with learning disabilities	3,803	4,750
People with physical disabilities	12,460	13,690
People with sensory impairments	748	963
Young carers	14	16
People who use mental health services	1,136	1,477
Disabled children	4,014	5,027
Disabled young people aged 16-17	368	326
Carers	3,438	5,435
People with an HIV/AIDS infection	193	169
People who misuse drugs/alcohol	20	37
Total	**33,760**	**41,623**

Source: CSCI (2006)

Many factors lie behind the policy emphasis on direct payments (and indeed more recently on individual budgets) (Fernandez et al, 2007). Social work theory has long emphasised independence and empowerment, giving such payments normative professional credibility. There is also a growing belief that such a policy can be cost-effective, although convincing evidence has yet to be assembled. The approach appeals both to the political Right because of its links to market mechanisms, and also to the Centre Left because of its connections with choice and accountability in public services. From the user perspective, direct payments are clearly attractive to many people because of the empowerment offered, and are clearly supportive of a rights-based agenda. A further reason for promoting direct payments is because they potentially engage people who might refuse to accept directly provided support on the grounds that they view receipt of council services as in some sense shameful, or because the quality of care is poor. It has also been argued that direct payments might help to break down barriers between social and health care, because the funding can be used within the 'grey area' between these systems (Lewis, 2001). And, of course, the policy has an inherent simplicity, being straightforward and in keeping with the modernisation of public services.

A number of reasons have been suggested for slow take-up (6, 2005; Fernandez et al, 2007). One reason is ignorance of their availability, among both people eligible for support and social care professionals, aligned to resistance among those who have responsibility for implementation. Risk aversion, conservatism and fear of loss of control are among the reasons hypothesised for the unenthusiastic attitudes of some care managers. There are also vested interests within the provider community – users given the freedom to choose what supports they will access may well decide not to purchase 'conventional' services from longstanding providers, throwing local social care markets into disequilibrium. Resource scarcity could be a further barrier, because there is not an inexhaustible supply of personal assistants, or support brokers, or low-level services that people may wish to access and purchase. The associated problem is that monetary levels of direct payment may simply be too small to allow people to access services that they wish to use. There may not be the availability of local community groups or support organisations to provide the reassurance to uncertain service users that the structures are in place for them to take on the (risky) responsibility of managing their own budgets. Clark et al (2003) found that older people in receipt of direct payments reported a number of benefits, but they also experienced difficulties in coping with the legal and administrative demands of handling their own funding. Indeed, there are understandable concerns about the vulnerability of direct payment users to financial exploitation.

There are a number of other implementation supports and challenges. Table 8.2 summarises the main such forces and brakes identified by over a hundred English local authorities that participated in a recent survey of direct payments policy and implementation (Davey et al, 2006). Not surprisingly, support, information, awareness, attitudes and training of staff and availability of personal assistants were all identified by responding local authorities as influential, whether as aiding or hindering factors.

Table 8.2: Factors aiding and hindering implementation of direct payments[a]

	%
Aiding factors[b]	
Effective direct payments support scheme	89
Training and support for frontline staff	86
National legislation, policy and guidance	82
Leadership within the local authority	81
Positive attitude to direct payments among staff	80
Demand from service users and carers for direct payments	78
Accessible information on direct payments for service users and carers	78
Local political support for direct payments	66
Central government performance monitoring	66
Targeted support within the direct payments support service	56
Direct payments developments fund award	56
Availability of people to work as personal assistants	55
Strong local voluntary sector	53
Hindering factors[c]	
Concern about managing direct payments among service users and carers	68
Resistance to direct payments among staff	65
Difficulties with the availability of people to work as personal assistants	63
Lack of demand from service users and carers for direct payments	40
Competing priorities for policy implementation	38
Inadequate training and support for frontline staff	38
Lack of accessible information on direct payments for service users and carers	32
Incongruence of direct payments policy with other local authority duties	31

Notes:

[a] Responses from 109 English local authorities.

[b] Percentages refer to the proportion of local authorities that cited each item as either 'critical', 'important' or 'helpful' in aiding implementation. Only factors described thus by at least half of all responding authorities are listed in the table.

[c] Percentages refer to the proportion of local authorities that cited each item as either 'critical', 'important' or 'unhelpful' in aiding implementation. Only factors described thus by at least half of all responding authorities are listed in the table.

Source: Davey et al (2006)

Not surprisingly in this context, there are very wide variations not just in rate of take-up and level of support by service user group, as we showed earlier, but also between local authorities across the country. We have explored the situational, policy and needs-related factors that appear to be associated with some of these differences in England (Fernandez et al, 2007). Strong connections were found to wider local authority approaches to the support of different client groups, as well as evidence that vested interests play a part. For example, local authorities that retained a larger in-house home care provider role were, other things being equal, supporting fewer older people through direct payments. This is entirely consistent with both risk aversion and protectionism. Similarly, authorities that funded a relatively high proportion of residential to community-based care, even after adjusting for local needs, were supporting fewer people on direct payments. Areas with lower population density had a greater take-up, suggesting that the difficulties of delivering conventional services might encourage authorities and users to take up direct payments. The supply of informal care was influential too, with direct payments take-up being lower in areas with a higher proportion of the local population providing informal care.

Individual budgets

Dissatisfaction with direct payments, particularly the restrictions that current regulations impose on how funding can be used, were one reason for the experimental introduction of individual budgets, which pull in a wider range of funding streams and give the individuals holding them considerably more freedom about how they are to be used.

Individual budgets are currently being piloted in 13 English local authorities. They bring together the resources to which an individual is eligible from, among other funding streams, local authority adult social care budgets, community equipment, housing adaptations, housing-related support through the Supporting People programme, the Independent Living Fund and Access to Work from the Department for Work and Pensions. An individual who is assessed as eligible for one or more of these forms of support is told the total amount available from these sources, and can then decide how to use their allocated resources to meet their personal care or other needs. The process is transparent, hands much more control to the individual budget holder, and clearly seeks to promote real, operational choice. The pilot programme is currently being comprehensively evaluated (Glendinning et al, 2006; Stevens et al, 2006).

The pilot sites are exploring a number of different ways of organising and implementing individual budgets (for older people, adults with physical and sensory impairments, adults with learning disabilities, mental health service users, and disabled young people moving from school to adult services). Within each pilot site, individual budget holders can choose a variety of funding mechanisms, including direct payments, brokerage arrangements or directly commissioned services.

One advantage is that individual budget holders do not necessarily have to employ staff themselves, as there is much more variety in the arrangements that are permissible. In contrast, direct payments do involve the employment of staff, which is one reason why some people might prefer individual budgets. Second, some people are currently ineligible for direct payments but do qualify for individual budgets. Other positive features are likely to include the choice and control afforded individuals to improve their quality of life; relief of some of the burden currently carried by family members; and greater flexibility to respond to changing needs. On the other hand, the individual budget arrangement is clearly a leap in the dark for everyone concerned, and many individuals will have little real idea when they start what an individual budget is and what it will mean for them personally in the longer term. The paperwork required may put off some people, particularly with the conflation of multiple funding streams. As with direct payments, the budget allocated to an individual may not meet their expectations, and may prove insufficient to allow them to employ the staff to meet their needs (if that arrangement is chosen), although this could simply be an example of unrealistic expectations rather than punitive rationing. There is also the issue that individual purchasers of services will not have anything like the market power currently enjoyed by local authority commissioners purchasing often thousands of hours of home care, or dozens of places in care facilities. A further difficulty could be the level of financial risk to which vulnerable people are exposed, including the risk of exploitation.

Conclusion

The adventurous experimentation with user control in social care in England is impressive. Hitherto, rather more cautious approaches to the 'choice agenda' have been attempted in, for example, the NHS. A number of features of social care and how it has been delivered have combined to support this more radical development. Not least among the influential factors has been that purchasers (commissioners) have had the upper hand in most social care markets for the past 15 years, whereas it is the providers who have the greater power in Britain's emerging healthcare markets. Knowing their local markets well, social care commissioners have been able to push through arrangements that empower service users. Similarly, while new governance arrangements in the NHS introduced *quasi*-markets, the arrangements for care home services for older people or for home care are more likely to resemble '*real*' contested markets that in principle make it easier for new commissioning channels to be introduced.

The comparative ease of market entry and exit in social care has undoubtedly been a factor. One reason is because social services are inherently less technically complex than healthcare. Market entry is more difficult in many areas of healthcare because of the high capital costs and the diseconomies of small scale. In turn, there is arguably less need for intervention to promote or protect competition in social care markets, although regulation is still needed to monitor and raise standards. Moreover, because most social care is not technologically complex, it is also more feasible and defensible to see service users taking control of purchasing. Ordinarily, users of social care services also tend to be engaged with services for a few years, gaining a degree of experience and a better understanding of their needs and how to meet them. Short-term care episodes, of a duration typical in the health system, are comparatively rare in social care. And finally, there is the long pedigree of social work commitment to the empowerment of disadvantaged individuals and groups, and the more recent practice of service user involvement in decision making, both of which make it a fairly natural development to introduce consumer-directed processes such as direct payments and individual budgets.

Building blocks for exciting change in social care are being put into place in England. Control is taking over from choice as the watchword of new social care initiatives. Progress on the ground towards genuine, informed choice and control has been slow until recently, but the continued encouragement of direct payments and the experimentation with individual budgets over the next two to three years will soon tell us what is feasible, effective and affordable.

References

6, P. (2005) 'The implementation of direct payments: independent variables and hypotheses from the literature', Working Paper, Nottingham: Nottingham Trent University.

Algozzine, B., Browder, D., Karvonen, M., Test, D. and Wood, W. (2001) 'Effects of interventions to promote self-determination for individuals with disabilities', *Review of Educational Research*, vol 71, no 2, pp 219-77.

Audit Commission (1997) *Take Your Choice: A Commissioning Framework for Community Care*, London: Audit Commission.

Audit Commission (2000) *Learning the Lessons from Joint Reviews of Social Services in Wales, 1999/2000*, Abingdon: Audit Commission.

Audit Commission (2004a) *Older People: Independence and Well-being*, London: Audit Commission.

Audit Commission (2004b) *Older People: A Changing Approach*, London: Audit Commission.

Baines, M., Brayshay, M., Norman, D., Roy, D., Wallis, M. and Walsh, M. (2001) *Making your Days Better: A Training Pack for People with Learning Difficulties*, Brighton: Pavilion.

Barnes, M. (1997) *Care, Communities and Citizens*, London: Longman.

Bland, R. (1999) 'Independence, privacy and risk: two contrasting approaches to residential care for older people', *Ageing and Society*, vol 19, no 5, pp 539-60.

Cabinet Office (2005) *Improving the Life Chances of Disabled People*, London: The Stationery Office.

Cambridge, P. and McCarthy, M. (2001) 'User focus groups and Best Value in services for people with learning disabilities', *Health and Social Care in the Community*, vol 9, no 6, pp 476-89.

Carr, S. (2004) *Has Service User Participation Made a Difference to Social Care Services?*, London: Social Care Institute for Excellence.

Challis, L. and Bartlett, H. (1998) *Old and Ill: Private Nursing Homes for Elderly People*, London: Age Concern Institute of Gerontology, King's College London.

CHI (Commission for Health Improvement) (2004) *State of Healthcare Report*, London: CHI.

Clark, H., Dyer, S. and Hartman, L. (1996) *Going Home, Older People Leaving Hospital*, Bristol: The Policy Press.

Clark, H., Gough, H. and MacFarlane, A. (2003) *It Pays Dividends: Direct Payments and Older People*, Bristol: The Policy Press.

Cope, C. (2003) *Fulfilling Lives: Inspection of Social Services for People with Learning Disabilities*, London: Social Services Inspectorate, Department of Health.

CSCI (Commission for Social Care Inspection) (2006) *The State of Social Care in England 2005-06*, London: CSCI.

Davey, V., Knapp, M., Fernandez, J.L., Knapp, M., Vick, N., Jolly, D., Swift, P., Tobin, R., Kendall, J., Ferrie, J., Pearson, C., Mercer, G. and Priestley, M. (2006) *Direct Payments: A National Survey of Direct Payments Policy and Practice*, London: PSSRU, London School of Economics and Political Science.

Davies, B. and Challis, C. (1986) *Matching Resources to Needs in Community Care*, Aldershot: Ashgate.

DETR (Department of the Environment, Transport and the Regions) (2001) *Quality and Choice for Older People's Housing: A Strategic Framework: Setting out a Vision for Older People's Housing and Housing-Related Support*, London: DETR.

DH (Department of Health) (1989) *Caring for People: Community care in the Next Decade and Beyond*, Cm 849, London: HMSO.

DH (1992) *Direction on Choice*, London: DH.

DH (2001a) *Valuing People: A New Strategy for Learning Disability for the 21st Century*, Cm 5086, London: DH.

DH (2001b) *The Journey to Recovery: The Government's Vision for Mental Health Care*, London: DH.

DH (2003) *Making Change Happen: The Government's Annual Report on Learning Disabilities 2003*, HC514, London: The Stationery Office.

DH (2004) *Valuing People: Moving Forward Together: The Government's Annual Report on Learning Disability 2004*, HC507, London: The Stationery Office.

DH (2005) *Independence, Wellbeing and Choice: Our Vision for the Future of Adult Social Care*, London: DH.

DH (2006) *Our Health, Our Care, Our Say*, Cm 6737, London: The Stationery Office.

DiMaggio, P. and Powell, W. (1983) 'The iron cage revisited: institutional isomorphism and collective rationality in organisational fields', *American Psychological Review*, no 822, pp 147-160.

District Audit (2002) *Rehabilitation Services for Older People*, London: District Audit.

Fernandez, J.L., Kendall, J., Davey, V. and Knapp, M. (2007) 'Direct payments in England: factors linked to variations in local provision', *Journal of Social Policy*, vol 36, no 1, pp 97-121.

Foord, M., Savory, J. and Sodhi, D. (2004) '"Not everything that can be counted counts and not everything that counts can be counted": towards critical exploration of methods of satisfaction methods measurement in sheltered housing', *Health and Social Care in the Community*, vol 12, no 2, pp 126-33.

Glendinning, C., Challis, D., Fernandez, J.L., Jones, K., Knapp, M., Manthorpe, G., Netten, A., Stevens, M. and Wilberforce, M. (2006) 'Evaluating the individual budget pilot projects', *Journal of Care Services Management*, vol 1, pp 123-8.

Glennerster, H. (1995) *British Social Policy since 1945*, Oxford: Blackwell Publishers.

Godlove-Mozley, C., Huxley, P., Sutcliffe, C., Bagley, H., Burns, A., Challis, D. and Cordingley, L. (1999) 'Not knowing where I am doesn't mean I don't know what I like: cognitive impairment and quality of life responses in elderly people', *International Journal of Geriatric Psychiatry*, vol 14, pp 776-83.

Harding, T. (1997) *A Life Worth Living*, London: Help the Aged.

Hardy, B., Young, R. and Wistow, G. (1999) 'Dimensions of choice in the assessment and care management process: the views of older people, carers and care managers', *Health and Social Care in the Community*, vol 7, pp 483-91.

Harris, J. (2000) *Choice and Empowerment for People with a Learning Disability*, Kidderminster: British Institute of Learning Disabilities.

Hatton, C. (2004) 'Choice', in E. Emerson, C. Hatton, T. Thompson and R. Parmenter (eds) *The International Handbook of Applied Research in Intellectual Disabilities*, London: John Wiley.

Healthcare Commission (2005) *Variations in the Experiences of Patients in England*, London: Healthcare Commission.

Holden, C. (2002) 'British government policy and the concentration of ownership in long-term care provision', *Ageing and Society*, vol 22, pp 79-94.

Kern, L., Vorndran, C., Hilt, A., Ringdahl, J., Adelman, B. and Dunlap, G. (1998) 'Choice as an intervention to improve behaviour: a review of the literature', *Journal of Behavioural Education*, vol 8, pp 151-69.

Langan, J. and Lindow, V. (2004) 'Mental health service users and their involvement in risk assessment and management', *Findings*, April, York: Joseph Rowntree Foundation.

LDTF (Learning Disability Task Force) (2004) *Rights, Independence, Choice and Inclusion*, London: Learning Disability Task Force.

Lewis, J. (2001) 'Older people and the health–social care boundary in the UK: half a century of hidden policy conflict', *Social Policy and Administration*, vol 35, pp 343-59.

Lewis, J. and Glennerster, H. (1996) *Implementing the New Community Care*, Buckingham and Philadelphia, PA: Open University Press, p 203.

Myers, F. and MacDonald, C. (1996) 'I was given options not choices: involving older users and carers in assessment and care planning', in R. Bland (ed) *Developing Services for Older People and Their Families*, London: Jessica Kingsley.

NIMHE (National Institute for Mental Health in England) (2003a) *Cases for Change: Policy Context*, London: NIMHE, Department of Health.

NIMHE (2003b) *Cases for Change: User Involvement*, London: NIMHE, Department of Health.

Office of Fair Trading (1998) *Older People as Consumers in Care Homes*, London: Office of Fair Trading.

Office of Public Management (1995) *From Margin to Mainstream: Developing User- and Carer-Centred Community Care*, York: Joseph Rowntree Foundation.

Oldman, C. (2000) *Blurring the Boundaries: A Fresh Look at Housing and Care Provision for Older People*, York: Joseph Rowntree Foundation.

Patmore, C. (2001) 'Improving home care quality: an individual-centred approach to quality and ageing', *Quality in Ageing*, vol 2, pp 15-24.

Quinn, A., Snowling, A. and Denicolo, P. (2003) *Older People's Perspectives: Devising Information, Advice and Advocacy Services*, York: Joseph Rowntree Foundation.

Reed, J., Cook, G., Sullivan, A. and Burridge, C. (2003) 'Making a move: care home residents' experiences of relocation', *Ageing and Society*, vol 23, pp 225-41.

Roberts, K. (2001) 'Across the health–social care divide: elderly people as active users of health and social care', *Health and Social Care in the Community*, vol 9, pp 100-7.

Robbins, D. (2004) *Treated as People: An Overview of Mental Health Services from A Social Care Perspective, 2002-04*, London: Social Services Inspectorate, Department of Health.

Ryan, A. and Scullion, H. (2000) 'Nursing home placement: an exploration of the experiences of family carers', *Journal of Advanced Nursing*, vol 32, pp 1187-95.

Secretaries of State (1989) *Caring for People: Community Care in the Next Decade*, Cmd 849, London: HMSO.

Social Services Inspectorate and Audit Commission (2004) *Old Virtues, New Virtues: An Overview of the Changes in Social Care Services Over the Seven Years of Joint Reviews in England 1996-2003*, London: Audit Commission.

Stalker, K. and Harris, P. (1998) 'The exercise of choice by adults with intellectual disabilities: a literature review', *Journal of Applied Research in Intellectual Disabilities*, vol 11, pp 60-76.

Stevens, M., Browning, D., Challis, D., Glendinning, C., Huxley, P., Knapp, M., Netten, A. and Manthorpe, J. (2006) 'Individual budgets: on the launch pad', *Journal of Intergrated Care*, vol 14, pp 23-31.

Walker, A. (1982) *Community Care: The Family, the State and Social Policy*, Oxford: Blackwell.

Ware, P., Matosevic, T., Hardy, B., Knapp, M., Kendall, J. and Forder, J. (2003) 'Commissioning care services for older people: the view from care managers, users and carers', *Ageing and Society*, vol 23, pp 411-28.

Wigley, V., Fisk, M., Gisby, B. and Preston-Shoot, M. (1998) *Older People in Care Homes: Consumer Perspectives*, Liverpool: John Moores University.

Williams, V. and Robinson, C. (2001) 'More than one wavelength: identifying, understanding and resolving conflicts of interest between people with intellectual disabilities and their family carers', *Journal of Applied Research in Intellectual Disabilities*, vol 14, pp 30-46.

Wright, F. (2003) 'Discrimination against self-funding residents in long-term residential care in England', *Ageing and Society*, vol 23, pp 603-24.

NINE

Neighbourhood renewal, mixed communities and social integration

Anne Power[1]

Introduction

This chapter examines the evidence to support a neighbourhood focus for delivering social policy. Howard Glennerster's work reveals the central importance of understanding how policy works in practice. He recognises neighbourhoods and their management as essential building blocks of applied social policy. His thinking about how we deliver social interventions on the ground has directly influenced efforts at neighbourhood renewal over the past 20 years. Here I present some findings on how neighbourhood renewal in practice addresses the problems of integration and urban recovery. The central questions are:

1. Why does the neighbourhood affect social conditions?
2. What is the evidence of progress in neighbourhood renewal?
3. Are more mixed urban communities likely to emerge through neighbourhood renewal?

Background – current research at CASE on neighbourhood renewal

This chapter draws on several long-run studies about low-income areas and their prospects. The Centre for Analysis of Social Exclusion (CASE) at the London School of Economics and Political Science has been tracking 12 highly disadvantaged areas, covering the different representative types of deprived neighbourhoods in England for the last eight years (Lupton, 2003). The Neighbourhood Renewal Unit (NRU) is trying to help in the recovery of up to 3,000 such areas, and our work feeds directly into the lessons from this process. Our work uncovers what is happening to policy on the ground.

We have conducted a parallel eight-year study, tracking the lives of 200 families in four of the 12 areas, two in east London and two in northern cities. These families are living in some of the most difficult conditions and we are trying to establish just what impact neighbourhood conditions have on families and children and whether interventions help (Mumford and Power, 2003). Whether families survive and flourish in these neighbourhoods is a litmus test of a humane city. The chapter also draws on a study over 25 years of 20 originally highly marginalised estates (Tunstall and Coulter, 2006).

The challenge and importance of neighbourhood renewal

There has been a broad consensus on the need for neighbourhood renewal since 1974. However, policies have gone through many upheavals and it was not until 1998 with the New Labour government that a decisive stamp was put on this issue under the title of *Bringing Britain Together*, a landmark report by the newly formed Social Exclusion Unit (SEU, 1998). The need to bring Britain together continues to ring true for many reasons even if the ways of doing it are still imprecise.

First, England is a heavily built-up country with 60% of the population living in major cities and at least another 25% of the rest in urban settlements of one kind or another. We all live in homes that are already built and in need of constant upgrading. At least 70% of the total stock requires reinvestment for energy efficiency reasons as well as simple 'wear and tear'; yet as we have shown the incentives for doing this are low and the barriers are high.

Second, we still have a very large legacy of council-built estates, about 10,000 in all, even after 25 years of the right to buy. Generally this has not changed the estate structure. Councils still own over two million properties in England and Wales with many more in Scotland and Northern Ireland. Over a million former council homes now belong to housing associations. Maintaining and improving this stock, creating mixed communities within them, and housing the people most in need of low-cost affordable housing, often low-income families with a lone parent, pose many challenges. Our long-run Joseph Rowntree Foundation-backed research on 20 unpopular estates shows how council estates can be renewed through intensive hands-on management, community involvement, the broadening of tenures, major reinvestment and a shake-up in ownership (Tunstall and Coulter, 2006). But it is an ongoing task. By the time work on creating 'decent homes' is completed, we will need to start on the next round of improvements. Reinvestment only rarely funds environmental improvements. Yet that is what residents often care most about. Repaired, predominantly the social rented housing estates risk sliding into decay again unless their overall environment and social conditions are addressed (ODPM, 2005).

Third, poor environmental conditions indicate the general decline of neighbourhoods, generated not just by the disincentives to reinvest in our homes but also by a withdrawal of street supervision, by the decay of street infrastructure and by the poor maintenance of urban parks, open spaces and play areas. In general we have allowed urban areas to become family unfriendly, child unfriendly, traffic prone and run down. These environmental signals generate high fear in communities, as recent police research is showing. The fear may be harder to combat than the real risk of trouble (Metropolitan Police, 2006). Some ground is being won on these issues but we are far from restoring neighbourhood conditions (Power, forthcoming).

Fourth, there is a serious risk to community cohesion through ethnic polarisation as the minority ethnic population has expanded numerically far more rapidly than the white population and the areas of original minority ethnic concentration have greatly expanded, generating fears of accelerating residential separation and certainly school separation (Power and Lupton, 2004). Many white families are leaving London in search of better schools and better social conditions. As a result, large numbers of inner London and particularly east London schools have become overwhelmingly minority ethnic schools (Burgess at al, 2005). This will not help to build cohesion in future generations.

Fifth, all building activity creates environmental impact even when carried out in the most sustainable way, and cumulatively over time, ecological chains can be disrupted through new housing developments that then have serious consequences for the survival of future generations. This carelessness for the future in the face of today's pressing needs will not be possible for long. The loss of biodiversity and species extinction can have extremely serious consequences for the food chain and for the survival of interdependent species, including humans (Wilson, 2002). Government, scientists, builders, insurers and communities are genuinely worried about the threat of floods, erosion, building on green belts, water stress, power supplies, road building, traffic congestion, infrastructure costs, the development impact of overgrowth, the distress of urban decline and the blanket impact of new housing. All of these issues drive the neighbourhood renewal agenda, which for optimists offers a way forward as socially necessary and environmentally a lifeline (Power, 2004).

The progress of neighbourhood renewal – tracking poor areas since 1998

CASE's findings from 12 high poverty areas offer detailed evidence of the impact of policy and the significance of neighbourhood renewal. These areas were among the 5% most deprived areas in the whole country when our studies began, consisting predominantly of social renting. The evidence from the 12 areas included here is based on Caroline Paskell's detailed work since 2003, and Ruth Lupton's research between 1999 and 2003. Table 9.1 shows the basic characteristics of the 12 areas our evidence describes.

Table 9.1: The 12 representative areas

Local authority	Area
Hackney	*West-City*[a] Mostly council-built housing Some pre-war housing Business, leisure and market area Ethnically mixed Inner city
Newham	*East-Docks* Mostly council-built housing Ethnically mixed, industrial sites, near business area Outer city
Knowsley	*Overtown* 1950s to 1960s council-built estates Some private housing Almost exclusively white Beyond city, built as overspill area
Nottingham	*Riverlands* 1960s to 1970s council-built estates Older private houses Sizeable Asian and black population Inner city
Newcastle	*Shipview* Inter-war council-built estates with more affluent older private housing Predominantly white Outer city
Sheffield	*The Valley* Small 1970s council-built estates, mostly pre-war private housing Ethnically mixed Inner city

(continued)

Table 9.1: (continued)

Local authority	Area
Blackburn	*High Moor* Mostly 1970s council-built housing Some private terraces Mostly white, plus Asian population Outer town
Birmingham	*Middle Row* 1950s to 1960s council-built estates Mostly private terraces Ethnically mixed, large Asian minority Inner city
Caerphilly	*Fairfields* 1970s council-built estates Older private housing Almost exclusively white Valley towns
Redcar	*Southside* Three 1900s to 1960s residential areas built to serve industrial plants Mixed tenure Almost exclusively white Beyond the city
Leeds	*Kirkside East* 1930s to 1940s council-built estates Some older private housing at edge Almost exclusively white Outer city
Thanet	*Beachville* Mostly 1900s private houses Small council-built estate Predominantly white, plus refugees Seaside town

Note: [a] These are codenames given in our 12-area study to assure anonymity for the areas.

Source: Paskell and Power (2005)

One of the most significant changes in these areas over the period 1991-2001 was in tenure. Low-income areas are strongly associated with high concentrations of council housing. In 1991, all of the areas bar two were dominated by council estates. Even in those, council renting was above the national average. By 2001, in six of the areas owner-occupation was more significant than social renting, even though social renting was above the national average in 11 of the 12 areas. Table 9.2 shows these changes in tenure.

Table 9.2: Tenure change in the 12 areas over 10 years (%)

Local authorities within which study areas are located	Social renting		Private renting		Owner-occupier	
	1991	2001	1991	2001	1991	2001
Hackney	74	61	8	12	17	24
Newham	68	51	7	13	25	32
Nottingham	52	61	15	11	33	24
Sheffield	52	42	7	11	40	44
Birmingham	55	34	8	14	35	46
Knowsley	57	52	4	5	37	38
Newcastle	61	55	5	5	33	38
Leeds	70	60	1	4	28	33
Redcar	45	41	3	5	51	52
Blackburn	53	36	9	6	38	53
Caerphilly	38	31	8	5	54	62
Thanet	18	17	24	20	58	58

Source: Paskell and Power (2005)

The table shows changes in all main tenures: decline in the proportion of social renting in 11 of the areas, with a steep fall in six of the 12 areas. In contrast, owner-occupation rose in 10 of the 12 areas. In one area owner-occupation increased by more than 10%; in three areas there was little change; one area had lost owner-occupiers due to demolition. The shift to owner-occupation through the right to buy had not led to as big an increase in owner-occupiers as expected due to the expansion of private lettings among new owner-occupiers. Private renting increased in seven of the areas, was stable in one and decreased in four. The change was less dramatic than for social housing; nonetheless it represented a significant shift in favour of private renting, often a direct consequence of the right to buy, with new right-to-buy owners letting out their property so they could move out and pay a second mortgage. There were reports of precarious private tenancies and their negative impact in some places.

Changing landlord structures

Government policy to shift council housing out of direct public ownership and management is now a cross-party agenda and has moved far beyond the right to buy. The transfer of council housing to alternative non-profit landlords and the creation of Arm's Length Management Organisations (ALMOs) where the council wishes to retain the stock but divest itself of direct management of rental homes have been instrumental in shifting the conditions within neighbourhoods in favour of extra investment and stronger management. Table 9.3 shows the changes in landlord structures.

Ten of the 12 areas are choosing one of three government options for change: transfer to a non-profit association, a private finance deal on a long lease to an alternative owner, or an ALMO. Birmingham is the one exception within the 11 English areas. Wales has somewhat different policies on council housing. Ironically, in Birmingham, many community groups have been struggling to achieve alternative forms of ownership (Power and Houghton, 2007). Changes in landlord structure attract investment on a bigger scale because private sector loans become possible and government underwrites some of the higher costs. Thus, within our 12 areas, 10 have changed their ownership structures and management arrangements, leading to higher capital investment and more local management and repair of the stock. This has significantly improved neighbourhood environments and housing.

Table 9.3: Changes in landlord structures in the 12 disadvantaged areas

Area	Transfer	Private finance initiative	ALMO
Hackney	Partial (2002)		
Newham		2000-12	
Knowsley	Complete (2002)		
Nottingham	Partial (2002)		
Newcastle			Planned (2004)
Sheffield			Implemented
Blackburn	Complete (2002)		
Birmingham	Considered and rejected	Considered and rejected	Considered and rejected
Caerphilly			
Redcar	Complete (2002)		
Leeds			Established (2003)
Thanet	Partial (1994)		

Note: Both Private Finance Initiatives and ALMOs retain public ownership; transfer involves changing ownership from public to non-profit, community-based or semi-private forms of ownership. In addition the right to buy for individual tenants has removed over 1.5 millions homes from council ownership.
Source: Paskell and Power (2005)

Local built environments

As a result of the changes in ownership and management, the quality of the local built environment and open spaces has improved. Table 9.4 shows environmental conditions in 1998. No area had a good environment. Four areas had little or no damage to buildings, but eight suffered visible vandalism. No area had well-maintained open spaces or communal environments.

All twelve areas had taken action on neighbourhood environments by 2004, either introducing wardens in seven cases or implementing neighbourhood management in five other cases, with some areas doing both. Under the impact of these measures, overall environmental problems have declined with visible environmental problems reduced by one third from the time of our first visits in 1998 (Paskell and Power, 2005). Many major regeneration programmes have also been in place on a virtually ongoing basis over a long timescale (Lupton, 2003).

Table 9.4: Quality of local environment, open spaces and buildings, based on visits in 1998

| Area | Environmental quality | |
	Natural	Built
Hackney	Some litter	Little vandalism or graffiti
Newham	Low-grade	Some vandalism and graffiti
Knowsley	Bland but clear	Some vandalism and graffiti
Nottingham	Little litter or rubbish	Much vandalism and graffiti
Newcastle	Gardens problematic, common areas clear	No vandalism or graffiti
Sheffield	Litter, rubbish, overgrown gardens	Poor upkeep and minor vandalism
Blackburn	Bland but no litter or rubbish	No vandalism or graffiti
Birmingham	Rats and rubbish, greenery removed	Poor maintenance, minor vandalism
Caerphilly	Rubbish, litter, bland open areas, vandalised	Extensive vandalism of empty homes
Redcar	Upgraded parks but open areas damaged	Severe vandalism, some arson
Leeds	Open areas damaged by joyriding and litter	Little vandalism or graffiti
Thanet	Litter, vandalism of open areas and plants	Extensive vandalism and graffiti

Source: Paskell and Power (2005) based on Ruth Lupton's visits.

These area improvements have instigated changes in demand. Eight of the 12 areas have rising demand, two in London and six elsewhere. Three areas have settled demand, sufficient to keep the stock occupied. In part, demand has risen as a result of demolition of the worst housing over the years (but three of the areas have precarious demand even though they are no longer in such great difficulty as before). Only one area has falling demand. The areas with weak demand are located on the very edge of declining urban areas, and they have yet to find a new economic rationale, given that they are within generally declining regions.

On the basis of research visits and the collection of evidence from the Census and other sources, we can place the 12 areas in one of the three categories of recovering, holding their own or declining. A few places have seemingly intractable problems of decline and marginality because they were built as peripheral council housing areas at a point where regional populations were declining, where local industry was disappearing and where jobs were being lost on a huge scale. This category applies to three areas: the outer Merseyside area; the outer Humberside area; and the former coalmining area in Wales.

Other areas had previously been classed as having intractable problems such as Newcastle, Sheffield and Blackburn. Five areas of this type have begun to show signs of recovery and in some cases they have recovered strongly. On the whole, they were located within the city but outside the inner core. Four inner city areas had experienced long periods of decline and were struggling with entrenched social problems, but on the whole they proved more responsive to change and were attracting some new investment alongside some new residents. None of the twelve areas was static, and the overall direction of change in a majority of areas was positive, even though they were far from stable or integrated into the wider city.

Based on recognisable signs of recovery measured by housing demand, house prices, employment and population change, the 12 areas were distributed as follows:

- four areas were *recovering*, all within inner cities;
- five were *holding their own*, showing some signs of recovery, or avoiding further decline, but not yet with a secure future. These five were within a main city although on the whole they were further out than the recovering areas.
- three areas were still *declining* or were stabilised at a low level. Their peripheral location, the oversupply of housing and the lack of jobs within the areas were major issues. This continuing problem was

accelerated by the overbuilding of cheap subsidised housing for owner-occupation, both within and near areas.

Overall, our evidence from the 12 areas shows that three factors help disadvantaged areas recover:

- low-level, ongoing intensive management and reinvestment;
- the diversification of ownership and management structures; and
- the care and updating of local environments.

In addition, significant investment in the physical stock can help raise its popularity and remedy intrinsic defects.

But strong interventions in precarious neighbourhoods involving large-scale demolition because of low demand, followed by large-scale building in spite of low demand, exacerbates the problem of depopulating vulnerable areas. Trying to remarket low-demand areas while fundamental structural problems of unemployment and the general oversupply of housing remain may not work. In contrast, inner-city declining areas with old street properties and mixed uses in more traditional urban settings recover more easily as a result of proximity to the centre, density of uses, more mixed job markets and some older potentially more attractive housing. These findings challenge the conventional wisdom of much current regeneration thinking, which is often strongly oriented towards high-cost, high-impact interventions rather than the restoration and upgrading of neighbourhood conditions.

Neighbourhood renewal is happening in many different forms

Our tracking of 12 deprived areas has given us an understanding of area transitions based on three main factors: location, management, and mixed styles and uses within clear street patterns. Our research in other low-income urban areas reveals some striking findings about how policy and practice are shifting in favour of neighbourhood renewal, mixed communities and social integration.

- *The 20 difficult council estates* that we have tracked since 1980 are now in a very different position from when we started. All of them have diversified their ownership and management structures although the vast majority are still predominantly council owned or socially rented. All estates now foster the right to buy and owner-occupation has risen although it is still under 20% on average. Selective demolition has made way for some new build housing association property and some private homes. The overall condition of estates has improved through diversification, investment and close attention to detailed management. However, as intensive management becomes more diluted because the estates have become more 'normal', it is unclear whether the improvements will continue. The process of reintegration, mixing and diversification is a long-term project and needs long-term management (Tunstall and Coulter, 2006).

- *The programmes to tackle low demand*, particularly in the North, which were first started in 1997 have begun to show real progress but not in the way that government expected or planned. To any objective observer market conditions in the North are radically different from eight years ago when our study, the *Slow Death of Great Cities* was published (Mumford and Power, 1999). House prices are now up to 10 times higher in the market renewal areas compared with then. Even steeper price rises have happened in some areas. Ordinary people who shunned such areas a few years ago are buying into extremely run-down, older terraced housing areas because they want to live there and because they provide affordable and potentially attractive houses. Community groups defend these areas, precisely because they value the homes and communities near to city centres even though they are unmistakeably run down. They like the heritage atmosphere and the proximity. Many traditional residents want to stay for all these reasons (Beck, 2005). *Boom or Abandonment*, our second study of these areas, reported very different conditions five years ago from conditions today (Mumford and Power, 2002). Neighbourhood management, reinvestment and infill building have turned East Manchester into an early market recovery area. Many northern and Midlands inner-city areas show similar signs of a potential for recovery.

- *The arguments in favour of ongoing large-scale clearance* on the grounds of obsolescence are often no longer borne out by evidence from the ground, and certainly the cost to the government of tackling areas of rapidly rising value as opposed to areas of low and decreasing value is undermining the original plans for large-scale clearance. As a result, demolition programmes are being seriously scaled back. The government has virtually dropped area demolition as a tool even if it is still tacitly allowing some agreed plans to proceed. Housing market renewal could become a pro-city, pro-existing neighbourhoods policy over the coming period if incentives are shifted in this direction (Power, 2005).

- *Our study of London in the Thames Gateway* (2003-04) highlighted the growth pressures on the environment and the urgency of regeneration and neighbourhood renewal in the near East End (Power et al, 2004). Our findings highlighted the huge infrastructure cost of new developments beyond the city and the underused capacity for infill development and upgrading within the city. The latter approach re-values and upgrades existing infrastructure, helps renew run-down communities and creates sufficient density of people to support good local facilities. Interestingly, the Olympic bid helps this alternative approach by drawing investment into the inner, built-up areas (Davidson and Power, 2007).

- *One size doesn't fit all*, our report on the future of council housing in Birmingham (Independent Commission on Future of Social Housing in Birmingham, 2003, 2006), proposed neighbourhood renewal, community-based housing organisations and mixed communities. Twenty-five community groups in Birmingham applied to exercise their right to manage in an attempt to gain control, while the city council determinedly held on to central control. The centralised approach to neighbourhood renewal risks penalising Birmingham's 70,000 tenants and damaging the renewal prospects of many inner-city neighbourhoods. It creates financial pressures on the city, highlights the weak management capacity of the city's housing service and the ominous distance between residents and the powers that be. Birmingham's resistance to community-based housing options for neighbourhood renewal has created a financial gap to maintain and regenerate estates, a gap in management to run them properly and a gap in community involvement by rejecting the idea of more diverse and mixed solutions to the problematic legacy of council housing (Power and Houghton, 2007). In the city, a number of independent 'beacon' neighbourhood projects such as Whitten Lodge, Bloomsbury, Castle Vale and Optima show what could be achieved through community-based approaches.

- *The importance of cities* is now widely recognised, partly under the impact of environmental constraints on new building, partly under the impact of the changing shape of the economy, partly under the beneficial impact of neighbourhood renewal and 'urban renaissance' policies. This changing agenda in favour of cities gradually helps neighbourhood renewal (Urban Task Force, 2005; ODPM, 2006).

- *The example of London* illustrates this process. Thirty years ago London was losing population faster than any other city in the country; it was more blighted by slum clearance programmes than any other city in the country; it was experiencing disorder and ethnic polarisation

(Jacobs, 1970). Because of the land constraints, the strict green belt, the sheer size of the city, and the return of dynamism to London's city centre and its economy, these problems have faded even if they have not gone away completely and new areas are taking their place. Within inner London, the renewal of older terraced property, the mixing of different ethnic communities and different tenures within the inner city are now considered assets rather than liabilities, as they still were 35 years ago, before the slum clearance era was over.

- *Low-level gentrification* may have a role to play. London now suffers from the opposite problem of gentrification and the overvaluation of property. By halting large-scale demolition in the early 1970s and giving incentives for renovating blighted, half-empty terraced housing, from the late 1960s to early 1980s, inner London recovered. London's experience will simply not transfer to other major cities in the country as it is the capital, but it is hard to escape the lessons that London offers. Parallel if not identical processes are now under way in other cities, and greater incentives for the renovation of decayed terraces within neighbourhood renewal programmes could reduce the unequal conditions between North and South. These could encourage 'low-level gentrification' or the gradual renewal of areas that have lost too much work through the investments of people in work.

Lessons from low-income areas

There are some key lessons from our detailed ground-level work that we can use to point the way forward. Based on findings from the 12 areas and the other studies referred to above, six issues that help an area to succeed can be identified:

- *Location*: Inner and central locations are more successful and recover faster than outer areas because quick transport links make a big difference to area recovery. On the whole, inner areas tend to be denser, older and more mixed because of proximity to the centre and step-by-step upgrading is often the only affordable and lasting approach.
- *Special regeneration programmes*: City Challenge, the Single Regeneration Budget, New Deal for Communities and other programmes have made a visible difference in most areas. It is possible to argue that the money could have been better spent, but it is equally possible to argue that it has had the same impact in most cases in improving the basic conditions of the areas. Generally they would have been

far worse without the aid of targeted programmes. However, there is some evidence from our research that a more incremental, less 'big bang' approach works faster and provides better value for money.

- *Selective demolition*: Using a 'scalpel', rather than a bulldozer, can make a very big difference in how quickly areas recover; small-scale, selective and carefully targeted demolition often helps. The selective removal of eyesores, of completely derelict buildings and of particular and specific properties that damage overall viability, can make a street viable and attractive again. This contrasts sharply with the large-scale clearances advocated under 'housing market renewal', which do not seem justified on the basis of changing demand, cost and environmental impact.

- *Intensive locally based management*: Incremental changes in management leading to the intensification of local services were found to have a generally positive impact on neighbourhood conditions. This approach won strong support from residents and was popular with locally based staff, since it made their jobs more rewarding and conditions more controllable.

- *Controlling neighbourhood conditions*: More localised, community-oriented policing and back-up police community support officers were also generally helpful. Recreating local supervision of local parks, open spaces and streets through the deployment of wardens and more intensive 'street services' made people and particularly families more confident about using the spaces.

- *Long time lags in neighbourhood renewal*: There are no easy ways of resolving all the problems that affect low-income areas. This complexity, the need for long-term sustained effort to achieve change and the requirement of multiple interventions creates concern over the value of regeneration programmes that come and go, while poor neighbourhood conditions persist. However, serious disturbances in France in 2005, following the virtual abandonment of area-targeted programmes there in the 1990s, suggests that a closer focus on disadvantaged areas is necessary. The government rationale for turning away from area-based programmes is that they create stigma and reduce incentives to integrate. However, the opposite may be true based on the experiences of neighbourhood renewal in this country. The focus of effort and measures is a prerequisite for normalisation, as the latest study of 20 estates suggests (Tunstall and Coulter, 2006). Areas can decline into extremely poor condition unless a targeted area approach keeps conditions manageable and residents involved in the attempts at improvement.

How can we apply these lessons?

England is by any measure a densely populated country, running level with the Netherlands, at the top of the European League. However, our urban population is significantly spread out in extensive suburbs and our cities have much underused capacity. Urban neighbourhoods need more households to make up for massive population losses since the 1950s, and a continuing shrinkage of average household size. They need schools, shops, cafes, restaurants and buses, which can only be supported at higher densities. Workplaces and services will only multiply if there is a critical mass of people within easy reach of neighbourhood centres. Urban recovery through more careful management conditions happens because people are attracted by old buildings; new uses are invented and services become viable again – such as buses in London.

The UK has a long track record of neighbourhood renewal and has demonstrated that it works. Prioritising the environmental deficits of run-down neighbourhoods is the most direct way to make them more attractive, thereby combating sprawl. We are running short of land, materials, water and energy; buildings are the single biggest user of energy and contributor to carbon and other waste in modern economies. Severe environmental limits on a global and European scale leave us with little choice but to recycle urban poor neighbourhoods. Therefore, the renewal of existing neighbourhoods is the most direct and affordable way of creating sustainable communities.

The role of mixed communities in neighbourhood renewal

We have argued that neighbourhood renewal is of pivotal importance both for the recovery of cities and for the sustainability of our small crowded country. It is also the obvious way to meet our expanding housing demand while maintaining social cohesion in the face of acute shortages, high prices and growing opposition to physical sprawl. By renewing existing neighbourhoods, we can create more mixed communities within them without building anew (Power, 2006).

Mixed communities are an unclear and changeable idea that so far defies an agreed definition. It helps to start with what they are not. A socially isolated housing area with poor environmental and social conditions is the main type of neighbourhood that mixed communities are designed to counter. The most marginal and precarious of our 12 areas reflect this reality. A mixed community implies mixed uses and services, rather than a mono-functional housing estate; but it also implies mixed tenure to include owner-occupation, private renting, housing associations and sometimes council housing. In order to ensure a variety of housing types and income groups a mixed tenure housing area will include people in work, and will attract people from diverse social backgrounds, incomes and ages. It will offer homes for different types of households, families, childless couples, single people, older people and young people. It is important for mixed-income communities to offer a mixture of styles, sizes of homes, and types of building with diverse spaces and functions within them. It will not just comprise streets and houses with private gardens; but also courtyards, shared gardens, patios and balconies within blocks of flats; parks, play areas, clusters of shops and cafes, places where people can meet and enjoy shared activity (Power et al, 2004).

One aspect of mixed communities that is not generally discussed is interethnic mixing. Over time and particularly in London and other cities with high proportions of minority ethnic communities, this will become increasingly important (Power and Lupton, 2004). But it has to be encouraged and supported to succeed. Neighbourhood management has a big role to play here too, by helping people to resolve problems locally and improve conditions.

The idea of mixed communities implies better, more stable, more attractive places with a working population, preventing the social isolation and poverty of ghettos. By definition a mixed community is going to be in better condition than the worst areas. It will not be at the bottom of the hierarchy of neighbourhoods, precisely because it attracts a wider range of people of different incomes and backgrounds. If, however, 'mixed communities' are taken to mean new-build schemes that draw away more ambitious households, then poorer families tend to get left behind and feel stranded. If better-off people in work can be attracted to neighbourhoods that are improving, those who already live there will benefit from the greater mixture. This form of 'low-level gentrification' is closely linked to neighbourhood renewal and generally helps it to take root. Therefore integrating new homes within existing communities and upgrading existing homes and neighbourhood conditions should go hand in hand within neighbourhoods in need of renewal.

The components of mixed communities

The core idea of a viable mixed community is that people in work, who like the area, will support local services, creating neighbourhood magnets that people recognise and value. Points of attraction draw people in and hold people together. A local bus stop, local shops, a well cared-for park, small supervised local play areas, a doctor's surgery are all the kind of public places that people need if they are to feel at home in their area and not alone. The social contact that results from local services provides the life-blood of communities (Rogers and Power, 2000).

The second idea relates to density of people. Isolation in lonely households is becoming a bigger problem as we splinter into smaller and smaller social units, particularly for young adults and older people. The need for proximity and interconnectedness relates to the number of people needed within a short geographical space to support local services – the magnets we just described. Mixed neighbourhoods must have enough people to keep the neighbourhood magnets working. The shrinking household size from four to just over two people since the Second World War means that a viable community requires nearly twice the number of households to maintain sufficient population; it is not possible to keep local shops or buses going with under 120 people per hectare or 50 homes. This implies a minimum density of 50 homes per hectare, which is at the moment 40% above typical urban densities (Power and Houghton, 2007). We have many successful models of this density of building: a Cornish traditional village; Victorian semi-detached houses in older inner-urban suburbs. Attractive, new model urban villages like Crown Street in Glasgow and Greenwich Millennium Village are built above this density. Their appeal lies in the harmony of their design, their sense of space and community, not crowded, but closely laid out, creating walkable, appealing neighbourhoods (Power, 2004).

The third issue is mixing incomes. It is easier to think of mixed communities as overlapping bands of income and types of activity rather than supposing that mixed communities can combine the most extreme luxury with concentrations of deep deprivation in subsidised social housing. There are some recent examples of 'mixed' developments providing affordable housing within a mixed tenure development, where the social housing is of vastly inferior quality and is built on the edge of the development, cut off from the main centre of gravity, standing out as a distinctive type of building. Developers try to meet their planning obligations by building very high-density, luxury flats separated from the 'social' part of their 'mixed' community. In the long run this internal 'segregation' within mixed communities seems unlikely to work and does not create a positive social environment (Silverman, 2006).

Any mixed development that actively seeks to integrate social housing within a largely private development must provide support across ethnic as well as income and age divides. Nurseries, primary schools and sports and health facilities can play a vital role in this mixing if the social provision can match the expectations of better-off households without putting up barriers for lower-income groups. There are examples such as the Greenwich Millennium Village, where the social housing is of as high quality as the rest the development and is far more integrated through closely recognised community and neighbourhood management and shared facilities such as the health centre and school (Silverman et al, 2006; Tunstall and Fenton, 2006).

Neighbourhood renewal is the logical foundation stone of mixed-income communities. In typical neighbourhood renewal areas, the aim is to attract and hold onto the more ambitious, better-qualified, in-work, younger households who are close to the existing community but want better conditions. Alternatively there are incomers who positively choose mixed urban neighbourhoods and want to contribute to neighbourhood renewal. Many of the groups fighting demolition plans in the North include this type of social mixture. Imaginative conversions like Chimney Pot Park in Salford attract 'low-level gentrifiers', people in work but socially committed to living in a low-income but mixed area (Power and Houghton, 2007).

Housing barriers to mixed communities

If we need to provide more homes, as plainly we do in many parts of the country, using available space within existing communities in order to integrate them into the existing urban fabric strengthens and upgrades existing services and conditions. Urban capacity studies are now revealing the huge flow of small infill sites scattered all over our inner cities, in need of attractive reuse to strengthen our decayed urban structures and provide much needed affordable housing (London Housing Research, 2005). These small, uncounted sites occur everywhere, including London. But there are many barriers to the development of *mixed communities* within the housing structures that we have. Below we discuss some of the most important that our work has identified.

High-demand areas create an inevitable affordability problem for poor people. They cannot gain access to market housing except in crowded, low-quality conditions. Therefore social housing has to be carefully targeted to the people in greatest need. This inevitably generates both polarisation by income and resentment from those who cannot get in. It can also create greater ethnic separation, if access to social housing is purely based on extreme need and homelessness (Dench et al, 2006). A needs-only-based system of allocation tends to prioritise relative newcomers over longer-standing residents since newcomers always have the greatest difficulty in getting a foot on the housing ladder, leading to the development of some estates housing predominantly minority ethnic groups.

In low-demand areas where there is a higher risk of investment being wasted, separation by income results from declining conditions. There the problem of oversupply drives people from seriously declining areas, pushing up demand for more and better-quality housing outside the existing built-up area. Neighbourhood decline and shortages of good-quality housing thus generate sprawl building and polarisation directly. This was one of the main findings of our work for the *Slow Death of Great Cities?* (Mumford and Power, 1999).

Unattractive neighbourhoods give a negative signal through their environmental conditions, persuading owners that it is better to leave than to reinvest in the area. They also deter incomers. Unattractive, run-down neighbourhoods and low-demand housing fuel each other in a constant spiral. Thus, run-down council estates are almost as common in some parts of London as they are in low-pressure northern cities (SEU, 1999; Bramley, 2000).

All existing homes run down year by year, bit by bit, the inevitable consequences of 'wear and tear'. The same applies to neighbourhoods. Over time there is a serious need to reinvest in existing homes and existing neighbourhoods. Yet we spend very little on major improvement of our existing stock, even though when we do, we find that it is considerably cheaper than new build. For low-income owner-occupiers there is a serious shortage of funds for reinvestment, particularly if they are older. Therefore the inevitable 'wear and tear' of buildings feeds into the problem of declining neighbourhoods, fuelling low demand (Power, 2006). This applies even in some poorer areas in the East End of London. Unless we adopt a continuous process of neighbourhood renewal, backed by reinvestment incentives in the existing stock, existing communities will continue to polarise and new 'mixed' communities will draw out the more fortunate and more ambitious.

The Value Added Tax (VAT) on virtually all repairs and improvements creates a major barrier to reinvestment in existing homes, particularly among lower-income households. This tax of 17.5% on work to existing homes contrasts sharply with the indirect subsidy to new build that is not only VAT-exempt but also receives new infrastructure effectively free of charge, through the Treasury. Thus a polarised choice emerges between existing run-down inner-city communities, where there is a high tax on repair, and new-build private estates on the edge of existing developments, which are tax-free. The Treasury does not know how to reduce the perverse incentives that VAT on repair creates, while retaining the large revenues it generates. Reducing VAT to 5% in neighbourhood renewal areas would be in line with the European Commission's minimum threshold rate and is allowed. It could be directly tied into energy efficiency and neighbourhood upgrading together, both targets set by government. A reduced tax would immediately signal an opportunity for renovation and would over time help to generate inward investment in homes.

Owning is seen as a much higher status tenure than renting in the UK (Barker, 2004). One way to upgrade neighbourhoods and create more mixed communities is to support affordable owner-occupation. Yet all of us some time in our lives need to rent. If there were an even playing field between owning and renting, with equal funding incentives and comparable conditions for comparable outlay, there would be a greater acceptance of the role of private renting in housing people of all incomes at different stages of their lives. Students take renting for granted and accept sharing and lower quality for a few years on grounds of cost, life style and independence. Encouraging more 'ad-hoc' renting is one way of ensuring more and cheaper housing as well as facilitating access to housing for newly forming households, new arrivals and so on. Private renting blends in with owner-occupation as long as landlords accept responsibility for management. The German housing market and subsidy system both favour renting, particularly private renting. As a result, a large majority of German households rent, with 40% of all households renting from private landlords. We cannot easily shift to a German housing system, but we can do a lot more to encourage well-managed, rented housing within better-managed households (Housing Corporation, 2006). A long-term management framework for mixed-tenure, mixed-income developments, comparable to other European countries, would help secure the goal of more mixed communities.

The idea of 'estates' is possibly the biggest barrier in turning 20th-century housing into more attractive, more mixed communities. Estates have been built as monolithic dormitory areas for particular types of people: private estates are often for families in work who can buy their homes; council and social housing estates are generally for lower-income, increasingly out of work, often marginal households, newcomers, lone parents, people on benefits. Estates are difficult structures within which to create mixed communities because they are usually built separately, under distinct tenure patterns and separate from ordinary streets. The larger the estate, the more so. Yet many new developments are being built in estates, whether private or social, because we have been extremely slow to adapt our design and building methods to a more mixed, more integrated approach. Estates are easy and cheap for developers since they are big, empty sites. Calling them 'mixed communities' will not overcome this problem. A more fine-grained, small-scale, 'infill' approach to new building, using street patterns that more readily blend uses, activities and people, would support mixed communities and would revalue and renew existing communities. Research supports this street-level approach on social interactions (Whyte, 1980; Gehl, 2003; Urban Task Force, 2005).

Some areas become so troubled that they seem almost unmanageable. Disorder creates an almost insuperable barrier to mixed communities. The most deprived council estates and the most run-down private housing areas experience such serious crime, drug problems, intense poverty and high levels of antisocial behaviour that it becomes hard to see how the physical place can survive the social disorder. These problems are a big driver of people leaving cities and leaving council housing, leading to the intense polarisation we see in the poorest areas. In the face of such extremes, neighbourhood renewal and new development within existing communities seem implausible approaches. But tight management, proper enforcement and social support can change this pattern (Power, forthcoming).

However, given that many poorer urban neighbourhoods have become too 'thinned out' to maintain social control, densifying them became a vital tool in re-establishing a sense of order; they have ample scope to absorb more homes. Focusing area improvements, renovation, local management and infill development within existing areas, with multiple small efforts over many years, can make the problem partly self-correcting (Paskell and Power, 2005). Our tracking of 12 highly disadvantaged areas shows that nine are improving or at least holding their own through combinations of these methods. As increasing land pressures and rapid growth in smaller households have reduced the opportunities for green field building, so existing areas have become more useful to meet supply problems. At the same time many of the new, smaller households do not want to move out into suburbs, thereby creating demand for higher-density, inner-city living (Nathan and Unwin, 2006).

Conclusion

There are signs, highlighted in the government's *State of the Cities* report (ODPM, 2006), that renewal is taking root more widely: New East Manchester; central Liverpool; the Jewellery Quarter and eastern regeneration area of Birmingham; the Ouseburn and Grainger Town in Newcastle; the Clydeside revival in Glasgow are all examples. This fact of renewal drives the rebirth of mixed communities within cities. Producing an affordable housing supply, renovating existing homes, and holding onto families within the city's limits are the biggest challenges of neighbourhood renewal and sustainable urban development, but bit by bit this is happening.

Jane Jacobs argued in *The Economy of Cities* (1970) that it is the people at the base of the urban hierarchy, struggling with the most live and acute problems, who have the strongest motivation to find solutions that work (PEP, 1987; Glennerster and Turner, 1991). Neighbourhood renewal is one such solution, invented by pioneering problem solvers in some of the most difficult housing areas in the early 1980s when the threat of social breakdown drove the creation of community-based solutions. This approach can help residents in today's more pressured urban areas to enjoy more peaceful, more orderly, more productive and more harmonious conditions. Given the social and environmental pressures on both cities and countryside, renewing the existing neighbourhoods that we use and damage so readily makes more sense than undermining both community cohesion and our historic urban infrastructure by repeating the mistakes of the past. The major lessons of neighbourhood renewal are to preserve, upgrade, manage and repopulate our priceless urban assets.

Notes

[1] I am deeply grateful to Caroline Paskell and Ruth Lupton for their work on the 12 areas, and to Jane Dickson, Laura Lane and Naomi Achie-Anku at the Centre for Analysis of Social Exclusion for help in producing the final document. I am grateful to the Economic and Social Research Council and the Joseph Rowntree Foundation for their support for many parts of this work. I would also like to acknowledge the support and advice of David Utting, Brian Robson and Peter Stowe in producing this chapter.

References

Barker, K. (2004) *Review of Housing Supply, Final Report Recommendations*, London: HM Treasury.
Beck, H. (2005) *Demolition Workshop Report*, London: LSE Housing.
Bramley, G. (2000) *Low Demand Housing and Unpopular Neighbourhoods*, London: Department of the Environment, Transport and the Regions.

Burgess, S., Wilson, D. and Lupton, R. (2005) *Parallel Lives? Ethnic Segregation in Schools and Neighbourhoods*, CASEpaper 101, London: LSE.

Davidson, R. and Power, A. (2007) *Families' and Children's Experience of Sport and Informal Activity in Olympic Areas of the East End*, Report to Sport England on the Olympics, CASEreport 35, London: LSE.

Dench, G., Gavron, K. and Young, M. (2006) *The New East End: Kinship, Race and Conflict*, London: Profile Books.

Gehl, J. (2003) *Life between Buildings*, Copenhagen: Danish Architectural Press.

Glennerster, H. and Turner, T. (1991) *PEP Evaluation*, London: Department of the Environment.

Housing Corporation, The (2006) *Neighbourhood and Communities Strategy*, London: The Housing Corporation.

Independent Commission on the Future of Council Housing in Birmingham (2003) *One Size Doesn't Fit All*, London/Birmingham: LSE/Birmingham City Council.

Independent Commission on the Future of Council Housing in Birmingham (2006) *One Size Still Doesn't Fit All*, London: LSE Housing.

Jacobs, J. (1970) *The Economy of Cities*, New York, NY: Random House.

London Housing Research (2005) *London Capacity Studies*, London: London Development Research.

Lupton, R. (2003) *Poverty Street: Causes and Consequences of Neighbourhood Decline*, Bristol: The Policy Press.

Metropolitan Police (2006) *Public Area-Based Consultations*, London: Metropolitan Police.

Mumford, K. and Power, A. (1999) *Slow Death of Great Cities? Urban Abandonment or Urban Renaissance*, York: Joseph Rowntree Foundation.

Mumford, K. and Power, A. (2002) *Boom or Abandonment: Resolving Housing Conflicts in Cities*, Coventry: Chartered Institute of Housing.

Mumford, K. and Power, A. (2003) *East Enders: Family and Community in East London*, Bristol: The Policy Press.

Nathan, M. and Unwin, C. (2006) *City People: City Centre Living in the UK*, London: Centre for Cities, Institute for Public Policy Research.

ODPM (Office of Deputy Prime Minister) (2005) *English House Condition Survey*, London: ODPM.

ODPM (2006) *State of the Cities Report*, London: ODPM.

Paskell, C. and Power, A. (2005) *The Future's Changed – Local Impacts of Housing, Environment and Regeneration Policy since 1997*, CASEreport 29, London: LSE.

PEP (Priority Estates Project) (1987) *PEP Guide to Local Housing Management*, vols 1-3, London: Department of the Environment.

Power, A. (2004) *Sustainable Communities and Sustainable Development: A Review of the Sustainable Communities Plan*, CASEreport 23, London: CASE/Sustainable Development Commission.

Power, A. (2005) *Sustainable Communities: Rescuing Abandoned Neighbourhoods and Restoring our Urban Environments*, Keele University Public Sector Lecture Series, 10 January, Keele: University of Keele.

Power, A. (2006) *Cities on the Edge*, United Nations Environment Programme World Conservation Monitoring Centre, 'Environment on the Edge 2005-06' lecture series, Cambridge: New Hall.

Power, A. (forthcoming) *City Survivors*, Bristol: The Policy Press.

Power, A. and Houghton, J. (2007) *Jigsaw Cities: Big Places, Small Spaces*, Bristol: The Policy Press.

Power, A. and Lupton, R. (2004) *Minority Ethnic Groups in Britain*, CASE-Brookings Census Briefs, no 2, London: LSE.

Power, A., Richardson, L., Seshimo, K. and Firth, K. with others (2004) *London Thames Gateway: A Framework for Housing in the London Thames Gateway*, vol 2, London: LSE Housing.

Rogers, R. and Power, A. (2000) *Cities for a Small Country*, London: Faber and Faber.

SEU (Social Exclusion Unit) (1998) *Bringing Britain Together*, London, Cabinet Office.

SEU (1999) Report of Policy Action Team 7: *Unpopular Housing*, London: Cabinet Office.

Silverman, E., Lupton, R. and Fenton, A. (2006) *A Good Place for Children? Attracting and Retaining Families in Inner Urban Mixed Income Communities*, London/York: Chartered Institute of Housing in association with the Joseph Rowntree Foundation.

Tunstall, R. and Coulter, A. (2006) *Turning the Tide*, York: Joseph Rowntree Foundation.

Tunstall, R. and Fenton, A. (2006) *In the Mix: A Review of Mixed Income, Mixed Tenure and Mixed Communities: What do we Know?*, London: The Housing Corporation/Joseph Rowntree Foundation and English Partnerships.

Urban Task Force (2005) *Towards a Stronger Urban Renaissance*, London: ODPM.

Whyte, W.H. (1980) *The Social Life of Small Urban Spaces*, Washington, DC: Conservation Foundation.

Wilson, E.O. (2002) *The Future of Life*, London: Knopf.

Part Three

Redistribution: between households;
over time; between areas

TEN

The restructuring of redistribution

David Piachaud

Introduction

By far the largest component of social policy in Britain measured in terms of government expenditure is the social security system. Despite many changes, this system was for over half a century recognisably the same as that proposed by Beveridge (1942). Over the past decade, however, that system has been radically restructured. Goals have been changed: the guiding mantra has become 'work for those who can, security for those who cannot' (DSS, 1998). The period since 1997 is also one in which tackling poverty has been given prominence. In 1999, the Prime Minister set out the goal of abolishing child poverty in a generation (Blair, 1999) and the reduction of pensioner poverty has also been a goal. 'Redistribution' has not, however, been a prominent New Labour term. No use of the word will be found in the Labour Party's General Election manifestos of 1997, 2001 or 2005. Yet a whole lot of redistribution has been going on, often in innovative ways.

The purpose of this chapter is to review and assess the changes that have occurred. The emphasis here is on both the structure of redistribution and its extent. The purpose is not to examine overall changes in inequality and poverty but rather to examine how the impact of government through benefits and taxes on the distribution of net money incomes has changed since 1997. The question of how these changes have affected behaviour will be touched on but is not the central focus.

What effect have the changes had on the extent of redistribution? That is the question that this chapter aims to answer.

Major changes in the structure and administration of redistribution, 1997-2006

The British social security system has shown a remarkable resilience, even though the department responsible for it has changed its name four times since 1948, most recently in 2001 to the Department for Work and Pensions. Although it had up to 1997 evolved in important ways, large parts still continued essentially unchanged. Since 1997 there have been the most fundamental administrative changes. These are summarised in Figure 10.1.

Most strikingly, large components of social security have been shifted into the tax system either taking the form of 'tax credits' or being administered by HM Revenue and Customs. The Conservative Chancellor of the Exchequer Nigel Lawson (1992) set out his view that the functions of taxing and spending should be kept entirely separate. Labour's Chancellor Gordon Brown has gone a long way in the opposite direction, bringing taxing and spending together. The five key principles that have guided tax-benefit integration were set out in 2000 as follows (HM Treasury, 2005, para 319):

1. to promote incentives to work, by reducing the tax burden on the low-paid and the number of low-income households on high marginal withdrawal rates;

Figure 10.1: Changes in organisation of redistribution, 1997-2006

1997	2006
Department of Social Security	**Department of Work and Pensions**
National Insurance contributions and benefits	Divided into:
Income Support	• Pensions Service
Disability Benefits	• Jobcentre Plus
Child Benefit	• Child Support Agency
Family Credit	• Disability and Carers Service
	National Insurance benefits
Inland Revenue	Pension Credit
Income Tax	Income Support (for non-pensioners)
	Jobseekers Allowance
HM Customs and Excise	Disability Benefits
Indirect taxes	
	HM Revenue and Customs
	Income Tax
	Indirect taxes
	National Insurance contributions
	Child Benefit
	Child Tax Credit
	Working Tax Credit

2. to ensure it is targeted on those who need it most, financial support should be assessed on a household basis where possible, while respecting the principle of independent taxation;
3. to tackle poverty, minimum levels of income should be guaranteed for the most vulnerable in society – the elderly, families, and those who cannot work because of illness or disability;
4. to reduce stigma and maximize take-up the income test should not be intrusive and the hassle of claiming should be minimized; and
5. to improve customer service and increase efficiency, the administration of tax and benefits should be modernized and brought closer together.

It is clear that assessing the redistributive effects of *only* social security or *only* tax and tax credits is wholly inadequate and misleading, although international comparisons often do this. Redistribution has been restructured and the new combination must be assessed together.

Why did this restructuring take place? The main participants have yet to publish their memoirs but a speculative explanation runs as follows:

For the conspiratorially minded, the origins, as of much else, may be traced to the Blair–Brown meeting in 1994 in the Granita Restaurant. What has not been in doubt is Chancellor Brown's dominance over taxation and social security policy. Secretaries of State Harman and Darling were, according to Browns' recent biographers (Bower, 2005; Peston, 2005), ruled by the Treasury. The independent-thinking Minister for Welfare Reform, Frank Field, was frustrated and soon departed. Brown had been much impressed by the Earned Income Tax Credit in the US and through the vehicle of tax credits wanted to increase pay packets relative to benefits for those out of work, a stance endorsed by the Taylor Report (HM Treasury, 1998). This led to the Working Families' Tax Credit, which was in effect an enhanced version of the old Family Credit with the administration transferred to the Inland Revenue (before its amalgamation into HM Revenue and Customs). Brown also raised Child Benefit for the first child by nearly one-quarter in real terms in 1999 and substantially increased Income Support rates for children. Following the phasing out of the married couple's allowance and the short-lived Children's Tax Credit, the Child Tax Credit was introduced in 2003: this combines a benefit for those on very low incomes that is related to the number of children and is sharply means tested and a family element that is not related to the number of children and is 'affluence tested' so that households on higher incomes (roughly the top 10%) are not eligible. In addition, for low-paid workers there is another means-tested benefit, the Working Tax Credit. Crucially, the new benefits have been defined as tax credits so that most of the cost is not counted as public expenditure, but rather as negative taxation.[1] In this way redistribution to families has been increased while apparently constraining public expenditure – a substantial political advantage for a prudent Chancellor.

It should be stressed that there was nothing wrong with this way of proceeding; it in effect evaded the arbitrary and meaningless distinction between (1) outgoings in the form of benefits and (2) tax expenditures in the form of tax allowances, tax credits or negative taxation – a distinction that had certainly constrained policy making in the past.

For pensioners, means-tested Income Support was renamed Minimum Income Guarantee and more recently Pension Credit (which is not a tax credit, although it sounds like one). This was increased faster than contributory, non-means-tested National Insurance Retirement Pension (which must wait probably until 2012 before being indexed in line with earnings following the government's response to the Pensions Commission (2005) recommendations – see Chapter Eleven).

The overall effect of these and other changes has been to give larger gains at lower income levels, as shown for families and pensioners in Figures 10.2 and 10.3.

Figure 10.2: Gains for families as a result of tax credits and other children's measures by 2005

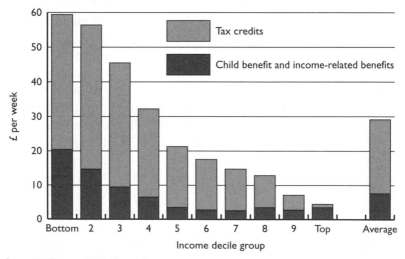

Source: HM Treasury (2005, Chart 6.1)

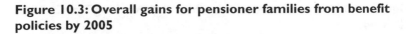

Figure 10.3: Overall gains for pensioner families from benefit policies by 2005

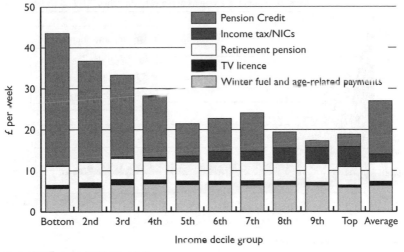

Source: HM Treasury (2005, Chart 6.5)

The combined effects have been described by the Chancellor as 'progressive universalism', with all getting something but the poor getting more.

Child benefits – a seamless system?

The restructuring of child support was explained by HM Treasury as follows (2002, para 2.3):

> The Child Tax Credit will create a single, seamless system of support for families with children, payable irrespective of the work status of the adults in the household. This means that the Child Tax Credit will form a stable and secure income bridge as families move off welfare and into work. It will also provide a common framework of assessment, so that all families are part of the same inclusive system and poorer families do not feel stigmatized.

The extent of support at different income levels is shown in Figure 10.4. The effectiveness of this structure of support for families in tackling child poverty is discussed in the penultimate section in this chapter. The structure itself has aroused little controversy and appears to enjoy the political support of the majority.

Figure 10.4: The structure of the Child and Working Tax Credits, 2003-04

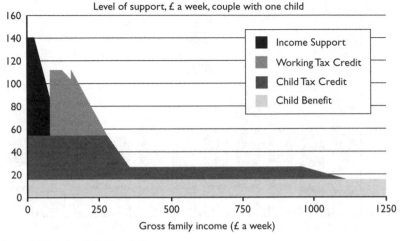

Level of support, £ a week, couple with one child

Legend:
- Income Support
- Working Tax Credit
- Child Tax Credit
- Child Benefit

Gross family income (£ a week)

Source: HM Treasury (2002, Chart 2.1)

The obvious extension of progressive universalism that some propose and many fear is progressive selectivity, ending all child support for higher income groups. But there is a strong case for retaining Child Benefit in terms of simplicity, take-up, payment to the mother for the child, stability and providing a ladder out of poverty, as Fran Bennett (2006) has argued. The current structure – highly means-tested child support at low income levels, then support that does not change as income rises, then gradual withdrawal at high income levels – may fit in with political realities, since there are relatively few at the lowest and highest income levels, and it may reconcile equity and efficiency concerns as well as possible. Yet, while there is a strong case for Child Benefit, it is a strange product of history that there are two systems – Child Benefit and Child Tax Credit – with two different names effectively concerned with the same objective. It is scarcely a seamless web.

Rights and responsibilities

Chancellor Brown put great stress on 'work for those who can'. Under the New Deals for the young and long-term unemployed there was to be 'no fifth option'. Perhaps surprisingly, there has been more talk than action. For the young and the long-term unemployed, there never really was a fifth option – those who refused to take available jobs or refused training places have always been subject to the sanction of benefits being reduced. For some, such as lone parents, there have been attempts to encourage employment by requiring claimants to attend interviews in order to be allowed onto benefit, and concern at the high levels of Incapacity Benefit recipients has led to recent reform proposals to extend such interviews (DWP, 2006a). But the sanctions for failure to take up 'suitable' jobs or training remain largely unchanged.

Thus far at least, there has been no major increase in conditionality of benefits such as has occurred in the US. There is no requirement to take employment for lone parents such as exists in the US, not even where all the children are of school age (although this is now proposed when children are over 11 in the 2007 Freud Review). There is no requirement to attend regular health checks in order to receive maternity benefits, such as exists in France – although to start receiving Sure Start Maternity Benefit registration with a doctor or midwife is required. There is no requirement on the unemployed to take drug tests and attend rehabilitation courses, such as exists in the US. Requirements to attend interviews and to sign jobseeker's agreements have been extended but overall there has been a cautious approach to conditionality.

Impact on incentives – unemployment and poverty traps

One of the concerns voiced before 1997, for example by the Commission on Social Justice (1994), was the discouragement of work due to the unemployment trap and the poverty trap. The unemployment trap – the small or non-existent gain in net income from employment relative to income out of work – has been addressed in a number of ways. First, the National Minimum Wage was introduced in 1999. (In this chapter the minimum wage is treated as a labour market measure rather than a redistributive measure). Second, in-work benefits particularly for the low paid have been substantially extended. Third, a reduced starting rate of Income Tax of 10 pence in the pound was introduced, with the claim that this helped the unemployment trap.[2] Fourth, benefits for the unemployed have only been indexed in line with prices. In aggregate these changes have certainly increased the financial gain from employment, as shown in Figure 10.5.

The poverty trap – the high effective marginal tax rate resulting from the cumulative impact of Income Tax, National Insurance contributions and the withdrawal of means-tested benefits and tax credits as earnings rise – has in some respects been eased. The numbers facing different

Figure 10.5: Gain to work for families with two children

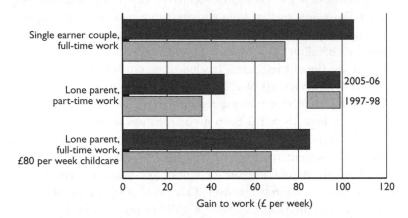

Note: Assumed levels of earnings are median for the couple family and National Minimum Wage for the one-parent families.
Source: HM Treasury (2005, Chart 4.3)

marginal rates are shown in Table 10.1. No longer are any facing marginal taxes of over 100% and the number facing marginal tax rates of over 70% has fallen from three-quarters of a million to one-quarter of a million. Yet the number facing rates of over 60% has greatly increased (most of them losing nearly 70 pence in the pound). Now nearly two million households on low incomes face a far higher effective marginal tax rate than those on the highest incomes. Thus, while the poverty trap has been alleviated in severity, it has been extended to yet more low-income households.

Table 10.1: The effect of the government's reforms on high marginal deduction rates[a]

Marginal deduction rate[b]	Before Budget 1998	2005-06 system of tax and benefits
Over 100%	5,000	0
Over 90%	130,000	30,000
Over 80%	300,000	165,000
Over 70%	740,000	235,000
Over 60%	760,000	1,730,000

Notes:

[a] Figures are cumulative. Before Budget 1998 based on 1997-98 estimated caseload and take-up rates; the 2005-06 system of tax and benefits is based on 2003-04 caseload and take-up rates.

[b] Marginal deduction rates are for working households in receipt of income-related benefits or tax credits where at least one person works 16 hours or more a week, and the head of the household is not disabled.

Source: HM Treasury (2005, Table 4.3)

While there is no clear evidence that this has had a large impact on behaviour, with a high efficiency cost, the equity of this situation remains a serious concern. What the government has failed to acknowledge is that this situation is the inevitable result of trying to boost the incomes of low-paid workers without either raising the general level of taxation or tackling inequalities in earnings, except at the very bottom through the minimum wage. It illustrates the intractable dilemma that seeking to reduce poverty while not reducing inequality is bound to scrunch up the bottom of the income distribution. Scrunched-up differentials are frequently unfair. Thus, while the poverty trap has been alleviated in severity, it has been extended to yet more low-income households.

Changing circumstances

If everyone was at a constant level of income and remained in a fixed family formation then redistribution would present few practical problems. There would be issues of equity and eligibility but eventually everyone might expect to get the correct level of benefits and to have any arrears or overpayment gently rectified. For better or worse, this is not the case and variations in circumstances have led to serious problems. The difficulties may be considered in relation to, first, fluctuating incomes and, second, fluctuating living arrangements.

Tax credits are in effect means-tested benefits and the amount payable depends on the level of income. This has not been a problem facing most households: for example, someone on median earnings can double their earnings without it affecting the amount of Child Tax Credit they receive. But for those on low incomes the amount of Child Tax Credit paid has been based on income in the preceding period with the proviso that if income rose more than a certain amount this should be reported and benefits would be reduced. Only at the end of the year has there been full adjustment for actual earnings. If there was a delay in reporting higher earnings, or they were not reported at all, or if adjustment took a long time, then the result was overpayment. Overpayment in turn led to attempts to recover the excess amount. In some cases recovery of overpayment led to loss of all tax credits and serious financial hardship. This became a very serious problem. The government responded first by attributing problems to teething troubles and then by raising the maximum increase in earnings that could be disregarded from £2,500 to £25,000 – a massive increase that was convenient if expensive (and in a few cases seriously inequitable).

The extent of the problem of fluctuating incomes was only revealed in research published long after the policy was introduced. Hills et al (2006) showed that:

> A quarter of the cases had 'erratic' or 'highly erratic reported incomes', with income during at least four four-week periods during a year differing by more than 15 percent from the annual average. (p 4)

They concluded that their findings illustrate a dilemma facing those administering systems such as tax credits:

> Such systems can be run on a basis of fixing payments for a while on the basis of past income. Alternatively payments can be adjusted to reflect current incomes. On the one hand, the degree of variation we show occurring within the year suggests that families' circumstances can change very rapidly, and that the justice involved in basing tax credits on past incomes would be rough. On the other hand, this degree of income variation makes administration of a system intended to adjust for it during the year very difficult. (p 7)

To cope with income fluctuations, a number of possibilities exist. Benefits can be adjusted on a continuous basis, in the same way that the PAYE system adjusts income taxation as income fluctuates. Or benefits can be fixed and the tax-take continually adjusted so that the *net* benefit varies with current income. Or benefits can be related to past income, using the previous year's tax statement as the crucial document, with no attempt to link benefits to current circumstances. The government has not followed any of these models. Rather it has introduced a system of means-tested benefits that are initially assessed using one time period but later adjusted using income in another. Having been unwilling to make a difficult choice, the result has been practical confusion and many people substantially and undeservedly messed about.

Changing personal relationships pose another serious problem, which has probably worsened over time. Since tax credits are assessed on the basis of joint family income, it is crucial who is included in the family. The clumping together of people in families, and their break-up, are therefore fundamental to entitlement – leaving aside the question of whether the system of taxes and benefits may have an effect on family formation and fission.

Until 1997, the trend in taxation had been towards individual taxation so that family relationships became less important; this was illustrated by the end of the child tax allowance and the decline of the married couple's allowance. This trend has been fundamentally reversed with joint assessment of the income of couples for tax credit purposes. This may well be more equitable in the sense that resources are used more effectively in terms of reducing poverty. But it makes partners more dependent on each other and may discourage family formation and encourage real or fictitious family fission.

The treatment of children is in contrast to the treatment of couples. With the original Working Families' Tax Credit, the government proposed that benefits be paid by employers into the main earner's pay packet in order to make it clearer that work pays.[3] Now Child Tax Credit is generally paid to the principal carer, in most cases the mother. Since children usually stay with the principal carer when families break up, this change is certainly to the benefit of children.

Reaching people

One of the claims for the restructured system of redistribution was that it would improve take-up and reduce stigma. Estimates of take-up rates are shown in Table 10.2.[4] Take-up has remained the same or worsened for means-tested social security benefits. The take-up of Child Tax Credit is now substantially higher than that of means-tested Family Credit. Tax credits, then, do seem to be reaching more of those eligible.

Whether stigma has been reduced is not known and it is only possible to speculate. The fact that Child Tax Credit is paid to most families may mean that those getting the child element feel less distinct from those better off. Perhaps dealing with HM Revenue and Customs is preferred to dealing with the old Department of Social Security.

Table 10.2: Take-up rates

	Caseload estimates (%)	
	1997-98	2003-04
Pensioners Income Support/Pension Credit	67-82	62-74
Non-pensioners Income Support	87-96	86-95
Jobseeker's Allowance (income based)	71-84	50-61
Family Credit/Child and Working Tax Credit[a]	67-70	87-91

Note: [a] Low-income working families with children receiving more than family element of Child Tax Credit.

Sources: DWP (2006b) and personal communication; HMRC (2006)

Perhaps the renaming of benefits, such as 'Pension Credit' for 'Income Support', results in less stigma. It does, however, seem probable that there is more confusion about entitlements since the system is generally more, not less, complex.

Levels of benefits

A, perhaps *the*, central objective of redistribution is to prevent poverty. Put in different, New Labour, language there were the twin goals of ensuring that those in paid work receive adequate incomes and providing security for those who cannot work. Has the new system provided security, or at least a poverty-level income? Since poverty – long denied under the Thatcher regime – is once more officially acknowledged, there is also a level that is treated as the poverty level – 60% of the median equivalised income level.[5]

The guaranteed minimum in the form of Income Support is compared with the poverty level in Table 10.3. The simple fact is that the social security system comes nowhere near providing the poverty level for those without any other resources. Indeed, because of the failure to keep Income Support rates in step with the rise in median incomes, the problem is for some groups getting worse. This dynamic problem is illustrated in Table 10.4, which shows the current basis for uprating benefits. (After the opprobrium of the 75 pence per week pension increase in 2000, these have not always been adhered to.)

What seems clear is that the tendency of the system to precipitate more claimants onto means-tested benefits has not been reversed. In terms of giving priority to poverty this may make sense, as Glennerster et al (2004) argued recently, but it drifts further and further from the conception of Beveridge's non-means-tested contributory-based system.

Table 10.3: Government poverty line and safety-net level, April 2005

	Poverty line (£)	Safety net (£)	Poverty gap (%)
Couple, aged 25, no children	193	88.15	54.4
Single, aged 25, no children	106	56.20	47.1
Couple, both aged 25, child (4 years old)	228	148.13	35.1
Single, aged 25, child (4 years old)	141	116.18	17.7
Couple, both aged 30, two children (5 and 11)	284	192.03	32.4
Single, aged 25, two children (5 and 11)	197	160.08	18.8
Couple, both aged 40, four children (8, 11, 13, 15)	416	279.83	32.7
Single, aged 40, four children (8, 11, 13, 15)	329	247.88	24.6

Source: CPAG (2005, Table 1)

Table 10.4: Current uprating formulae

Child Benefit	Inflation
Child Tax Credit	
Child element	Average earnings
Family element	None
Working Tax Credit	Inflation
Retirement Pension	Inflation
Pension Credit	Average earnings
Other National Insurance and Income Support rates	Inflation

Source: House of Commons Library (2005)

Changes in taxation

The whole taxation system is far beyond the scope of this chapter. But, since the tax system has become a key component of the attack on poverty, it makes no sense to examine only tax credits and ignore other changes in taxation. Here we consider briefly estimates of the combined effects of direct and indirect personal taxes and benefits. Apart from the introduction of tax credits, the Income Tax system has seen the abolition of the married couple's allowance (except for pensioners) and the additional personal allowance. Aside from the (soon to be abolished) small reduced rate band,[6] the basic rate has been reduced – a paradoxical step for a government with some concerns about inequality – and, the higher rate has been unchanged at 40% – although numbers paying the higher rate have substantially increased. When other direct taxes – National Insurance contributions and Council Tax – are included, direct taxes have on average risen slightly as a proportion of gross income, as shown in Table 10.5. The top quintile group experienced a slightly higher than average increase in

Table 10.5: Taxation by income level

	Taxes as a % of gross income by quintile group of households					
	Bottom	**2nd**	**3rd**	**4th**	**Top**	**All**
1996-97						
Direct taxes	10.2	12.9	17.6	20.6	23.3	19.8
Indirect taxes	27.3	22.0	18.9	16.3	11.8	16.1
All taxes	37.4	34.8	36.5	37.0	35.1	35.9
2004-05						
Direct taxes	9.6	13.0	17.7	21.2	24.7	20.5
Indirect taxes	26.8	19.6	17.3	14.8	10.8	14.8
All taxes	36.4	32.6	35.0	36.0	35.6	35.3

Sources: Stuttard (1998, Table B); Jones (2006, Table 3)

direct taxes. But indirect taxes –VAT, alcohol, tobacco, petrol taxes and others – continue to have a steeply regressive effect. The combined effect of direct and indirect taxes is that, while the overall impact is roughly proportional, the highest proportionate burden continues to be borne by the bottom quintile group.

One important caveat should be noted. These are average tax burdens and some taxes, notably alcohol and tobacco duties, are far from evenly distributed. Tobacco duty in particular is a highly regressive tax; higher taxes may deter some from smoking – it has declined in middle and higher income groups – but there remain hard-core addicts on low incomes who are, in effect, taxed into poverty. Their situation is not reflected in the average figures.

Overall redistributive effects

What has been the overall effect of the restructuring on redistribution? This may appear a straightforward question but on closer examination it is not so simple.

On any journey, one can distinguish the direction and the distance. Both must be known to locate the destination. Similarly, one can in principle distinguish the structure and the extent of redistribution.

It would be convenient to be able to separate (1) the effects of changes in the *structure* (or methods or system) of redistribution, which of course reflect changing priorities, from (2) the effects of changes in the *extent* (or amount or volume) of redistribution, which also reflect political priorities. Yet in practice this separation seems impossible. Tax credits, for example, change both the structure and the extent of redistribution.

What has therefore been done is compare the effectiveness of the old and the new structures and rates in reducing poverty. This is done by comparing the extent of poverty based on original income with the extent of poverty after taxes and benefits. Poverty is measured both in terms of the head count of poverty – the number below the poverty level – and the mean poverty gap – the average amount by which households fell below the poverty level. The data used are those on which the Office for National Statistics' estimates of the effects of taxes and benefits are based, published in *Economic Trends*; these data are now derived from the Expenditure and Food Survey.

The results for the whole population are shown in Table 10.6. Overall, the effectiveness of redistribution in reducing the extent of poverty – whether measured by numbers in poverty or the mean poverty gap – increased between 1996-97 and 2004-05. The proportion taken out

Table 10.6: Overall redistributive effects

	1996-97	2004-05
Proportion of households in poverty (%)		
Based on original income	37.7	35.9
Based on disposable income	19.7	15.9
Proportion taken out of poverty	47.8	55.8
Mean poverty gap as proportion of poverty level (%)		
Based on original income	28.0	25.1
Based on disposable income	4.5	3.9
Proportion of poverty gap closed by redistribution	84.0	84.6

Note: Poverty level is 60% of median equivalised disposable income (before housing costs). Mean poverty gap is mean of whole population (including those not in poverty). It therefore indicates the extent of poverty overall rather than the severity of poverty of those below the poverty line.

Sources: Author's analysis of Office for National Statistics datasets derived from the Family Expenditure Survey 1996-97 and Expenditure and Food Survey 2004-05:

- Office for National Statistics, Effects of Taxes and Benefits on Household Income, 1996-1997 [computer file]. Office for National Statistics [original data producer(s)]. Colchester, Essex: UK Data Archive [distributor], November 1998. SN: 3948

- Office for National Statistics, Effects of Taxes and Benefits on Household Income, 2004-2005 [computer file]. Office for National Statistics [original data producer(s)]. Colchester, Essex: UK Data Archive [distributor], August 2006. SN: 5446.

Data are Crown Copyright. The Office for National Statistics and the UK Data Archive bear no responsibility for the analysis or interpretation.

of poverty has increased from 48 to 56%. The mean poverty gap that is closed by redistribution has gone up, but by less than the decline in the head count of the poor. This difference is because many of those in direst poverty have had smaller improvements in their relative position than those closer to the poverty level.

The effects of the changes in redistribution on different types of household are shown in Table 10.7. The biggest increase in effectiveness is among households with children with 43% taken out of poverty in 2004-05, compared to 27% in 1996-97; the effectiveness of redistribution in reducing the poverty gap has also increased. There have been increases in effectiveness in reducing the head count of poverty for both employed and retired households, but not in reducing their mean poverty gap. For single, non-retired people redistribution has become markedly less effective at preventing poverty or reducing the mean poverty gap.

Overall, this evidence shows that the restructuring of redistribution since 1996-97 has made it more effective in achieving the intended goals. On the other hand, there remains a very long way to go before child poverty, let alone poverty among older people, disabled people or those seeking jobs, has been eliminated.

Table 10.7: Redistributive effects by household type

	1996-97	2004-05
Proportions taken out of poverty (%)		
Households with children	27.1	43.1
Employed households	34.4	41.8
Households with retired members	61.2	66.1
Single, non-retired	48.8	46.0
All households	*47.8*	*55.8*
Proportion of poverty gaps closed by redistribution (%)		
Households with children	76.7	81.3
Employed households	69.5	64.5
Households with retired members	89.9	89.2
Single, non-retired	83.0	79.6
All households	*84.0*	*84.6*

Note and sources: As Table 10.6.

Conclusions

The results presented in the previous section suggest there has been some progress in reducing poverty. This reduction in poverty is substantially the result of the restructured and enhanced redistribution.

This conclusion mirrors that of Sefton and Sutherland (2005) who were confident that 'changes in the tax-benefit system have strongly favoured the poorest households'; but they added that, in relation to inequality, 'it is probably too early to judge whether the small progress made under New Labour is "scratching the surface" of the problem or whether it does indeed represent the beginning of a new trend towards greater equality' (p 249).

This conclusion is also borne out by international comparisons. Stewart (2005), comparing UK experience with that of other countries, concluded that:

> Efforts to bring down the rate of child poverty have had a positive impact on the UK's ranking in Europe, and the UK has also made the most progress of EU countries in bringing down the overall poverty rate.... The package of tax credits and benefits for lower-income households with children appears now to be among the most generous in the industrialized world.... However....Almost all households dependent on income support are likely to remain well below the poverty line (pp 319-20).

To sum this up – in a phrase that would gain New Labour approval in terms of its length but not for its inclusion of a verb – 'redistribution works'.

On the figures up to 2004-05, inequality too has declined, although only in recent years. The Gini coefficients for household income distribution fell between 2001-02 and 2004-05 from 53 to 51% for original income and from 36 to 32% for disposable income (Jones, 2006). A considerable part of the decline in inequality of disposable income is due to the restructuring of redistribution. Whether the small decline will be maintained in the face of the orgy of greed exemplified by recent City bonuses and top chief executive officer salaries remains to be seen. As on innumerable topics, a much longer perspective is brought by Howard Glennerster (2006) in a recent paper that examines changes in the distribution of incomes from 1937 to 2005.

Problems and issues remain that have not been solved simply by having more redistribution. First, the entire system is mightily confused. It is hard to describe it as a coherent system. What was once the sphere of the Department of Social Security is now divided between two major departments with many new benefits and other changes.[7] It is a structure that is probably less comprehensible and it is certainly less contributory. Yet, if it does a better job in reducing poverty, does anything else matter?

In general redistribution has become more income-related or targeted. This may seem self-evidently desirable – redistribution that went to all equally would be no redistribution at all. Yet the concentration on the poorest – or more particularly the poorest with children, especially those in work – does present problems when contrasted with a wider redistribution involving higher tax rates. Concentrating on the poorest is in effect the cheapest way of reducing poverty and it may have undesirable equity and efficiency effects. Many more now gain very little from extra earnings due to high effective marginal tax rates – and they may end up worse off if they become 'time-poor' as a result of increased working time. Whether the adverse incentive effects reduce work effort and create more dependence on benefits remains an open question.

A major change in the structure of redistribution has been the increased role of HM Revenue and Customs. This raises questions about administration and the treatment of people in or close to poverty. Put simply these are not the usual clientele of HM Revenue and Customs; whereas proceeding in units of 365 days may be entirely appropriate for Income Tax, many people budget weekly, fortnightly or monthly (and some from day to day). Shifting to a system that in effect ignores intra–annual changes has posed serious problems for many recipients of tax credits, as well as for administrators and ministers.

The increased role for the tax system, especially at low income levels, may have increased the public and political acceptability of redistribution on the scale that has occurred. If this is so, it is very important. But it is not clear if it is so.

The perception of those who benefited may have been improved if they see themselves as part of the tax system rather than as 'claimants'. On the other hand, those left out of the new world of tax credits, which include the millions still relying on Income Support, may feel worse off as they become yet more residualised.

A serious long-term political question concerns the diminished role of the Department for Work and Pensions. In the past it has acted as an effective voice of the poor in Cabinet, challenging the Treasury on benefit levels. With a Chancellor in control who is concerned about poverty this may make little difference. But Chancellors move on and a future Chancellor may not have the same concern. At that time the loss of political voice for people living in poverty may have very serious consequences.

While redistribution was being restructured, it was being written out of the New Labour script. Whether this was good or bad is a matter of judgement. It could be said to have helped poor people because it has concealed an increase in redistribution. If the extent of redistribution to the poor tends to be exaggerated – since the poor receive their small share very explicitly whereas those better off tend to gain from services like subsidies to commuter trains that are less visible – then obscuring what has happened may have helped poor people. On the other hand, as Sefton (2005, p 114) has argued:

> The very scale of the challenge suggests that the current approach of 'quiet redistribution' or 'redistribution by stealth' is unlikely to get us much further than the real progress already made and may even become counterproductive. The low-key nature of many recent changes to the tax and benefit system have led to a lack of public recognition of the government's progress in reducing poverty.

One of the requirements to 'make social policy work' is that welfare should be popular. As the Prime Minister Tony Blair said, 'if people lose faith in welfare's ability to deliver, then politicians have an impossible job persuading hard-pressed taxpayers that their money should go on a system that is not working' (Blair, 1999, p 12). Whether the restructuring of redistribution that has occurred has increased the popularity of the welfare system is an important question to which there is as yet no clear answer.

Much has then been achieved by the increase in redistribution since 1997. The changes in the structure of redistribution may have contributed to political acceptability but it is not clear that they have contributed to the coherence and comprehensibility of the redistributive system. The changes have largely helped those in paid work; they have done a little, but not much, to achieve the goal of 'security for those who cannot work'.

What is far from clear is where we go from here if child poverty is to be halved, halved and halved again to match the lowest levels in Europe. More of the same is not an option.

Notes

[1] Only where the tax credit paid exceeded Income Tax payable was the tax credit counted, for public sector accounting purposes, as additional expenditure.

[2] A claim that stands no scrutiny since the low paid would benefit more by raising the tax threshold and abolishing the reduced rate band.

[3] As recommended in the Taylor Report (HM Treasury, 1998). After protests, Working Families' Tax Credit could be claimed and paid to either person in a couple with children, not necessarily via the pay packet.

[4] Only 'case-load' estimates are shown. Estimates of take-up based on expenditure are not shown because the latter are not available for both years on a comparable basis.

[5] Questions of definition, such as whether poverty should be measured before or after housing costs, are important but not directly relevant here.

[6] In the 2007 Budget it was announced that the 10 pence band will be abolished from 2007-08 onwards, but with the revenue used to cut the basic rate, rather than increase tax allowances.

[7] Space has not allowed discussion of disability benefits, the Social Fund, the Child Support Agency, asset-based welfare or numerous other important components of the redistributive system.

References

Bennett, F. (2006) *Child Benefit: Fit for the Future*, London: Child Poverty Action Group.

Beveridge, W.H. (1942) *Social Insurance and Allied Services*, Cmd 6404, London: HMSO.

Blair, T. (1999) 'Beveridge revisited: a welfare state for the 21st century', in R. Walker (ed) *Ending Child Poverty: Popular Welfare for the 21st Century*, Bristol: The Policy Press.

Bower, T. (2005) *Gordon Brown*, London: HarperCollins.

Commission on Social Justice (1994) *Social Justice: Strategies for National Renewal*, London: Vintage.

CPAG (Child Poverty Action Group) (2005) *Media Briefing on the Pre-Budget Report*, London: CPAG.

DSS (Department of Social Security) (1998) *A New Contract for Welfare: The Gateway to Work*, Cm 4102, London: The Stationery Office.

DWP (Department for Work and Pensions) (2006a) *A New Deal for Welfare: Empowering People to Work*, Cm 6730, London: The Stationery Office.

DWP (2006b) *Income-Related Benefits Estimates of Take-up in 2003/2004*, London: DWP.

Freud, D. (2007) *Reducing Dependency, Increasing Opportunity: Options for the Future of Welfare to Work*, Leeds: Corporate Document Services.

Glennerster, H. (2006) *Tibor Barna: The Redistributive Impact of Taxes and Social Policies in the UK 1937-2005*, CASEpaper 115, London: London School of Economics and Political Science.

Glennerster, H., Hills, J., Piachaud, D. and Webb, J. (2004) *One Hundred Years of Poverty and Policy*, York: Joseph Rowntree Foundation.

Hills, J., Smithies, R. and McKnight, A. (2006) *Tracking Income: How Working Families' Incomes Vary through the Year*, CASEreport 32, London: London School of Economics and Political Science.

HMRC (HM Revenue and Customs) (2006) *Child Tax Credit and Working Tax Credit Take-Up Rates 2003-2004*, London: HMRC.

HM Treasury (1998) *Work Incentives*, The modernisation of Britain's tax and benefit system, no 2, London: HM Treasury.

HM Treasury (2002) *Child and Work Tax Credits*, The modernisation of Britain's tax and benefit system, no 10, London: HM Treasury.

HM Treasury (2005) *Tax Credits: Reforming Financial Support for Families*, The modernisation of Britain's tax and benefit system, no 11, London: HM Treasury.

House of Commons Library (2005) *2006 Benefit Uprating*, SN/SG/3819, London: House of Commons.

Jones, F. (2006) 'The effects of taxes and benefits on household income, 2004-05', *Economic Trends*, May.

Lawson, N. (1992) *The View from No. 11*, London: Bantam.

Pensions Commission (2005) *A New Pension Settlement for the Twenty-First Century*, Second Report of the Pensions Commission, London: The Stationery Office.

Peston, R. (2005) *Brown's Britain*, London: Short.

Sefton, T. (2005) 'Inequality and redistribution under New Labour', *Benefits*, vol 13, no 2, June, pp 109-14.

Sefton, T. and Sutherland, H. (2005) 'Inequality and poverty under New Labour', in J. Hills and K. Stewart (eds) *A More Equal Society? New Labour, Poverty, Inequality and Exclusion*, Bristol: The Policy Press.

Stewart, K. (2005) 'Changes and inequality and poverty in the UK in an international context', in J. Hills and K. Stewart (eds) *A More Equal Society? New Labour, Poverty, Inequality and Exclusion*, Bristol: The Policy Press.

Stuttard, N. (1998) 'The effects of taxes and benefits on household income, 1996-97', *Economic Trends*, April.

ELEVEN

Pensions, public opinion and policy

John Hills

'The trouble with the British is that they want European-level services with US levels of tax.' This quotation, from *Wall Street Journal* coverage of the UK General Election of 2001, was used by Howard Glennerster (2003, p 199) to illustrate one of the besetting difficulties facing UK policy makers. The problem is that, in reality, 'someone has to pay', as he headlined an early section of his book on *Understanding the Finance of Welfare*. Pensions policy, and the current debate on how we cope with future pressures on pensions, illustrate both the difficulties associated with what may be unrealistic expectations and the unavoidable choices in working out who pays for a substantial part of the welfare state.

In May 2006, the government published wide-ranging proposals for the long-term reform of Britain's pensions system, hailing them as 'a radical reform and the most important since Beveridge' (House of Commons Work and Pensions Committee, 2006, p 10). Some historians demurred.[1] The Fowler reforms of 1988 were similarly described – as have been many other social welfare reforms in the previous 50 years. More to the point, the reforms associated with Barbara Castle that brought in the State Earnings Related Pension Scheme (SERPS) in the late 1970s could justifiably have been described in these terms. What is notable about the latest batch of reforms is that, with one crucial addition – the introduction of a low-cost system of additional funded pension accounts into which people will be automatically enrolled unless they opt out – their main effect is eventually to *return* the UK's pension system towards a flat-rate state pension system of a kind that would have been completely recognisable by Beveridge or the post-war Attlee government that introduced the reforms based on his proposals.[2]

Nonetheless, the latest reforms do represent one of the most radical social policy changes for a generation, and with all-party backing for their main structure and a wide – if not universal – expert consensus behind them, the prospects currently look promising for their survival for longer than the typical UK pension system of the last quarter century. A key to this will, however, be whether public opinion will ultimately accept the painful realities the reforms crystallise, or whether we slip back to hankering after the hope that someone else will pay.

This chapter looks at the evidence on what the public wants from pensions, and at how people react when confronted with the potential ways of achieving it. The first section discusses why it became apparent that wide-ranging pension reform was necessary. The next section describes the recommendations made by the Pensions Commission (of which the author was a member) in 2005, the government's reaction to them, and the reforms that are now being put into legislation. Subsequent sections discuss public attitudes to pensions in general, public views of the trade-off between the fundamental choices in tackling the pensions problem, and then specific views of how entitlement to state pensions should be 'earned'. For social policy to 'work' and reforms to stick, ultimately requires sustained public support. The conclusion discusses the long-term prospects for survival of the reforms in the light of these findings.

Changing perceptions of the pensions problem

There has been a remarkable change in both government and public perceptions since the Labour government came into office in 1997. In its first pensions Green Paper (DSS, 1998), the emphasis was on tweaking the inherited structure. The aspiration was that in the long run, pension flows would switch from an alleged 40% of the total coming from the private sector and 60% from the state to the reverse.[3] In this way, the same share of Gross Domestic Product (GDP) (or even a falling one) for state pensions could be spread among a much larger number of future pensioners in the middle of the century, without their relative living standards falling. With the private sector assumed to be coming in to fill the gap, the government said that the flat-rate 'basic' state pension (as established following Beveridge) could continue to be price-linked, as it has been since 1981. While the consequently ever-falling relative value this implied for the basic pension would leave a problem for low-paid workers, the rules of what had been SERPS and became the State Second Pension would be tweaked to make them more generous to the low paid, theoretically allowing them to avoid the need for means-tested top-ups in retirement.[4] There was no need to change State Pension Age. Part of the way that the switch from 40:60 to 60:40 in the contribution of the private sector would be achieved would be through sending people annual pension statements. The optimistic assumption at the time was that on realising quite how low their entitlements were, particularly from the state, at least some people would decide that they needed to save more.

Subsequent reforms to means-tested assistance for today's pensioners created the two-part Pension Credit. This both improved the value of the means-tested minimum for pensioners (the Guarantee Credit) and introduced an additional element (the Savings Credit), which assisted those just above the minimum level, removing some of the 100% effective marginal tax rates people had faced on retirement income (but at the cost of extending shallower withdrawal over a wider income range).

The distance between the assumptions of that Green Paper and the May 2006 White Paper (DWP, 2006a) is considerable. What has changed? Five factors stand out. First, there have been substantial revisions to both public and private sector actuarial forecasts of future longevity. As recently as the 2002 population projections of the Government Actuary, the implicit assumption was that the continual improvements in age-specific mortality of recent decades would slow and then stop. Male life expectancy at 65 would, on the central projection, rise from about 17 years in 2002 to about 19 in 2050. The most recent projections made in 2005, suggest that the figure is already over 18 years, and would approach 24 by 2050 (PC, 2005, Figure 1.38). This – and the equivalent improvements for women – are good news for individuals, but represent a major headache for pension providers, whether public or private.

Second, in the late 1990s, both companies and the government assumed that generous private sector 'defined benefit' (DB) pension promises (for instance, those based on a percentage of final salary) were backed by adequate funds. The private sector had used apparent surpluses in their funds to finance restructuring through early retirement deals in the early 1990s, and the incoming Labour government could withdraw tax credits for pension fund investment income in 1997 without thinking that the system was unsustainable. The stock market crash after 2000 punctured this 'irrational exuberance'. At the same time, both tighter regulation and lower inflation rates meant that pension providers had less room for manoeuvre in controlling their costs (for instance, through letting the real value of pensions in payment fall, as they had in the 1970s when there was a similar stock market fall).

Third, in reaction to both developments, the private sector started to retreat from the old DB schemes, telling new recruits that they would instead be members of 'defined contribution' (DC) schemes, where employees took the risks on both investment performance and future longevity. On average, that need not necessarily have implied a cut in generosity, but in fact contribution rates to DC schemes are far below the effective value of the old DB promises. Crucially, companies then found that they did not seem to suffer any great labour market (recruitment or retention) penalty from this change. As they realised that the old system was more expensive and far riskier than they had assumed, but did not seem to be valued by potential workers, the retreat from DB became a flood. While, so far, most existing members of private DB schemes have maintained their rights to accrue new rights for further years of work in the same way, some companies have already ended such new accruals, and many expect the most of the rest of the private sector to follow.

Fourth, far less was being contributed to funded pension schemes than official and private statistics had suggested. As recently as the 2004 national accounts *Blue Book*, the Office for National Statistics (ONS) believed that the inflow of new savings into funded pension schemes had risen from 4% of GDP in the early 1990s to 6% in 2002.[5] In fact, the flow had remained at just under 4% of GDP throughout the period (PC, 2004, Figure 3.49). One of the problems was that the considerable 'churning' of *existing* private pension funds between one provider and another was being classed by the insurance companies as 'new business', and so by ONS as new saving, when it was nothing of the sort.

Finally, levels of public trust in pension providers had plummeted (Taylor-Gooby, 2005). People had heard of private companies, such as Allied Steel and Wire, which had gone bankrupt without enough money in their pension funds to honour the promises made to their workers (although those who had already retired were partly protected). The difficulties of the Equitable Life insurance company in meeting the promises it had made to different kinds of investor were constantly in the news. Prospective returns on DC schemes plunged following the stock market collapse and the adjustment of annuity rates to improved life expectancy forecasts. People had not forgotten the Maxwell pension scandal of the early 1990s or 'pension mis-selling' in the 1980s. And people knew that the basic state pension was steadily losing its relative value. Faced with all this, instead of reacting to poorer than expected pension rights by saving more, many people appeared, in the words of another contributor to the volume, Nicholas Barr, to be 'like rabbits trapped in the headlights' – aware that there was a problem, but unable to work out a safe way to turn.

While realisation of some of these developments lay ahead – indeed it partly emerged as a result of the Commission's work – the government was sufficiently concerned in 2002 to establish an independent Pensions Commission, chaired by Adair (now Lord) Turner. The brief of the

Commission was to review the adequacy of private pension saving in the UK, and advise on appropriate policy changes, including whether there was a need to 'move beyond the voluntary approach'. We started work in early 2003, produced a first report laying out the problems as we saw them in October 2004, a second report with our main conclusions and analysis in November 2005, and a short final report commenting on some of the issues arising in the debate on our recommendations in April 2006 (PC, 2004, 2005, 2006).

From the outset it was clear that to understand the adequacy of private pensions and the impact of policies towards them, the interface with state pensions had to be taken into account. This determines both the starting point from which private pensions could build towards an adequate level of provision, and the incentives (and perceived incentives) for people to build private provision on a voluntary basis. In the event, our recommendations and the government's response in its May 2006 White Paper (DWP, 2006a) covered both private and state pensions.

Faced with developments of the kind sketched above, combined with the large gaps in existing coverage of pensions beyond the state's minimum for many low-paid workers, those working for small- or medium-sized firms, and for many women with interrupted paid work careers, the findings in the Commission's first report (PC, 2004, pp x–xiii) were clear:

- While the state had been planning to provide decreasing support for many people to control expenditure in the face of an ageing population, the private sector had not been developing to offset the state's retreating role. Instead it was in significant decline.
- Given present trends, many people would face what they would see as inadequate pensions in retirement. While some would be well-provided for, many would not be: pension right accrual was both deficient in total and increasingly unequal.
- Women in particular have much lower pension rights than men, with the state system based on assumptions about family structure that have ceased to be valid. An effective pension system for the future should be one where the vast majority of women accrue pension rights, both state and private, in their own right.
- There are big barriers to the success of a voluntary pension system, including inherent barriers of inertia in making complex decisions, high costs of individually sold pension products, and the bewildering complexity of the UK pension system, state and private combined.

- Means testing within the state system both increases complexity and reduces the incentives to save created by the tax system. The scope of means testing would grow over time if recent indexation approaches had continued (with the basic pension price-linked, but the minimum given by Pension Credit earnings-linked).
- Given all of this, it was unlikely that the present voluntary system combined with the present state system would solve the problem of inadequate pension savings.

Fundamentally, any country faced with the demographic challenge of an ageing population and the impending retirement of the 'baby boom' generation has to choose between four options (or some combination of them):

- pensioners will become poorer relative to the rest of society;
- taxes/National Insurance contributions devoted to pensions must rise;
- savings must rise; or
- average retirement ages must rise.

The Commission found the first of these options unattractive given the UK's already internationally low level of pensions, but that there were significant barriers to solving the problem through any one of the other three options alone. The fourth section of this chapter discusses public views of this fundamental choice.

The current pension reforms

The Commission's main report in November 2005 proposed a series of reforms to achieve a mixture of the latter three responses:

- introduction of a low-cost, funded, National Pension Savings Scheme (NPSS), with employees automatically enrolled into this or good-quality existing employer schemes. People would have the right both to opt out and to make additional contributions above the automatic minimum;
- this should be underpinned by a less means-tested, more universal, flat-rate state pension than would result from unchanged policies. The cost of this, in the face of the demographic challenge, implied facing the reality of the need for *both* public spending on pensions as a share of national income *and* state pension ages to rise in the long run;

- as a corollary of the last point, and indeed of increasing life expectancy, a series of measures was needed to facilitate later and more flexible retirement.

The first of these, the NPSS, was designed to put right a market failure: the problems of a competitive system where individual pension policies are sold to potential buyers. To provide low-cost savings and high coverage, we suggested using the 'soft compulsion' of automatic enrolment to harness the power of inertia in a positive direction, the evidence being that participation in 'opt out' schemes of this kind is much higher than in 'opt in' schemes. At the same time, a national system would remove many of the costs of current provision for those outside large occupational schemes. Default *minimum* contributions to the NPSS would be set at about 8% of earnings between the tax threshold and an upper limit:

- 4% from the employee's net pay;
- 1% from tax relief (if they are basic rate taxpayers); and
- a 3% compulsory employer matching contribution.

Additional contributions would be allowed (up to twice this amount for a median earner), contributions would be collected through the PAYE system or a newly created Pension Payment System, and funds would be invested on individuals' instructions (generally in funds bulk-bought at low cost, including a 'default scheme' for those who did not make an explicit choice). We did not propose a general reform of tax relief for pension contributions, but suggested that the government should examine the case for a specific regime for the NPSS, giving a single rate of upfront matching payments (instead of tax relief on contributions and tax-free lump sums on retirement).

The state system proposals had five elements:

- building on recent reforms, by accelerating the evolution of the State Second Pension to become flat-rate, with improved carer credits;
- indexing the Basic State Pension to average earnings growth over the long term (preferably from 2010), and moving *accruals* of future rights onto a universal, individual basis;
- maintaining the recent progress that had been made in reducing pensioner poverty through the improved generosity of Pension Credit, but limiting the future spread of means testing (by freezing the real value of maximum Savings Credit);

- accepting that this kind of structure required increases in both the State Pension Age and the level of public spending as a share of GDP in the long-run, with a trade-off between the two. We suggested a 'range for debate' in which, given current life expectancy projections, the State Pension Age (SPA) would rise from 65 in 2020 to between 67 and 69 in 2050, with public spending on pensions and other benefits to pensioners rising from about 6.2% of GDP today to between 7.5 and 8.0% of GDP depending on by how much SPA rose;
- 'ideally' paying the full Basic State Pension to all those aged over 75 on an individual basis.

In the light of the continuing wide differences in life expectancies by social class, we suggested that such reforms should be accompanied by an agenda that facilitated later working and gradual, rather than sudden, moves into retirement. This could involve: a focus on occupational health *earlier* in working lives and on the education and training of older workers; allowing earlier claim of Guarantee Credit than the SPA (for instance, this could stay at 65 as the SPA rose above it); removing the default retirement age of 65 currently allowed by anti-age discrimination legislation; improving knowledge of the advantages of deferring state pensions (then paid at a higher level) and allowing people to claim part of their state pension while deferring the rest of it, supporting, for instance, a transitional move into part-time work; and incentives for employers to hire post-SPA workers (such as reduced employer National Insurance contributions).

The government's initial response was mixed. While the then Prime Minister, Tony Blair, and the then Secretary of State for Work and Pensions, John Hutton, welcomed the architecture of the proposals as 'basically right', newspaper reports suggested that the Treasury had major reservations about the potential cost of the state sector reforms. This was not so much the cost in the long run – the Commission's projections of long-run public spending of between 7.5 and 8% of GDP were little higher than the Treasury's own projections of spending under current arrangements (*if* the minimum given by the Guarantee Credit continued to be linked to earnings, although there was then no commitment to this). Rather, the problem was in the 2010s. Without reform, spending on pensioner benefits was expected to *fall* as a share of GDP between 2010 and 2020, as the effects of the already planned increase in women's SPA to 65 worked through. Under the Commission's proposals, spending would remain much the same share of GDP over this early period.

A six-month period of consultation followed, not just with representative and expert bodies – most of which, whatever their views on particular details, backed the proposals – but also through a major 'deliberative polling' exercise in March 2006, National Pensions Day, organised by Opinion Leader Research (OLR) for the Department for Work and Pensions. Results from this are discussed below. At the end of this, in May 2006, the government produced its first White Paper (DWP, 2006a). This accepted the Commission's main recommendations, and promised legislation, in the form of a Pensions Bill in the 2006-07 parliamentary session. Key elements of this, and variations from the Commission's recommendations, were:

- establishment by 2012 of a system of 'personal accounts', into which people would be automatically enrolled, but with the question left open as to whether these would be run along the lines of the Commission's NPSS or through an industry-based competitive model. Contribution rates would be as outlined above. In its second White Paper (DWP, 2006b), it proposed that personal accounts should be run largely along the lines of the Commission's proposed NPSS;
- a return to earnings-indexation of the Basic State Pension from 2012, 'subject to affordability and the fiscal position ... but in any case by the end of the [next] Parliament' (p 17). The Guarantee Credit would be assumed to be earnings-linked as well, and the State Second Pension and Savings Credit reformed much as proposed by the Commission;
- State Pension Age would rise in three steps, to 66 between 2024 and 2026, 67 by 2036 and 68 by 2046, towards the top of the range suggested by the Commission;
- instead of the move towards residence-based accruals of rights to the basic pension, the existing contributory system would stay, but with the number of years of contributions or credits required for a full payment reduced to 30 from April 2010 (see penultimate section).

The White Paper said little new about ways in which extended working lives and more flexible retirement could be supported.

Crucially for its potential long-term viability, this package attracted all-party support,[6] including for what might previously have been seen as controversial elements, such as the increase in SPA and compulsory employer-matching contributions to personal accounts (if employees do not opt out). Criticism has mainly centred on the vagueness around the date for the return to earnings-indexation of the basic pension, and on whether the reforms will take enough people out of means testing (Pensions Policy Institute, 2007).

The public and pensions: great (but short) expectations

Ultimately, policy makers have to yield to public preferences, unless they can change them. A problem for pensions policy is that levels of understanding are so low and have, if anything, deteriorated in recent years. Table 11.1 shows that the proportion of the population claiming even a 'reasonable, basic knowledge' of pensions fell from 53% in 2000 to 47% in 2005. At the same time, the proportion who had given 'a lot of thought' to arrangements for income in retirement had fallen from 35 to 26%, and the proportion thinking that it was mainly their own or their family's responsibility to ensure people have enough money to live on in retirement had fallen from 50 to 37%. More than half now lay the last responsibility at government's door.

Some of the attitudinal evidence collected for the Commission suggests that people are not so much trapped in the headlights, as wilfully shutting their eyes to the oncoming problem. Just over half

Table 11.1: Knowledge and views of pensions issues (%)

	2000	2005
(a) Self-reported knowledge		
Good knowledge	13	12
Reasonable, basic knowledge	40	35
Knowledge is patchy	28	31
Know little or nothing	18	20
Don't know	1	2
(b) Thought given to arrangements for income in retirement		
A lot of thought	35	26
Some thought	36	36
Very little thought	17	23
Not thought about it at all	12	15
(c) Whose responsibility for ensuring people have enough money to live on in retirement?		
Mainly the government	42	55
Mainly a person's employer	4	4
Mainly a person themselves and their family	50	37
Don't know/No opinion/None of these	4	3

Source: PC (2005, Appendix figures D6-D8) (based on 1,304 responses in 2000 and 855-875 responses in 2005)

(52%) agreed with the statement that, 'I'd rather make sure that I had a good standard of living today than put aside money for my retirement', with only 42% disagreeing (PC, 2005, Appendix figure D.10). At the same time, when asked what income level they were aiming at in retirement, 19% wanted 'plenty of money to afford food, housing, living expenses and luxuries' and a further 38% 'enough to afford basic food, housing, and living expenses and to treat themselves about every week'. Two-thirds of those with a private pension, but even just over half of those with *no* pension had one or other of these aspirations. Only 12% of the population saw their aim as being no more than 'enough to afford basic food, housing, and living expenses'. Remarkably, nearly half of those who said they aimed at 'plenty of money to afford food, housing, living expenses and luxuries' also said that they would rather have a good standard of living today than save for retirement (PC, 2005, Appendix figures D.20 and D.21).

How much people thought such standards of living would need by way of income in retirement varied widely. The median response when people were asked what would be the 'minimum' net income in retirement, if they retired today, was £210 per week; the median amount needed for a 'comfortable' net income was about £310 per week. The answers people gave to such questions varied with income level, but by no means in proportion: comparing those with high incomes in a range about three times as high as those in a low income range, median responses to the 'minimum' income question rose from about £190 to £240 per week, and those for a 'comfortable' income from £260 to £350 per week (PC, 2005, Appendix figures D.23 and D.25).

The answers were, however, very varied around these median figures. Part of this may reflect the difficulty for those far from retirement to think about such questions. But part reflects genuinely varied preferences. This – combined with widely varying situations in terms of other assets, accrued pension rights, expectations of inheritance and so on – was one of the reasons why the Pensions Commission did not favour a move to a system of full compulsion designed to ensure, for instance, that everyone retired with a retirement income equal to two-thirds of their pre retirement gross income. Instead, the proposals were designed to produce for someone with median earnings, a replacement rate of around 30% from state pensions, a further 15-18% from the NPSS, and the potential for voluntary NPSS contributions that would double this, taking the total replacement rate to 60-66%. Even this would be well below the aspirations of many. In 2005 earnings terms, this system corresponds to gross incomes of around £195 per week for those with a fairly full working history making the default level of contributions to the NPSS, up to £285 per week for those making the maximum voluntary additions. The former is a little below the median view of a 'minimum' income in retirement; the latter is just short of the median view of a 'comfortable' income.

When retirement savings were discussed with focus groups convened for the Commission, people recognised that they were not saving enough for retirement, but opposed compulsion, even though they felt that encouraging people to save more without compulsion would not overcome barriers to saving. As we suggested, 'there did appear to be some contradiction between participants wanting to make their own decisions, but also wanting to be told what to do because they did not always feel they could make the right decisions' (PC, 2005, Appendix D, p 108). The approach of 'soft compulsion' through automatic enrolment with the right to opt out may be the best way of coping with such conflicting feelings. Indeed, when the options were explained in the much larger deliberative polling exercise with more than 1,000 participants on National Pensions Day, 72% favoured the idea of automatic enrolment with the choice to opt out, 20% full compulsion with no right to opt out, and only 8% leaving things as they are on a voluntary basis (OLR, 2006, Chart 13).

One of the problems in designing – and selling – such policies is that people's expectations of their own longevity have lagged behind the views of actuaries and demographers. As Table 11.2 shows, the Commission's surveys confirmed other research (O'Brien et al, 2005) suggesting that younger cohorts simply do not anticipate the increase in their own life expectancy that actuaries now predict: people judge things by what happened to their grandparents and parents. The difference between people's expectations of how long their retirements might be combined with when they expect to retire generates anticipated life expectancies that are three to four years below the Government

Table 11.2: Differences between average derived estimates of life expectancy and Government Actuary's Department forecasts by current age (years)

Age	Men	Women
16-25	7.4	10.3
26-35	6.2	8.7
36-45	4.5	6.6
46-55	4.0	7.1
56-65	3.4	4.1

Source: PC (2005, Appendix figure D6) (based on 2005 Omnibus Survey and GAD 2004-based estimates of life expectancy)

Actuary's most recent projections for survival beyond 65 for those aged 56-65, but six to nine years below them for those aged 26-35.

As a result it is hard to persuade people quite how expensive pensions are likely to be to provide, whether through funded or through tax-financed systems. Current best expectations are that men and women retiring today can look forward to spending a third of their adult lives in retirement (PC, 2005, Figure 1.44). Funding one year in retirement for every two years of working age is a very expensive proposition, however you meet the costs. But if people's expectations are of a shorter retirement, voluntary retirement provision is likely to be inadequate, and systems that really do meet the cost will look very expensive to them.

Public opinion and the four unavoidable options

In the Commission's focus groups, participants were asked to award points between the 'four unavoidable options' in response to an ageing population described above. They were asked to do this both before and after detailed discussion of each option, its advantages and (more commonly) disadvantages. The amount of adjustment required for each option to solve the future problem by itself was set out. For instance, if all the adjustment were to be achieved through 'poorer pensioners' and none through the other three options, relative pensioner incomes would have to fall by 30%. Alternatively, if it were all achieved only by later retirement, average retirement ages would have to rise from 63 to 70. As Table 11.3 shows, among the 70 participants involved in the groups, the detailed discussion changed the overall balance of opinion little. People favoured about half of the adjustment coming from saving more, most of the rest coming from higher taxes or working longer, and very little coming from pensioners becoming poorer.

This was a rather small group, of course. Parallel analysis of relevant questions asked in the 2004 British Social Attitudes survey by Phillips

Table 11.3: Focus group allocation of points between the four options (average points out of 20)

	Pre-discussion	Post-discussion
Having to pay into a pension or other savings	10	10
Increasing taxes/National Insurance	5	6
Work longer	3	3
Poorer pensioners	2	1

Source: PC (2005, Appendix figure D4) (based on responses from 70 participants)

and Hancock (2005) came to similar conclusions. They found views that 'effectively rule out public support for the suggestion that pensioners in future should have to live on less money' (p 188). But while there was partial support for better pensions paid for by higher taxation, 'even among those who want extra money spent on pensions, there is no great appetite for more taxes' (p 188). They only found limited support for the suggestion that people should work longer and retire later, while although the suggestion that people should save more is popular *in principle*, many of those not doing so at present said they could not afford to do so. When asked unprompted (and before the Pensions Commission reports and associated intense media coverage around pension reform), there were,

> various contradictions in people's views and behaviour which mean that we have not found clear support for any one of the propositions suggested by the Pensions Commission. It is, however, likely that some combination of more taxation, more private savings and later retirement will be necessary.... But support is very tentative ... if any future pensions policy is to square this circle, substantial changes in the public's attitudes and behaviour will be required. (Phillips and Hancock, 2005, p 189)

The National Pensions Day exercise explored whether people's views did change when the issues were explained in the way laid out by the Commission. Table 11.4 shows participants' views at the start and end of the day on five issues related to the four options. They are suggestive in terms of the need for a continuing active debate, particularly when thinking about the option of later retirement. Interestingly, opinion hardened during the day *against* the option of poorer pensioners, even with it being carefully spelt out that this was in relative terms, 'compared with the rest of society'. By the end of the day only one in six thought that this would have to be part of the solution. By contrast, support for both a higher share of taxes going to pensions and for people having to save more grew from over two-thirds to four-fifths or more. Most strikingly, at the start of the day, more people were against people having to work for longer than in favour. By the end of the discussions, 57% were in favour and only a third against. At both the start and end, four-fifths thought that employers will have to contribute to employee pensions.

Table 11.4: National Pensions Day views of potential solutions to the pensions issue in the UK (%)

	Pre-debate		Post-debate	
	Agree/ strongly agree	Disagree/ strongly disagree	Agree/ strongly agree	Disagree/ strongly disagree
Pensioners will have to get poorer compared with the rest of society	24	59	16	78
A greater share of taxes will have to be spent on pensions	68	15	80	11
People will have to save more for their retirement	70	19	88	7
People will have to work for longer	42	45	57	33
Employers will have to contribute to employee pensions	81	8	84	7

Source: OLR (2006, Charts 3-7)

Table 11.5 shows that these preferences translated into a distribution of points (in this case from a total of 10) that was slightly more balanced between the three favoured options than in the earlier focus group exercise. Again, the idea of relatively poorer pensioners attracted very little support. A greater share of taxes and saving more attracted roughly equal support on average, and an increase in average retirement age about half as much. Opinion Leader Research also ran an online debate between February and March 2005 asking similar questions and with some of the same material available. Although, unlik
e the National Pensions Day participants, they did not form a nationally representative sample, the 5,000 participants gave a very similar balance of answers.

All this suggests that the basic strategy of a balance between greater public spending, greater savings, and later retirement, while avoiding the outcome of relatively poorer pensioners, is one that can command public support – but that support becomes firmer when people get the opportunity to debate the issues.

Table 11.5: Support for the four options (average points out of 10)

	National Pensions Day	Online debate
Pensioners becoming poorer compared to rest of society	0.4	0.7
Greater share of taxes spent on pensions	4.1	4.0
Saving more	3.6	4.2
Increase in average retirement age	2.1	2.2

Source: OLR (2006, Charts 16 and 37)

The (strange) survival of the contributory principle

In theory, the bulk of British state pensions spending is based on social insurance principles – entitlement depends on a 'contribution record'. As Beveridge put it in 1942:

> Benefit in return for contributions, rather than free allowances from the State, is what the people of Britain desire.... Payment of a substantial part of the cost of benefits as a contribution irrespective of the means of the contributor is the firm basis of a claim to benefit irrespective of means. (Beveridge, 1942, para 21)

Elaborate records are kept of how many years people have made – or have been 'credited' with – enough contributions, and entitlements depend on these.

However, over time this system has been eroded by governments of both Left and Right. From the Left, attempts have been made to correct the way in which those with interruptions to their paid work careers (particularly women with caring responsibilities) are excluded from a full entitlement through extending systems of credits for those in approved circumstances. For the Right, a non-means-tested system has always had the drawback that some spending will go on those who do not 'need' it, leading to policy changes that reduced the value of National Insurance-based pensions against means-tested ones. The end result has been a system where benefits *mainly* depend on the fact of having made contributions, but people can receive 'contributory' benefits without having made contributions, and can be ruled out of entitlement despite having made contributions (Hills, 2004).

It is easy to mock the end result, and one of the important currents in the recent pensions debate has been whether this ill-understood and complex system should be swept away and the present basic and second state pensions replaced with a single 'Citizens Pension', a flat-rate pension with entitlement depending only on a minimum number of years of recent residence in the UK. Despite the important arguments in its favour, the Pensions Commission rejected this approach, although we did recommend moves essentially in that direction. We suggested that:

- future *accruals* of rights to the *basic* pension should move onto a residence basis;
- *payment* of a full basic pension should 'ideally' be made automatically to those over 75, in particular to improve rights to a full pension for women with incomplete records;
- the State *Second* Pension should be retained, but over time become flat rate (more quickly than under current arrangements), with a wider group of carers credited into entitlement to it.

A major consideration in putting forward this kind of halfway house was the treatment of accrued rights. Governments avoid explicitly reneging on accrued pension rights,[7] and it seems unlikely that any would simply tell those receiving or expecting, say, large State Second Pension payments (reflecting past earnings), that they would now get a much lower flat-rate pension. But if such accrued rights were respected (even if future accrual of State Second Pension stopped) and the basic pension replaced with a simple more generous Citizens Pension, the better off would be large gainers (and some with low incomes would not gain as a result of loss of means-tested benefits). To moderate (but not eliminate) the distributional consequences of this (and its significant immediate cost), one can imagine a system of 'offsets', under which those with existing entitlements above the new Citizens Pension would have no increase in receipts. But where we start from is complex. Some people have low State Second Pension entitlements because they 'contracted out' of entitlement in return for paying lower National Insurance contributions. It would be unfair if they were treated as generously as those who had the same incomes, but had paid in more. Again, one can imagine systems that deal with this. However, as one adds to the list self-employed people (who have also paid much lower National Insurance contributions), women who chose to pay reduced contributions, those who have deliberately paid extra voluntary contributions to 'buy back' lost years, and so on, not only does complexity grow, but so do the potential difficulties of explaining why some people's bygones are bygones, but others are not and so will be 'offset'.

A second issue is the length of residence period that should count. New Zealand runs a Citizens Pension system based on just a few years of residence. But within the European Union, with transferability of state pension rights, setting, say, 10 years as the minimum could lead to workers who move around the Union being entitled to a full UK pension, as well as having fairly full entitlements to state pensions elsewhere. But if the criterion is longer residence – say 30 or 40 years – it becomes impossible to apply the rule retrospectively: we simply do not know who was resident in the UK for how long over such periods looking backwards.

Such problems – as well as a judgement about the ability of different reforms to gather widespread support – led to the Commission's proposals. But in this area, the government is taking a somewhat different approach. It rejected the ideas of basing future accruals to the basic pension on residence or of automatic payment of the full amount at 75. Instead, from April 2010, the number of years needed for full entitlement to the basic pension will fall to 30, and a wider group of carers will accrue credits towards the second pension. These proposals hold on more to the idea of a 'contributory pension' more closely than the Commission – under what ministers have called the 'something for something' principle – although their ultimate effects on entitlements are not so different. The much battered 'contributory principle' lives on.

Part of the reason for this is its apparently enduring popularity with the public, and the resonance of the idea of 'something for something'. On the other hand, the 'something' for which one gets something, is not simply paid work, as can be seen from the National Pensions Day results summarised in Table 11.6. First, after discussion of the issues involved, participants were in favour of the idea that any 'years spent living in the UK' should count towards entitlement to a basic pension. Exactly half agreed or strongly agreed with this residence-based principle, but a substantial minority (35%) disagreed.

In discussion, participants articulated precisely the key arguments for and against the residency principle (OLR, 2006, pp 31-33):

> I agree with residency. I feel it is fairer. How much you get is proportional to how long you live here ... everyone has a right to a pension.

> Women, parents and carers would benefit and get a better deal.

But on the other hand:

> [It] would be unfair if people who had never worked got the same as someone who works all their life.

Table 11.6: National Pensions Day views of what years should count towards state pension entitlement

	Strongly agree	Agree	Neither	Disagree	Strongly disagree	Don't know
Towards the basic state pension						
Years spent living in the UK	21	29	12	21	14	2
Towards the additional state pension						
Caring for sick, older or disabled people	49	45	3	2	1	-
Paid work	53	38	4	3	1	1
Caring for children	40	44	7	7	2	-
Long-term sick or disabled	20	53	9	7	1	-
Voluntary work	20	51	15	12	2	-
Unemployed but actively seeking work	7	32	21	25	14	1

Source: OLR (2006, Charts 8-10)

> You could sit in the house for 40 years.... Why should we work when someone else gets the same who doesn't do anything. It's not fair. Pensions should be a reward for working.

> I don't believe that the Government would be able to keep track of who is here. I would feel like there would be a big brother state if we kept track.

The lower half of Table 11.6 shows people's responses when they had discussed various categories of people who should accrue entitlement to an additional pension in excess of the basic pension (effectively the State Second Pension, but very few people recognise the term). What leaps from the table is how long the list is, and how strong the support for some categories. 91% think that paid work should lead to additional entitlement, but *more* think the same for caring for sick, older or disabled people, and more than 70% think so for those caring for children, for those who are sick or disabled themselves and for those doing voluntary work. Only the unemployed miss out, although even here, as many think they should get the additional pension (39%) as disagree. When one thinks of the proportions of the population covered by one or other of these categories, this is getting close to 'all must have prizes', with rather few exceptions – those 'sitting in the house for 40 years' and so on. Less pejoratively, one could interpret this as a desire for a 'participation pension' reflecting Tony Atkinson's (1995) ideas of a wider basis than paid work for entitlement to a basic income, but stopping short of universal entitlement.

One interpretation is that the public would support the mix proposed by the Commission: a residence basis for a basic pension, but with an additional entitlement for a widened range of other activities. The support for the residence principle is, however, both narrow and limited to a basic component. It is certainly hard to see strong support for a simple integrated Citizens Pension in such results. And the government's judgement (supported by the Conservative opposition) is that the idea of extra for 'deserving' groups and thus 'something for something' justifies retention of a modified contributory basis whatever the critiques that it amounts to a complicated way of ruling out a very small number from full entitlement.

Conclusion: making decisions for the long term

One of the desirable features of a pension system is that it should be stable. People need to know what the rules of the game will be in the future when they are making decisions about how much to save or when to retire, and they will be very unhappy if such rules are changed after they make those decisions. But the UK pensions system has been anything but stable in recent years. For current reforms to endure in a way that can rebuild confidence in pension saving, they have to be built on a consensus that will outlast one particular government. For that to be true, they have to command public support now, and that support has to last.

One of the encouraging features of the public consultations is that when the problems are explained to people, they do come to clear and generally consistent conclusions about the best ways forward. Around a thousand people took part in National Pensions Day debate, many reacting – perhaps to their own surprise – with enthusiasm to the idea of spending a day discussing pensions. It is hardly practical for such an exercise to be repeated for the entire electorate, but if current reforms are to stick, politicians will have to find some way of reminding the electorate what has been decided on pension reform and why. Ironically, the *lack* of controversy around the reforms may be a problem here. In the first half of 2007, the Pensions Bill, containing what would previously have been seen as dramatic proposals such as raising SPA, was proceeding through Parliament with very little media coverage of its reform elements,[8] reflecting the all-party support for its key elements. At some point, its contents will start to affect people's lives: the reasons for the reforms will then need to be explained all over again and may come as a shock.

Thinking about future pressures on social spending it is hard to avoid cliches about the need to make hard choices, and this is particularly the case with pensions policy. We simply cannot have it all, in the way suggested by some attitudes towards what people want by way of a pension but are expecting to pay through tax or pension contributions. Steering a way through this involves some politically tricky compromises. What is essential for those decisions to endure is that we make them with our eyes open. This requires careful analysis and explanation. Here social policy research and analysis – exemplified by Howard Glennerster's own continuing work (already long after the age to which SPA will rise as late as 2046) – has an important role to play.

Notes

[1] See, for instance, the Epilogue to Pemberton et al (2006).

[2] Albeit at a much less generous level than was needed to avoid reliance on the national safety net minimum, then known as National Assistance (Glennerster and Evans, 1994).

[3] If one allows for the proportion of 'private pensions' that are in fact paid to public sector workers, the value of tax concessions, and the way in which part of private pensions represents private funding of compulsory pension contributions (under 'contracting out'), the truly private part of the system was, and remains, far smaller than 40% of the total.

[4] But even this would have been true only at the point of retirement, and for those with relatively full contribution histories (Rake et al, 1999).

[5] Even this was already a substantial downward revision from earlier figures.

[6] See the House of Commons debate on 27 June 2006 and the report of the House of Commons Work and Pensions Committee (2006).

[7] Although changes to indexation rules from those previously expected can be argued to have this effect, albeit less visibly.

[8] Although there was controversy around the terms of the Financial Assistance Scheme for people whose employer had failed, leaving an inadequately funded pension scheme.

References

Atkinson, A.B. (1995) *Incomes and the Welfare State*, Cambridge: Cambridge University Press.

Beveridge, W.H. (1942) *Social Insurance and Allied Sevices*, Cmd 6404, London: HMSO.

DSS (Department of Social Security) (1998) *A New Contract for Welfare: Partnership in Pensions*, Cm 4179, London: The Stationery Office.

DWP (Department for Work and Pensions) (2006a) *Security in Retirement: Towards a New Pensions System*, Cm 6841, London: The Stationery Office.

DWP (2006b) *Personal Accounts: A New Way to Save*, Cm 6975, London: The Stationery Office.

Glennerster, H. (2003) *Understanding the Finance of Welfare*, Bristol: The Policy Press.

Glennerster, H. and Evans, M. (1994) 'Beveridge and his assumptive worlds: the incompatibilities of a flawed design', in J. Hills, J. Ditch and H. Glennerster (eds) *Beveridge and Social Security: An International Retrospective*, Oxford: Oxford University Press.

Hills, J. (2004) 'Heading for retirement? National Insurance, state pensions and the future of the contributory principle in the UK', *Journal of Social Policy*, vol 33, no 3, pp 347-71.

House of Commons Work and Pensions Committee (2006) *Pension Reform*, Fourth report of session 2005-06, HC 1068-I, London: The Stationery Office.

O'Brien, C., Fenn, P. and Diacon, S. (2005) *How Long do People Expect to Live? Results and Implications*, Nottingham: Centre for Risk and Insurance Studies, University of Nottingham.

OLR (Opinion Leader Research) (2006) *National Pensions Day: Final Report*, London: DWP.

PC (Pensions Commission) (2004) *Pensions: Challenges and Choices*, First report of the Pensions Commission, London: The Stationery Office.

PC (2005) *A New Pension Settlement for the Twenty-First Century*, Second report of the Pensions Commission, London: The Stationery Office.

PC (2006) *Implementing an Integrated Package of Pension Reforms*, Final report of the Pensions Commission, London: The Stationery Office.

Pemberton, H., Thane, P. and Whiteside, N. (eds) (2006) *Britain's Pensions Crisis: History and Policy*, Oxford: Oxford University Press for the British Academy.

Pensions Policy Institute (2007) *Will the Pensions Bill Solve the Problems of State Pensions?*, PPI Briefing Note, no 36, London: Pensions Policy Institute.

Phillips, M. and Hancock, R. (2005) 'Planning of retirement: realism or denial?', in A. Park, J. Curtice, K. Thomson, C. Bromley, M. Phillips and M. Johnson (eds) *British Social Attitudes: The 22nd Report: Two Terms of New Labour: The Public's Reaction*, London: Sage Publications.

Rake, K., Falkingham, J. and Evans, M. (1999) *Tightropes and Tripwires: New Labour's Proposals and Means-Testing in Old Age*, CASEpaper 23, London: London School of Economics and Political Science.

Taylor-Gooby, P. (2005) 'Uncertainty, trust and pensions: the case of the UK reforms', *Social Policy and Administration*, vol 39, no 3, pp 217-32.

TWELVE

Distributing resources

Tony Travers

The distribution of resources within the British welfare state has a profound effect on the provision of services from place to place and from individual to individual (see Chapter Ten). During the 20th and 21st centuries, British governments and social scientists have debated, evolved and analysed systems of resource distribution that are at least as sophisticated as any used within other developed democracies. As a result of such policy evolution, the research community (if not politicians) in Britain is relatively well equipped to devise and administer distribution systems with particular social or economic objectives.

However, there is evidence that policy towards resource distribution is now changing. The high watermark of equity-driven allocation formulae has almost certainly passed. Having used academic and other research to inform the evolution of such formulae over 40 years, it now appears that other considerations – notably the desire to have smooth and predictable allocations – are beginning to dominate policy making. The implications of a shift from equity-driven resource allocation to a system with flat-rate changes from year to year will be significant.

To understand the changes currently under way, it is necessary to examine the long history of resource allocation mechanisms in Britain. The allocation of resources in local government, the NHS and various sectors within education is a matter of ongoing political interest. The publication of the report of the Lyons Inquiry into local government in March 2007 was a further step along the long road of policy evolution. Howard Glennerster has long been a leading expert in health service resource allocation and has been a member of the NHS Advisory Committee on Resource Allocation.

Background: the evolution of distribution mechanisms

It is impossible to make sense of contemporary resource distribution mechanisms in Britain without an understanding of their history. A book written to celebrate the intellectual contribution of Howard

Glennerster is a particularly apt place to consider this history and the place of London School of Economics and Political Science (LSE) within it. A number of the LSE's senior members, from Sidney Webb onwards, have set the terms of the debate concerning the need for universal welfare provision across the country and also of how to secure fair funding of such provision throughout the evolution of the contemporary welfare state.

Sidney and Beatrice Webb wrote as early as 1897 that they saw a need for government intervention to reduce the gross geographical and personal inequalities existing in Britain. Glennerster et al, writing in 2000, stated the Webbs believed that 'the unfettered operation of the market produced such degradation in some areas that the nation state was put in danger and its effective operation undermined' (Glennerster et al, 2000, p 10). The Webbs went on to write in great detail about local government, which, at this time, provided virtually all social welfare services.

Many of Sidney Webb's radical, social democratic, precepts still underpin debates about resource distribution in Britain in the early years of the 21st century. In his 1911 book *Grants in Aid: A Criticism and a Proposal* he argued that grants in aid were necessary on four grounds. First, they would prevent extreme inequality of burden between one district and another. Second, they would help central government to encourage efficiency and economy of local administration. Third, they would allow the wisdom and experience of central departments to cascade into smaller councils. Finally, grants-in-aid would enforce a 'national minimum' in the provision of local services that would reduce the risk of damaging social spillover effects from one place to another.

In this 1911 book, Sidney Webb set the terms of the debate right up to the 2000s. LSE staff and others have, in the intervening period, undertaken elaborate statistical analyses that have provided both the justification for action and the intellectual basis for a number of formulae that distribute resources around the country. R.H. Tawney, an LSE academic, set his ideals in terms of equality rather than a bare national minimum level of provision. Ellison (1994) quotes Tawney drawing out the distinction between equal provision, equal outcomes and need, thus moving beyond the notion of simply levelling households or individuals up to a basic minimum receipt from the state. Instead, Tawney envisaged a system where the government attempted to secure similar public service outcomes for people in different circumstances. There are clear steps from Webb, via LSE figures such as Richard Titmuss and William Beveridge, to the state's contemporary efforts to ensure that individuals from different backgrounds have an equal chance in terms of, say, going to university or of achieving equivalent health outcomes.

The contemporary, heavily researched, statistical understanding of how needs vary and can be measured was significantly evolved at LSE by Bleddyn Davies in his 1968 book *Social Needs and Resources in Local Services*. The increased sophistication of social science research during the 1950s and 1960s, allied to the development of computing, allowed researchers to measure differences between individuals and areas in compelling detail. Governments, ever searching 'evidence-based' policy, could hardly ignore the statistical detail placed before them about the differences between places within Britain.

Local government, which was the key institution in the early evolution of education, health, social housing and personal social services, had received grants since the 19th century. However, such grants represented only a small proportion of expenditure and, originally, were not intended to equalise between authorities to compensate them for differences in spending needs: they were generally paid as a percentage of centrally certificated spending. The resulting gross inequalities were what the Webbs had in mind in their works cited above.

The Webbs were not alone. In a minority report to the 1901 Royal Commission on Local Taxation, Lord Balfour and his supporters proposed that grants should be paid on the basis of a needs formula, coupled with the equalisation of taxable capacity (Travers, 1986). This proposal was close to Sidney Webb's ideal, although no action to enact grants based on such principles was taken until the 1929 Local Government Act. This legislation was, in part, based on a complicated formula that took account of each authority's population weighted by the number of children under five, unemployment, sparsity and rateable value.

A further, major step towards the modern form of equalisation was next taken in the 1948 Local Government Act: all authorities with a rateable value (that is, the tax base) below the national average would be compensated by the grant system to the point where no council fell below the average. Subsequent legislation in 1958 produced a further shift towards general grants based on formulae that were intended to compensate councils for differences in their service requirements and population make-up (Foster et al, 1980). By this time, the post-war National Health Service (NHS) and council housing were subject to their own funding regimes that were separate from the generality of local government.

From the late-1960s onwards, Whitehall started to develop new and more complex methods for measuring service needs and allocating resources. The creation of universal health and education services, plus massive expansion of social housing and personal social services in the post-1945 period, posed major questions for government and social science research. These services, backed up by a complex social security system, became the 'welfare state' in its modern form.

The state has continued to develop services in such a way as to take account of different needs and resources, although in recent years new objectives have been added to those originally outlined by Webb. Julian Le Grand has commented that governments face problems in the provision of public services such as healthcare, education, social services, housing and transport. Objectives not only cover equity or fairness, but must also cope with market failures such as externalities, poor information among users/consumers and increasing returns to scale (Le Grand, 2002).

Le Grand (2002, p 15) explained that:

> Equity may be defined in different ways according to the service: thus health care may be provided in such a way as to promote equality of access, equal treatment for equal need, and/or greater equality of health itself; education so as to further equality of opportunity; housing so as to ensure a minimum standard of provision; and so on.

For a further discussion of this issue, see Tania Burchardt's discussion in Chapter Three. Le Grand then went on to describe several manifestations of market failure that require government intervention beyond the achievement of equity objectives. There is no doubt that the debate about 'quasi'-markets within public services has provided an influential post-modern addition to the long-evolved literature on the subject.

Commenting in 2004, Howard Glennerster summarised the long sweep of the history of the evolution of the British welfare system in the following terms:

> Poor relief took less than 1 per cent of the GDP in 1696 and rose to 2 per cent by 1800. The numbers concerned rose from about 3.5 per cent of the population in 1700 to 8 per cent by mid century and 14 per cent by 1800. It was the consequent cost and the very existence of a national legislative framework that attracted the attention of leading

social scientists of the day.... The concern was not just with the misguided actions of a few burghers.... It was a national issue. (Glennerster et al, 2004, p 65)

This analysis neatly summarises the way in which Britain, as an increasingly centrally governed unitary state, has evolved systems to help poor households and, during the 20th century, created universal services that have sought to override the failures and parsimony of parochial interests. This approach, accurately summarised by Glennerster, has had the effect of influencing the very shape of British democracy. This issue will be considered in more detail at the end of this chapter.

The scale of the contemporary welfare state in the UK

The British welfare state operates within an overall public spending total that, as a proportion of Gross Domestic Product (GDP), falls below the levels found in a number of comparable European countries. However, public expenditure has moved significantly – both up and down – in the years since the mid-1970s. Table 12.1 shows taxation as a proportion of GDP in a number of Organisation for Economic Co-operation and Development (OECD) countries in 2004, while Table 12.2 shows public expenditure as a share of GDP for the UK over the period since 1975.

It is important to understand the scale of resources available to the state as an indicator (however crude) of how far the British taxpayer is willing to finance the provision of public services. Britain is close to the OECD average for taxation as a proportion of GDP, but lies well below countries such as France, Italy or Sweden. On the other hand, taxation is higher in Britain in proportion to GDP than in Germany

Table 12.1: Total tax revenue as a percentage of GDP, 2004

Canada	33.0
US	25.4
Finland	44.3
France	43.7
Germany	34.6
Italy	42.2
Netherlands	39.3
Spain	35.1
Sweden	50.7
UK	36.1

Source: OECD (2005)

Table 12.2: Public expenditure in the UK as a proportion of GDP, 1975-76 to 2005-06

	Total (%)	Welfare (%)
1975-76	49.9	
1976-77	48.8	
1977-78	45.8	
1978-79	45.3	
1979-80	44.8	
1980-81	47.3	
1981-82	48.1	
1982-83	48.5	
1983-84	48.2	
1984-85	48.0	
1985-86	45.6	
1986-87	44.1	
1987-88	42.1	23.4
1988-89	39.4	23.3
1989-90	39.7	22.1
1990-91	40.0	23.0
1991-92	42.3	25.1
1992-93	44.2	26.9
1993-94	43.4	26.8
1994-95	43.0	26.6
1995-96	42.3	26.3
1996-97	40.6	25.7
1997-98	38.9	24.4
1998-99	38.1	23.8
1999-00	37.2	23.8
2000-01	38.0	24.1
2001-02	38.7	25.0
2002-03	39.6	25.5
2003-04	40.8	26.6
2004-05	41.7	27.2
2005-06	42.7	27.7

Note: 'Welfare' = expenditure – as % of GDP – on housing, health, education and social security. Data only available in a consistent form after 1987-88.

Source: HM Treasury (2006, Tables 3.1 and 3.4)

or the US. This propensity to pay tax, in turn, should probably be seen in the context of wider expectations about social justice and equity in the delivery of public services.

Public expenditure as a share of the UK economy has fluctuated significantly in the period since the mid-1970s. Having reached almost 50% in 1975–76, the figure fell back during the Callaghan Labour government. Under Mrs Thatcher's Conservatives, the figure rose and then fell sharply, before rising and falling under the Major government.

In the first three years of Tony Blair's Labour government, public expenditure continued to drop – as a share of the economy – to its lowest figure for a generation. Subsequently, since 2000-01, it has risen back towards 43%.

The switchback pattern of public expenditure as a share of GDP is evidence of the different policies adopted by successive governments since 1976. Mrs Thatcher was determined to 'roll back the frontiers of the state' and, after an initial jump in spending within the economy (because of a deep recession), it fell in line with her policies. This pattern was repeated under John Major and then reversed during the Blair years. New Labour maintained the Tories' public expenditure plans for 1998-99 and 1999-2000 – causing spending to fall as a proportion of GDP – and then added significantly to spending, particularly on health and education in the period after 2000-01.

The welfare state and resource allocation mechanisms must fit within this curiously bumpy pattern of overall public expenditure as a part of the whole economy. The funding available for NHS, local government and education funding formulae has been squeezed in some periods and increased in others. The smaller the real terms increase in resources within a formula, the more difficult it will generally be to redistribute from one area to another. Similarly, buoyant levels of funding over a longer period make it possible, in principle, to bring about a significant redistribution of money. The scale and direction of change of public expenditure totals therefore have important implications for the distribution of resources.

The evolution of distribution mechanisms

Health

Insofar as there was publicly funded health provision in Britain in the period before the NHS was created in 1948, it was financed from local rates. As the discussion above has shown, local government finance gradually evolved in such a way as to take account of differences in social and demographic characteristics and tax capacity. But there was a very wide range of provision and local tax burdens varied enormously. The NHS was funded by central government, but proceeded on a last-year-plus basis, embedding past spending patterns into the 1950s and 1960s. Some areas fared badly from this approach (Glennerster et al, 2000).

Access to health services was geographically patchy, leading to a growth in academic and professional interest in the issue. By the end of the 1960s, work was being undertaken on a formula to allocate resources, based partly on population and partly on crude measures of demand. A more sophisticated distribution formula was developed by the Resource Allocation Working Party (RAWP), which worked during the mid-1970s. The distribution of resources based on the RAWP formula led to significantly greater geographical equality in the distribution of resources.

However, losing areas (generally in London) criticised the RAWP-based distribution. A decade after RAWP, the system was reviewed. The then Conservative government sought to improve the 'fairness' of the measurement of need. Although a number of changes were made that reduced the impact on London and the south of England, the system of needs-based formulae remained in place. Even at the height of the Thatcher revolution, the idea that health resources should be allocated about the country on the basis of a formula that took detailed account of indicators such as multiple deprivation and mortality rates was not challenged.

Subsequently, there has been a continuing programme of statistical research into the factors that most appropriately measure spending needs in health (Carr-Hill et al, 1994). The University of York, in particular, has become a key centre for such measurement and analysis. Labour continued to review the method of resource allocation (DH, 2005, 2007) and have made changes to the pattern of distribution. But the basic idea of a complex, research-based, distribution mechanism has continued directly from the 1960s to the present day. There is a continuing political consensus that NHS resources should be distributed across England using a needs-based formula.

Education and skills

Like health, education funding started life within local government and has subsequently evolved into a number of different national resource allocation mechanisms. During the late 19th and early 20th centuries, there were percentage grants to underpin schools funding within local government. These percentage grants, plus some general grant funding, provided support for ratepayers until the major reforms of 1958, which increased the use of 'general' grants, which were not linked to individual services.

Subsequent grant arrangements, introduced in 1967-68, 1974-75, 1981-82 and 1990-91 continued to place education alongside other services such as social services, highways and the environment within a single general grant (Travers, 1986). Advanced further education (the polytechnics and other higher education) and then further education were transferred from local to central control during the 1980s. Schools continued to be underpinned by the Rate Support Grant until 1989-90 and, from 1990-91, by the Revenue Support Grant. Schools funding was fundamentally reformed in 2006-07, removing it from the wider system of local government finance.

The distribution formulae that were developed within local government from the 1960s onwards included factors intended to measure educational needs (Ministry of Housing and Local Government, 1966). Pupil numbers, social needs, sparsity and ethnicity were used within formulae that attempted to attribute causal links between social and demographic factors and the need to spend. Regression analysis was often used in the continuous programme of work on expenditure needs assessment.

From 1989-90, local authorities were required to develop local funding formulae to allocate resources from town halls to individual schools. This was a radical new use for distribution formulae and was intended to allow schools greater autonomy under the Conservative government's local management of schools (LMS) policy (Wallace, 1992). New funding allocation mechanisms were also developed for advanced further education (initially by the Polytechnics and Colleges Funding Council and latterly by the Higher Education Funding Council for England) and for further education and skills (currently in the hands of the Learning and Skills Council).

Education saw the radical evolution of local government-based funding formulae for schools during the 1960s, 1970s and 1980s. New distribution arrangements – based on principles radically different from those used for schools – were invented for the ex-polytechnics and for further education. From 1989, each authority had its own funding formula to distribute money to individual schools.

From 2006-07 onwards, there has been a ringfenced Dedicated Schools Grant (DSG), which is now allocated from the centre to each authority (see Chapter Five for more detailed discussion). Councils must then allocate their DSG, via their local funding formula, to schools. Authorities may not allocate less than the DSG. Schools funding now has its own, separate, funding mechanism, which will be subject to limited change from 2008-09. Moreover, the government now believes that deprivation should predominantly be dealt with at the local authority level (DfES, 2006). A further review of schools' funding will take place before 2011-12, possibly including an entirely new formula for schools.

Housing

Social housing, unlike health and education, is only partly the subject of grant allocations. Tenants must pay rent for properties and therefore may make a substantial contribution towards the cost of their homes. As in health and education, local government was the original provider of social housing. For example, the London County Council (of which Sidney Webb was a member) undertook its first slum clearance scheme as early as 1890 at Boundary Street, with an estate of council-built flats replacing the demolished homes. Before the First World War, the London County Council had a rule that ensured rents had to meet all charges (including capital), with no cost to the rates (Gibbon and Bell, 1939).

Central government did offer subsidies to local authority and private house-building in an attempt to build 'homes fit for heroes' after the 1914-18 war. Such subsidies took the form of £x per home for a fixed number of years and were intended to stimulate provision (Malpass and Murie, 1987). A similar enthusiasm for public house-building can be seen after the Second World War. Government support was used by authorities and house-builders who were willing to undertake schemes, rather than according to any needs-based principles. By the 1960s and 1970s, efforts were being made by central government to control the construction of new units and to allocate resources fairly by formula (Hills, 1998).

Local authorities started to subsidise rents from the rates, creating a second stream of taxpayer support for tenants. Moreover, the large council house-building programmes of the 1950s and 1960s had left councils with very different debt burdens. The 1972 Housing Finance Act attempted to establish equalised 'fair rents' across all council housing in England and Wales (Glennerster et al, 2000). These rents would rise until they matched regulated private-sector rentals. The poorest tenants were to be protected by a rent rebate scheme. By this time, three different kinds of subsidy and control were in use: for construction, for rent regulation and via social security.

Subsequent governments reformed the system several times. Labour in the late 1970s restored councils' freedom to subsidise rents from the rates. The Conservatives ended this practice in the 1980s. Labour first encouraged house-building with percentage grants and then imposed capital controls on authorities. Mrs Thatcher's Tories then radically reduced the role of local authorities in social home construction and shifted virtually all house-building to housing associations. The 1979-97

Conservative governments also encouraged tenants to buy their homes at a discounted price through its right to buy policy.

Remaining subsidy for council housing was paid so as to achieve a number of different objectives in parallel. These purposes include the need to provide grant towards accumulated housing debt, the need to hold rents to a 'fair' or reasonable level, the need to underpin the finances of the poorest households and, importantly, the need for public expenditure control. Incentives are a key element in the overall design of the system (Glennerster et al, 2000).

The fact that virtually all new social housing construction from the 1980s onwards was channelled through housing associations created the need for a second stream of grant support. Funding was paid by The Housing Corporation to registered social landlords. Originally subsidy was a matching grant to encourage new homes although at the end of the 1980s the government became increasingly concerned with the need to control costs and moved to fixed capital grants. Housing associations set rents so as to fund their accumulated debt, subject to de facto government rent increase limits.

Overall, housing finance has equity objectives built into it at several points. But, unlike health and education, there is not a single formula that seeks to measure and then equalise for differences from place to place (and thus, indirectly, from individual to individual). Housing policy has, arguably, been significantly politically contested over the years, leading to radical lurches in policy.

Local government

When Sidney Webb wrote his lengthy works about local government in the early 20th century, many welfare services were in their infancy. Moreover, councils were the public institution where most government provision had evolved. In the intervening 100 years, national government has assumed the role of guarantor and/or direct provider of a number of services. Health provision, which originated in local authorities, charities and the private sector, was 'nationalised' with the creation of the NHS. Education remained a 'national service locally administered' until the creation of a separate ringfenced grant in 2006-07. Even now, local government still has an important role in schools' provision. Housing has been partly nationalised, although many councils remain substantial social landlords.

More generally, local government is still a key public provider, including welfare provision such as personal social services. Many other local public services, including libraries, police, regeneration and leisure have welfare aspects. Local government is underpinned by the Revenue Support Grant (RSG), which provides extensive equalisation of both spending needs and taxable capacity.

British local government funding systems attempt to equalise between authorities to a significantly greater extent than those in most other countries (Bramley, 2002). There are detailed formulae for social services, highways, police, fire, environment, protective and cultural services and for capital finance (ODPM, 2005). As within the NHS, years of research and analysis have contributed to the formulae now in use. The resulting distribution of grant ensures the poorest councils spend significantly more than the most affluent ones.

The arrangements for local government funding are conspicuously complex. Whereas within a professionally driven service such as the NHS the complexity of the funding formula appears to be an accepted consequence of efforts to achieve equity, the RSG is more problematic. Local authorities are elected. The fact that they receive the bulk of their funding via formulae that cannot be fully understood even by those who operate the system is, to say the least, problematic.

Local government finance has been the subject of two major reviews within the past generation. In 1976 the Layfield Committee provided a comprehensive overview of the whole system of local authority funding, including detailed studies of needs-related grant arrangements (DoE, 1976). From 2003 to 2006, the Balance of Funding Review (ODPM, 2004) and then the Lyons Inquiry (2007) once again considered the future of local government finance.

Both Layfield in 1976 and Lyons in 2007 accepted the underlying principles of the British approach to public service funding. Equalisation of spending needs and resources were an important element in ensuring the fair operation of the local government finance system. However, both the Balance of Funding Review and the Lyons Inquiry appeared prepared to consider the possibility of moving away from full equalisation in an attempt to allow greater local autonomy.

The regions

Throughout the period from the 1950s to the present day, policy makers and commentators have debated the need (or otherwise) for regional policy within Britain. The 1964-70 Labour government pursued policies designed to shift economic activity away from the prosperous South East towards the North. The 1974-79 government took unsuccessful steps to introduce devolution to Scotland and Wales. In 1994, the Conservatives introduced 'government offices' within the nine English regions. The Blair government created a devolved Parliament for Scotland and created an Assembly for Wales.

In England, the 1997 Labour government introduced city-regional government for London, creating a directly elected mayor and assembly. Subsequent efforts to introduce a regional assembly for the North East of England were rejected by the electorate in the autumn of 2004. Nevertheless, indirectly elected 'chambers' have been created in the eight English regions outside London, with powers over spatial planning, transport and housing.

In 2004, the Treasury announced that regions would receive funding for these services (HM Treasury, 2004), albeit on the basis of a bid-based system. The allocation of resources to regions, thus far at least, has been on the basis of centrally assessed bids prepared in the light of Whitehall advice. Little by way of the 'equity' drivers considered in the evolution of health, education and housing funding has been included in this new sphere of centrally determined funding. This change may yet be an indicator of a long-term-shift away from traditional needs-based funding formulae towards specific and bid-based systems.

The Barnett formula

Devolution to Scotland and Wales highlighted the use of the so-called Barnett formula to determine the balance of funding between England and the other countries of the UK. In reality, this arrangement is more a convention than a formula. It is named after Lord (Joel) Barnett who, as Chief Secretary to the Treasury in the 1974-79 Labour government, determined a method for allocating equivalent changes to spending programmes for Scotland, Wales and Northern Ireland to any that are made in England (House of Commons Library, 1998). As 'England' expenditure programmes go up or down, so those for Scotland, Wales and Northern Ireland will rise and fall, taking account of population differences.

The Barnett formula is not a needs-based calculation. In effect, it freezes the ratio of spending in England and the other countries within the UK in relation to each other. An exercise was undertaken in the late 1970s that attempted to use needs formulae to assess the relative spending needs of each country within the UK (McCrone, 1999). The results, which suggested that Scotland, Wales and Northern Ireland were marginally overfunded, were not used for resource distribution. Subsequently, the Treasury Committee of the House of Commons argued, in a 1997 report, that a new needs formula should be generated to inform the distribution of resources within the UK

(House of Commons Treasury Committee, 1997). No action was taken. Subsequently, there have been academic calls for a UK-wide needs-based resources distribution formula (McLean and McMillan, 2003)

Within Scotland and Wales, equalisation arrangements within local government and resource distribution mechanisms in the health service have broadly followed the pattern adopted in England. That is, equity and equalisation have been key objectives of the resource allocation mechanisms used.

The impact of Britain's unique approach

The Blair government has moved sharply and deliberately towards a policy of delivering, as far as possible, equal outcomes for individuals in different circumstances. Thus, in the 2005 White Paper *Higher Standards, Better Schools for All* (DfES, 2005, p 20), the government stated:

> Breaking cycles of underachievement, low aspiration and educational underperformance is vital for our economic future. We must ensure that all children have the same chance in life – with success based on hard work and merit, not wealth and family background.

Similar expectations have been determined within health, with the intention of narrowing the differences between indicators recorded in different areas and between individuals.

Although contemporary British local authorities (and other units of public service provision) are large in population terms, they display considerable differences in terms of social and demographic variations. Despite the efforts of governments and social policy interventions (including the resource distribution mechanisms discussed in this chapter), the differences between areas with the highest levels of assessed expenditure needs or deprivation and those with the lowest levels are often greater in England/Britain than in other developed countries.

The Gini coefficient, published by the United Nations, provides a measure of variations in personal income inequality in different countries. Among the developed nations, the US has a relatively high Gini coefficient, suggesting relatively wide levels of personal income differentiation. Australia, Ireland, Italy, New Zealand and the UK fall in an 'upper middle' group in such terms, with smaller differences in Canada, France and Spain and even lower ones (suggesting greater income equality) in Belgium, Denmark, Finland, Germany, Japan, Norway and Sweden.

The extent of inequality will, unless there is an equal distribution of less well-off people from authority to authority, have significant implications for efforts to equalise for authority-to-authority variations in spending needs and taxable capacity. Thus, in a country with limited income variation (particularly if the rich and poor are mixed in each area) it could be argued that there would be less need for equalisation than in a country where there are bigger income disparities (especially if the poor are disproportionately located in some areas).

Pressures on equalisation mechanisms of the kind used in the NHS, education and local government will also depend on political and societal expectations about 'fairness' and equity. A country with modest expectations concerning the equal availability of public services (for example the US), would expect few demands for inter-tier equalisation or redistribution arrangements. However, in countries where variations in public service availability or perceptions of 'fairness' are politically salient issues, as appears to be true in England/Britain today, demands for efforts to achieve the equitable delivery of services or outcomes are likely to be intense.

It is therefore easy to see why grant arrangements for health, education and local government are more apparently stressed in England than in many other countries. Personal income inequality remains relatively significant (despite efforts to reduce it in recent years) while demands for public services that achieve equal outcomes have grown. 'Postcode lotteries' are, without doubt, considered a bad thing within the British political system. This expectation that the outcomes of schools, hospitals and other public services should as far as possible be equal means that the public services should, logically, compensate for the significant differences in individuals' backgrounds that result from wide personal and territorial income variations.

Politicians have behaved in recent years as if they believe the British electorate does not want a radical reduction in levels of income variation. Although there has, as other chapters in this book show, been an effort to narrow these income differentials, they remain relatively wide by comparison with many developed countries. However, the same voters are judged to want public services that treat people equitably and, indeed, to move towards public service outcomes that are equal. NHS, education and local government resource distribution systems are an element in the solution of this problem: they are supposed to provide councils with sufficient resources to avoid 'postcode lotteries'.

The UK is, arguably, in a unique position. Public service formula-based grant and equalisation arrangements, taken with other public provision, must compensate health authorities, schools and councils sufficiently to allow them to deliver services that are expected to overcome disadvantages caused by low income and other factors. Yet the scale of income and deprivation differences is such that delivering 'fair' outcomes will always be stressed and prone to failure.

Conclusion – political demands and pragmatic limitations

For over a century, there have been demands that public services in Britain should be funded in ways that take account of differences in the need to spend and, within local government, taxable capacity. As the earlier paragraphs of this chapter have shown, a number of public services have been funded since the 1960s or 1970s using allocation mechanisms that explicitly take account of spending need. Indeed, there appears to have been a wide acceptance across British politics that such needs-based distribution formulae should be used.

As a result, the highest expenditure on public services such as health and education tends to be in poorer areas. Hackney or Manchester spend significantly more in schools than, say Richmond or Stockport. Outcomes, of course, are not equal in different areas and authorities, or among individuals in different circumstances. It is not really possible to show that public services treat individuals or areas in a similar way.

The evolution of funding formulae in Britain has almost certainly passed its zenith. There is evidence, particularly within education and local government, of moves towards bid-based and specific-purpose grants – often in support of new initiatives. Such funding is often allocated on the basis of judgements within central government rather than by formula. The local government funding formula has been frozen in recent years while year-on-year allocations of grants to councils have been heavily 'damped'. That is, gains and losses to individual councils have been tempered by overriding any redistribution that should, according to the formula, take place.

Schools funding in 2006-07 and 2007-08 was, to a significant degree, allocated between local authorities as a ringfenced grant on the basis of the previous year's spending plus a flat-rate percentage per pupil. Allocations made in this way are less and less likely to take account of different social needs. Indeed, predictability and simplicity now appear to be more important than social equity to many contemporary administrators and institutions. This change has almost certainly been encouraged by the move to devolve power to individual schools and other micro-institutions (see Chapter Five). Smaller bodies are less easily able to absorb large changes in their year-to-year resources.

In education and health, there has also been a significant shift towards 'quasi-market' mechanisms where resources follow individual pupils or patients exercising choice between institutions (Le Grand, 2003; Chapter Seven, in this volume). Of course, it is still possible to take account of different expenditure needs while operating choice-driven systems, although incentives for those delivering services will be different from those in a purely needs-based resource allocation system. Indeed, such changed incentives for producers are a key objective of moving to quasi-market mechanisms.

There are other potential challenges to the relatively pure form of expenditure-needs-driven resource allocation systems that evolved in England/Britain during the 20th century. In the report of the Balance of Funding review (ODPM, 2004), which considered the future of local government finance, the possibility of moving away from full equalisation was briefly discussed. The interim report of the Lyons Inquiry (2005) into local government went further, suggesting that local government performance might be improved if authorities were able to retain part of any growth in their local tax base. Such a change would, within local government at least, move away from the near-full equalisation of resources that currently operates.

In his final report, published in March 2007, Lyons effectively acknowledged that the pursuit of extensive resources and needs equalisation has had the effect of undermining local incentives to promote development – albeit in the service of the objective of delivering 'fairness' and equity (Lyons Inquiry, 2007, pp 317-46). Such a charge might be made more generally for the kind of resource distribution mechanisms that have gradually moved away from the massive geographically-based inequalities of the 19th century towards today's more equal arrangements for government service delivery. What is not known is the extent to which the evolution of needs and resources-driven allocation mechanisms has (or has not) contributed to the achievement of particular outcomes for individuals or the areas in which they live. Looking ahead, Lyons recommended that there should be a rather less equity-driven resource allocation than in the past, although with equalisation still remaining as a feature of the local government grant system. In addition, the desire to deliver stability will mean that grants are less redistributive and that mechanisms may be seen as producing a new kind of 'fairness' where flat-rate annual increases are the norm.

Nevertheless, in the increasingly complex and fractured society that appears to be emerging in Britain, it is likely that public welfare services will continue to be funded by mechanisms that retain elements of the needs-driven systems that have been used since the 1950s. The scale of redistribution already built into existing levels of funding means it would take some time fully to move away from the existing pattern of resource allocation. Moreover, it appears likely that new demands will be made of distribution systems, for example the need to facilitate the 'quasi-market'; the delivery of efficiency; the need to change behaviour in relation to the environment; or the need to provide different incentives for particular neighbourhoods. Resource distribution in the 21st century is likely to evolve beyond the settled model of the latter years of the 20th. Public services will change accordingly.

References

Bramley, G. (2002) *Report of Inquiry into Local Government Finance*, vol 3, Local Government Committee, 6th Report 2002, SP Paper 551, Session 1 (2002), Edinburgh: Scottish Parliament.

Carr-Hill, R.A., Hardman, G., Peacock, S., Sheldon, T.A. and Smith, P. (1994) *A Formula for Distributing NHS Revenues Based on Small Area Use of Hospital Beds*, York: University of York.

Davies, B. (1968) *Social Needs and Resources in Local Services*, London: Michael Joseph.

DfES (Department for Education and Skills) (2005) *Higher Standards, Better Schools for All: More Choice for Parents and Pupils*, Cm 6677, London: The Stationery Office.

DfES (2006) *Child Poverty: Fair Funding for Schools*, London: DfES and HM Treasury.

DH (Department of Health) (2005) *Resource Allocation: Weighted Capitation Formula (fifth edition)*, London: DH.

DH (2007) *Options for the Future of Payment by Results: 2008/09 to 2010/11*, London: DH.

DoE (Department of the Environment) (1976) *Local Government Finance Report of the Committee of Inquiry*, Cmnd 6453, London: HMSO.

Ellison, N. (1994) *Egalitarian Thought and Labour Politics*, London: Routledge.

Foster, C.D., Jackman, R. and Perlman, M. (1980) *Local Government Finance in a Unitary State*, London: George Allen & Unwin.

Gibbon, G. and Bell, R.W. (1939) *History of the London County Council 1889-1939*, London: Macmillan.

Glennerster, H., Hills, J., Piachaud, D. and Webb, J. (2004) *One Hundred Years of Poverty and Policy*, York: Joseph Rowntree Foundation.

Glennerster, H., Hills, J. and Travers, T. (2000) *Paying for Health, Education and Housing: How Does the Centre Pull the Purse Strings*, Oxford: Oxford University Press.

Hills, J. (1998) 'Housing: a decent home within the reach of every family?', in H. Glennerster and J. Hills (eds) *The State of Welfare: The Economics of Social Spending*, Oxford: Oxford University Press.

HM Treasury (2004) *Devolving Decision-Making: A Consultation on Regional Funding Allocations*, London: The Stationery Office.

HM Treasury (2006) *Public Expenditure Statistical Analyses*, Cm 6811, London: The Stationery Office.

House of Commons Library (1998) *The Barnett Formula*, Research Paper 98/8, London: House of Commons.

House of Commons Treasury Committee (1997) *The Barnett Formula, Second Report*, Session 1997-98, HC 341, London: The Stationery Office.

Le Grand, J. (2002) 'Models of public service provision: command and control, networks or quasi-markets?', in Public Services Productivity papers presented at a seminar held at HM Treasury, 13 June 2002, London: HM Treasury.

Le Grand, J. (2003) *Motivation, Agency and Public Policy: Of Knights and Knaves, Pawns and Queens*, Oxford: Oxford University Press.

Lyons Inquiry (2005) *Lyons Inquiry into Local Government Consultation Paper and Interim Report*, London: The Stationery Office.

Lyons Inquiry (2007) *Place-Shaping: A Shared Ambition for the Future of Local Government, Final Report*, March, London: The Stationery Office.

McCrone, G. (1999) 'Scotland's public finances from Goschen to Barnett', Fraser of Allander *Quarterly Economic Commentary*, vol 24, no 2, pp 30-46.

McLean, I. and McMillan, A. (2003) 'The distribution of public expenditure across the UK regions', *Fiscal Studies*, vol 24, no 1, pp 45-71.

Malpass, P. and Murie, A. (1987) *Housing Policy and Practice (2nd edition)*, Basingstoke: Macmillan Education.

Ministry of Housing and Local Government (1966) *The Rate Support Grant Order 1966*, HoC Paper 252, Session 1966-67, London: HMSO.

ODPM (Office of the Deputy Prime Minister) (2004) *Balance of Funding Review: Report*, London: ODPM.

ODPM (2005) *Local Government Finance Report (England) 2006/07*, HC 858, Session 2005-06, London: The Stationery Office.

OECD (Organisation for Economic Co-operation and Development) (2005) *Revenue Statistics 2005*, Paris: OECD.

Travers, T. (1986) *The Politics of Local Government Finance*, London: George Allen & Unwin.

Wallace, G. (1992) *Local Management of Schools: Research and Experience*, Clevedon: Multilingual Matters.

Webb, S. (1911) *Grants in Aid: A Criticism and a Proposal*, London: Longmans.

Appendix: Bibliography of Howard Glennerster's publications

2007

British Social Policy: 1945 to the present, Oxford: Blackwells.
Tibor Barna: The Redistributive Impact of Taxes and Social Policies in the UK, 1937-95, CASEpaper 115, London: London School of Economics and Political Science.

2006

'Situation de la protection sociale au Royaume-Uni en 2005: évolution positive', *Revue Belge de Securite Sociale*, vol 48, no 4, pp 797-817.
'A capital start: but how far do we go?', in W. Paxton, and S. White with D. Maxwell (eds) *Citizen's Stake: Exploring the Future of Universal Asset Policies*, Bristol: The Policy Press.
'Capital poor', *The Journal of Poverty and Social Justice*, vol 14, no 1, pp 27-31.
'Why so different? Why so bad a future?', in H. Pemberton, P. Thane and N. Whiteside (eds) *Britain's Pension Crisis: History and Policy*, Oxford: Oxford University Press and the British Academy.

2005

'The health and welfare legacy', in A. Seldon and D. Kavanagh (eds) *The Blair Effect, 2001-5*, Cambridge: Cambridge University Press.
(with A. McKnight and R. Lupton) 'Education, education, education: an assessment of Labour's success in tackling education incqualities', in J. Hills and K. Stewart (eds) *A More Equal Society?*, Bristol: The Policy Press.

2004

'Mrs Thatcher's legacy: getting it in perspective', in N. Ellison, L. Bauld and M. Powell (eds) *Social Policy Review 16: Analysis and Debate in Social Policy*, Bristol: The Policy Press.

(with J. Hills, D. Piachaud and J. Webb) *One Hundred Years of Poverty and Policy*, York: Joseph Rowntree Foundation.

2003

Understanding the Finance of Welfare: What Welfare Costs and How to Pay For It, Bristol: The Policy Press (also Korean edition).

'Paying for welfare', in P. Alcock, A. Erskin and M. May (eds) *The Student's Companion to Social Policy*, Oxford: Blackwell.

British Social Policy: Howard Glennerster's Selected Works, B. Li (ed)

(Translated into Chinese) Beijing: Commercial Press (Shangwu Yinshuguan).

2002

'United States poverty studies and poverty measurement: the past twenty-five years', *Social Service Review*, vol 76, no 1, pp 83-107.

'United Kingdom education 1997-2001', *Oxford Review of Economic Policy*, vol 18, no 2, pp 120-36.

(with J. Sparkes) 'Preventing social exclusion: education's contribution', in J. Hills, J. Le Grand and D. Piachaud (eds) *Understanding Social Exclusion*, Oxford: Oxford University Press.

2001

'The international perspective', in P. Alcock, H. Glennerster, A. Oakley and A. Sinfield (eds) *Welfare and Wellbeing: Richard Titmuss' Contribution to Social Policy*, Bristol: The Policy Press.

'Social policy', in A. Seldon (ed) *The Blair Effect: The Blair Government, 1997-2001*, London: Little Brown.

United Kingdom Education 1997-2001, CASEpaper 50, London: London School of Economics and Political Science.

2000

(with J. Hills and T. Travers) *Paying for Health, Education and Housing: How Does the Centre Pull the Purse Strings?*, Oxford: Oxford University Press.

(with A.B. Atkinson and N. Stern) *Putting Economics to Work: Volume in Honour of Michio Morishima*, STICERD Occasional Paper 22, London: London School of Economics and Political Science.

British Social Policy Since 1945 (2nd edition), Oxford: Blackwell.

US Poverty Studies and Poverty Measurement: The Past Twenty-Five Years, CASEpaper 42, London: London School of Economics and Political Science.

1999

'A third way?', in H. Dean and R. Woods (eds) *Social Policy Review 11*, Canterbury: Social Policy Association.

'Which welfare states are most likely to survive?', *International Journal of Social Welfare*, vol 8, no 1, pp 2-13.

'The elderly: a burden on the economy', in *Centrepiece*, London: Centre for Economic Performance, London School of Economics and Political Science.

(with R. Lupton, D. Noden and A. Power) *Poverty, Social Exclusion and Neighbourhood: Studying the Area Bases of Social Exclusion*, CASEpaper 22, London: London School of Economics and Political Science.

(with D. Piachaud) 'Age of reason', *The Guardian*, 23 June.

1998

'Competition and quality in health care: the UK experience', *International Journal for Quality in Health Care*, vol 10, no 5, pp 403-10.

'Social policy in the UK: creating a new social contract', monograph no 5 in series *Toward a New Public Philosophy: A Global Re-evaluation of Democracy at Century's End*, New York, NY: Carnegie Council on Ethics and International Affairs.

'Tackling poverty at its roots: education', in C. Oppenheim (ed) *An Inclusive Society: Strategies for Tackling Poverty*, London: Institute for Public Policy Research.

'A reply to "Things can only get better"', *Policy & Politics*, vol 26, no 4, pp 477-8.

'L'assistenza ai grandi anziani: soluzioni pubbliche e soluzioni private', *Prospettive Sociali e Sanitarie*, vol 28, no 5, pp 1-11.

(ed with J. Hills) *The State of Welfare* (2nd edition), Oxford: Oxford University Press.

'Solutions for long-term care', *New Economy*, vol 5, no 1, pp 24-9.

'Alternatives to fundholding', *International Journal of Health Services*, vol 28, no 1, pp 24-9.

(with D. Billis) 'Human services and the voluntary sector: towards a theory of comparative advantage', *Journal of Social Policy*, vol 27, no 1, pp 79-98.

1997

Paying for Welfare: Towards 2000, Hemel Hempstead: Prentice Hall.
'Paying for welfare', in P. Alcock, A. Erskin and M. May (eds) *The Student's Companion to Social Policy*, Oxford: Blackwell.
(with J. Le Grand, N. Mays, J.A. Mulligan, N. Goodwin and J. Dixon) *Models of Purchasing and Commissioning: Review of the Research Evidence: A Report to the Department of Health*, London: King's Fund.
'What have we learned and unlearned on the welfare state programme: what next steps', in *Managing the Cost of Transfer Programmes*, Public Management Occasional Papers No 16, Paris: OECD.

1996

(ed with F.W. Schwartz and R.B. Saltman) *Fixing Health Budgets: Experience from Europe and North America*, Chichester and New York, NY: Wiley.
'Future funding structures for social policy: information implications', in J. Steyaert (ed) *Information Technology and Human Services, More than Computers*, Utrecht: Netherlands Institute for Care and Welfare.
(with A. Cohen and V. Bovell) *Alternatives to Fundholding*, Welfare State Programme Discussion Paper, no 123, London: STICERD, London School of Economics and Political Science.
'The big trade-off revisited', Paper presented at The Industry Commission Conference on Equity, Efficiency and Welfare held in Melbourne, November, Melbourne: Industry Commission.
'Fixed budgets for fundholding general practitioners in the UK', in F.W. Schwartz, H. Glennerster and R.B. Saltman (eds) *Fixing Health Budgets: Experience from Europe and North America*, Chichester and New York, NY: Wiley.
'Vouchers and quasi-vouchers in education', in M. May, E. Brunsdon and G. Craig (eds) *Social Policy Review 8*, London: Social Policy Association.
(with J. Lewis) *Implementing the New Community Care*, Buckingham: Open University Press.

1995

Social Policy in Britain since 1945, Oxford: Blackwell.

(with J. Dixon) 'What do we know about fundholding in general practice?', *British Medical Journal*, vol 311, pp 727-30.

'Opportunity costs', *New Economy*, May, pp 110-14.

'La contractualisation au sein du service national de sante au Royamme-Uni', *Revue Française D'Administration Publique*, No 76, Octobre-Décembre, pp 641-8.

'Le développement des quasi-marchés dans la protection sociale', *Revue Française D'Economie*, vol 10, no 3, pp 111-34.

(with R. Bennett and D. Nevison) 'Regional rates of return to education and training in Britain', *Regional Studies*, vol 29, no 3, pp 279-95.

(with R. Bennett and D. Nevison) 'Investing in skill: expected returns to vocational studies', *Education Economics*, vol 3, no 2, pp 99-117.

'The life cycle: public or private concern', in J. Falkingham and J. Hills (eds) *The Dynamics of Welfare: The Welfare State and the Life Cycle*, Hemel Hempstead: Prentice Hall.

(with J. Falkingham and N. Barr) 'Education funding: equity and the life cycle', in J. Falkingham and J. Hills (eds) *The Dynamics of Welfare: The Welfare State and the Life Cycle*, Hemel Hempstead: Prentice Hall.

'Internal markets: context and structure', in M. Jerome-Forget, J. White and J.M. Wiener (eds) *Health Care Reform through Internal Markets*, Washington, DC: Brookings Institution.

(with J. Le Grand) 'The development of a quasi-markets in welfare provision in the United Kingdom', *International Journal of Health Services*, vol 25, no 2, pp 203-18.

1994

'La politique sociale', in J. Leruez (ed) *La Grande-Bretagne à la fin du 20ème siècle*, Paris: La documentation Française.

'Health and social policy', in D. Kavanagh and A. Seldon (eds) *The Major Effect*, London: Macmillan.

(with M. Matsaganis, P. Owens and S. Hancock) 'GP fundholding: wild card of winning hand?', in R. Robinson and J. Le Grand (eds) *Evaluating the NHS Reforms*, London: King's Fund.

(with M. Matsaganis) 'The English and Swedish health care reforms', *International Journal of Health Services*, vol 24, no 2 pp 231-51.

(with M. Matsaganis) 'The threat of 'cream skimming' in the post-reform NHS', *Journal of Health Economics*, vol 13, pp 31-60.

'New challenges for management accounting: issues in health and social services', *Financial Accountability and Management*, vol 10, no 2, pp 131-41.

(with M. Evans) 'Beveridge and his assumptive worlds: the incompatibilities of a flawed design', in J. Hills, J. Ditch and H. Glennerster (eds) *Beveridge and Social Security: An International Retrospective*, Oxford: Clarendon Press.

(with M. Barr and J. Falkingham) *Funding Higher Education*, London: London School of Economics and Political Science.

(with M. Matsaganis and P. Owens) *Implementing GP Fundholding*, Milton Keynes: Open University Press.

'Impact and future of general practitioner fundholders', in M. Burrows, R. Dyson, P. Jackson and H. Saxton (eds) *Management for Hospital Doctors*, Boston, MA: Butterworth/Heinemann.

(with N. Barr) 'European schooling systems and financing: lessons for the United States', in R.J. Thornton and A.P. O'Brien (eds) *The Economic Consequences of American Education*, Connecticut, CT: JAI Press.

1993

'The economics of education: changing fortunes' in N. Barr and D. Whynes (eds) *Current Issues in the Economics of Welfare*, London: Macmillan.

(with T. Turner) *Estate Based Housing Management: An Evaluation*, London: HMSO.

'Paying for welfare: issues for the 1990s', in R. Page and N. Deakin (eds) *The Costs of Welfare*, Aldershot: Avebury.

'The UK health reforms', in D.P. Chinitz and M.A. Cohen (eds) *The Changing Roles of Government and the Market in Health Care Systems*, Jerusalem: The JDC-Brookdale Institute and the State of Israel Ministry of Health.

(with M. Matsaganis) 'The UK health reforms: the fundholding experiment', *Health Policy*, vol 23, pp 179-91.

(with M. Evans) *Squaring the Circle: The Inconsistencies and Constraints of Beveridge's Plan*, Welfare State Programme Discussion Paper, no 86, London: STICERD, London School of Economics and Political Science.

1992

Market Type Mechanisms and Health Services in the UK, Occasional Papers in Public Management: Market Type Mechanisms Series, no 2, Paris: OECD.

'Are measures of quality of life likely to be useful instruments of social policy?', in A. Hopkins (ed) *Measures of the Quality of Life and the Use to which such Measures may be Put*, London: Royal College of Physicians.

'GP fundholding in the United Kingdom: is it working?', *Pharmaco Economics*, vol 3, no 1, pp 10-13.

(with R. Bennett and D. Nevison) *Learning Should Pay*, London: London School of Economics and Political Science.

(with R. Bennett and D. Nevison) 'Investing in skill: to stay on or not to stay on', *Oxford Review of Economic Policy*, vol 8, no 2, pp 130-45.

(with M. Matsaganis and P. Owens) *A Foothold for Fundholding*, King's Fund Institute Research Report, no 12, London: King's Fund.

Paying for Welfare: The 1990s, Hemel Hempstead: Harvester Wheatsheaf.

(with R. Bennett and D. Nevison) *Investing in Skill: Expected Returns to Vocational Education*, Welfare State Programme Discussion Paper, no 74, London: STICERD, London School of Economics and Political Science.

1991

(with A. Power and T. Travers) 'A new era for social policy: a new enlightenment or a new leviathan?', *Journal of Social Policy*, vol 20, no 3, pp 387-414.

'Quasi markets for education?', *The Economic Journal*, vol 101, no 408, pp 1268-76.

(ed with J. Midgley) *The Radical Right and the Welfare State: An International Assessment*, Hemel Hempstead: Harvester Wheatsheaf.

1990

'Social policy since the Second World War' and (with W. Low) 'Education and the welfare state: does it add up?', in J. Hills (ed) *The State of Welfare*, Oxford: Oxford University Press.

'The costs of hospital closure: reproviding services for the residents of Darenth Park Hospital', *Psychiatric Bulletin*, no 14, pp 140-3.

(with P. Owens) *Nursing in Conflict*, London: Macmillan.

1989

(with N. Barr and J. Le Grand) 'Working for patients: the right approach?', *Social Policy and Administration*, vol 23, no 2, pp 117-27. (Also published as written evidence to the House of Commons Social Services Committee.)

'Swimming against the tide', in M. Bulmer, J. Lewis and D. Piachaud (eds) *The Goals of Social Policy*, London: Allen and Unwin.

'What commitment to welfare', *Social Security*, no 39.

(with W. Low) 'Changed Climate for education managers', *Public Money*, Spring, pp 17-23.

1988

(with P. Owens) *The Nursing Management Function after Griffiths: A Second Interim Report 1986-87*, London: North West Thames Health Authority and London School of Economics and Political Science.

(with N. Barr and J. Le Grand) *Reform and the National Health Service*, Welfare State Programme Discussion Paper, no 32, London: STICERD, London School of Economics and Political Science.

'A requiem for the Social Administration Association', *Journal of Social Policy*, vol 17, no 1, pp 83-4.

1987

'Goodbye Mr Chips', *New Society*, 9 October, pp 17-19.

(with P. Owens) 'Aiming for the top', *Nursing Times*, vol 83, no 23.

(with P. Owens) 'A word in your ear', *Nursing Times*, vol 83, no 25.

1986

(with P. Owens) *The Nursing Management Function After Griffiths*, London: North West Thames Regional Health Authority and London School of Economics and Political Science.

1985

(with N. Korman) *The Closure of a Hospital: The Darenth Park Project*, Occasional Papers in Social Administration, London: Bedford Square Press.

Paying for Welfare, Oxford: Blackwells.

1984

'Programme budgeting', in J. Midgley and D. Piachaud (eds) *Fields and Methods of Social Planning*, London: Heinemann Educational Books.

(with J. Le Grand) 'Financing students', *New Society*, December, pp 421-2.

1983

'Client group budgeting', *Public Money*, December, pp 25-32.

(with N. Korman and F. Marslen-Wilson) 'Planning and practice: the participants' views', *Public Administration*,

vol 61, no 3, pp 253-64.

(with N. Korman and F. Marslen-Wilson) *Planning for Priority Groups*, Oxford: Martin Robertson.

(ed) *The Future of the Welfare State: Remaking Social Policy*, London: Heinemann.

'A new start for Labour', in J.A.G. Griffiths (ed) *Socialism in a Cold Climate*, London: Unwin Paperbacks.

1982

'Social planning: a local study', *Final Report of an SSRC Funded Report*, London: London School of Economics and Political Science.

'Barter and bargains', *Health and Social Services Journal*, June.

1981

'From containment to conflict? Social planning in the Seventies', *Journal of Social Policy*, vol 10, part 1, pp 31-51.

'Social service planning in a hostile environment', in C. Hood and M. Wright (eds) *Big Government and Hard Times*, Oxford: Blackwell and M. Robertson.

'The role of the state in financing recurrent education: lessons from European experience', in M.J. Bowman (ed) *Collective Choice Education*, Boston, the Hague and London: Kluwer.

(with K. Russell, S. Benson, C. Farrell, D. Piachaud and G. Plowman *Changing Course: A Follow-up Study of Students Taking the Certificate and Diploma in Social Administration at the London School of Economics and Political Science, 1949-1973*, London: Department of Social Administration.

1980

'Public spending and the social services, in M. Brown and S. Baldwin (eds) *The Year Book of Social Policy in Britain 1979*, London: Routledge and Kegan Paul.

'Prime cuts: public expenditure and social services planning in a hostile environment', *Policy & Politics*, vol 8, no 4, pp 367-82.

1979

'The determinants of public expenditure', in T. Booth (ed) *Social Policy and the Expenditure Process*, Oxford: Blackwell and M. Robertson.

1977

'The year of the cuts', in K. Jones, M. Brown and S. Baldwin (eds) *Year Book of Social Policy 1976*, London: Routledge.

'The existing system of finance', in *The Finance of Education*, Buckingham: Open University Press.

1976

(ed) *Labour's Social Priorities*, London: Fabian Society.

'In praise of public expenditure', *New Statesman*, pp 252-4.

1975

Social Service Budgets and Social Policy, London: Allen and Unwin.

'Social services in Great Britain: taking care of people', in D. Thurz and J.L. Vigilante (eds) *Meeting Human Needs*, London: Sage Publications.

1973

(with E. Hoyle) 'Education policy and education research', in W. Taylor (ed) *Research Perspective in Education*, London: Routledge.

'A tax credit scheme for Britain?', *Journal of Human Resources*, vol 8, no 4, pp 422-35.

1972

Willing the Means: An Examination of the Cost of Reforming our Education System, London: Council for Educational Advance.

'Education and inequality', in P. Townsend (ed) *Labour and Inequality*, London: Fabian Society.

1970

'The finances of the direct grant schools', *Public Schools Commission Second Report*, vol ll, London: HMSO.
(with G. Wilson) *Paying for Private Schools*, London: Allen Lane.

1968

'The Plowden research', *Journal of the Royal Statistical Society*, Series A, vol 132, part 2, pp 194-204.
'A graduate tax', *Higher Education Review*, vol 1, no 1, pp 26-38 (reprinted with commentary, *Higher Education Review*, vol 35, no 2, pp 25-40).
(ed) *Planning Education for 1980*, London: Fabian Society.
'The Finances of Public Schools', Appendix 12, Public Schools Commission, *First Report*, vol 2, London: HMSO.

1967

(with A. Peacock and R. Lavers) *Educational Finance – Its Sources and Uses in the UK*, London: Oliver and Boyd.

1966

Graduate School, London: Oliver and Boyd.

1964

(with R. Pryke) *Public Schools*, London: Fabian Society.

1962

National Assistance: Service or Charity?, London: Fabian Society.

1959-64

Publications by the Labour Party to which he contributed:
Labour Party Local Government Handbook, London: Labour Party.
Towns for Our Times, London: Labour Party.

The Years of Crisis: Report of the Labour Party's Study Group on Higher Education, London: Labour Party
(ed) *Twelve Wasted Years*, London: Labour Party.

Index